ULI HESSE

Uli Hesse is an expert on German football and the author of *Tor! The Story of German Football*, which was shortlisted for the William Hill Sports Book of the Year Award. He writes for *FourFourTwo*, *ESPN* and the *Blizzard*.

ALSO BY ULI HESSE

Tor!: The Story of German Football

ULI HESSE

Bayern

Creating a Global Superclub

YELLOW JERSEY PRESS
LONDON

1 3 5 7 9 10 8 6 4 2

Yellow Jersey Press
20 Vauxhall Bridge Road,
London SW1V 2SA

Yellow Jersey Press is part of the Penguin Random Housegroup of companies
whose addresses can be found atglobal.penguinrandomhouse.com

 Penguin
Random House
UK

First published in paperback by Yellow Jersey Press in 2017
First published in trade paperback by Yellow Jersey Press in 2016

www.vintage-books.co.uk

A CIP catalogue record for this book is
available from the British Library

ISBN 9780224100113

Printed and bound by Clays Ltd, St Ives plc

Penguin Random House is committed to a sustainable future
for our business, our readers and our planet. This book is made
from Forest Stewardship Council® certified paper

MIX
Paper from
responsible sources
FSC® C018179

"Be not afraid of greatness:
Some are born great,
Some achieve greatness,
and some have greatness thrust upon 'em"
  – William Shakespeare, *Twelfth Night*

CONTENTS

INTRODUCTION

The money's rarely great and the working hours are often an imposition, but writing about football is still the best job in the world. Unless, that is, you have to talk to a player who is suffering from a major injury.

Such players are usually grumpy, sometimes even in a foul mood. They hate not being able to play. They fear they will lose their place in the team. They are bored with all those long hours spent in the company of physios. They miss the dressing-room camaraderie. They are irritable in a way we all would be irritable if we were scanning our bodies for small signs of improvement every waking minute.

So I braced myself for the worst when the door opened and into the room stepped a footballer who had been sidelined by a broken ankle for more than three months. I needn't have worried. Philipp Lahm wore a very broad grin as he extended a hand to say hello.

In fact, the captain of Bayern Munich's 2013 Champions League-winning side (and the captain of Germany's 2014 World Cup-winning team) was in such a jolly mood that we both forgot we were supposed to talk about football. Instead we spoke about his latest passion, golf, and then I asked him if it was true that he had a snooker table at home. He said it was, which sparked a discussion about eight-ball pool versus snooker.

Then I remembered something.

'Oh,' I said, 'I almost forgot to send greetings and best wishes from Franz Roth.'

Bayern have boasted a vast number of star players over the decades, but astonishingly often it has been an unsung hero who has come to the rescue at crucial moments in the club's history. So it was with Franz Roth – who holds the unusual distinction of having scored deciding goals in no fewer than three European finals for Bayern (in 1967, 1975 and 1976).

Lahm's face lit up. 'Oh, that's nice, thank you,' he replied. 'How is he doing?'

Lahm was born five years after Roth left Bayern to see out his playing career in Austria. So I asked him if he knew Roth well. He replied that they weren't close or anything but that they would run into each other now and then and were very aware of what the other had achieved. Then he slowly said: 'This is one of the biggest and most successful clubs in the world, but at the same time it feels like a large family. That is the truly great thing about Bayern.'

This is a sentiment you hear often from people who have played for Bayern, who used to coach here or have worked for the club in some other capacity. And it's true. If you spend some time at Bayern's clubhouse in Giesing, the simple and unglamorous borough of Munich where Bayern have trained since 1948, and have had their headquarters since 1971, your chances of running into a former player are high.

Karl-Heinz Rummenigge (chairman), Uli Hoeness (president until his tax-evasion scandal in 2014) and Franz Beckenbauer (honorary president) are merely the ones you read about most often. You might also find Paul Breitner and midfield workhorse Wolfgang Dremmler, both now working in the scouting department. Former goalkeeper Walter Junghans is part of the reserve team's coaching staff, as Gerd Müller used to be until he finally lost his fight against Alzheimer's in late 2014. Another former shot-stopper, Raimond Aumann, is Bayern's long-time supporter liaison officer. When Hans Pflügler, who played in the 1982 and 1987 European Cup finals for Bayern, finished his first-team career at thirty-two years of age in 1992, he soldiered on for another five years in the reserves (practically the Under-23 team) to teach the club's hopefuls the ropes. Now he works in Bayern's merchandising department.

Family ties even extend to the children of former players. Max Breitner, Paul's son, works in the press department. Uli Hoeness's daughter Sabine is involved in Bayern's celebrated club museum. Franz Beckenbauer's older brother Walter runs an ad agency, which produces Bayern's club magazine, and his son, Stephan, played for the reserves and then coached and scouted in the youth set-up until a terminal illness claimed his life in August 2015.

Yes, the homely, familial, warm Bayern Munich really does exist. It's not just a façade. There is a deep-rooted cliché in Germany that says Bayern's fans are merely glory hunters, customers more than supporters. But when I first spent time at the club to research a cover story for *FourFourTwo* magazine a few years ago, Uli Hoeness told us: 'Many clubs don't have a philosophy, they are driven by investors who only want success. In their effort to get to the top, they pay only little attention to the fans, the people. But for Bayern, involving these people plays a central role. It always comes as a shock to those who don't think this is possible, but for our fans and members, this is more than just a club. It's home. It's a surrogate family.' His face and his voice left no doubt as to how sincerely felt those words were.

However, this friendly, inviting Bayern Munich is not, of course, the only Bayern Munich. There is another club. One that annoys and enrages. It's tempting to argue that the resentment that follows Bayern wherever they go in Germany has to do with their exalted position. Bayern have celebrated twenty-six national championships in Germany. The next most successful teams, Nuremberg and Borussia Dortmund, have lifted only eight each. Bayern have won the DFB-Pokal, the German FA Cup, eighteen times. The second-best team, Werder Bremen, have won it just six times. Since the end of the 1970s, when Borussia Mönchengladbach fell by the wayside, Bayern have had no real national rival, only teams that manage to compete with them for a limited period of time before running out of steam. It stands to reason that this situation annoys a lot of people.

But the antagonism is much older than that. Bayern have divided opinion – and very strongly so – long before they became an all-conquering powerhouse. As early as 1968, when the club hadn't yet won a single Bundesliga title, Sepp Maier was attacked by a fan after an away game at Hannover 96. 'I'm going to kill you, you Bayern pig!' the man cried, lifting his umbrella to hit the goalkeeper. (Maier knocked him out cold with an uppercut.) In a country whose football was so deeply steeped in regionalism, not to say parochialism, that a nationwide league had only been formed five years earlier, it was highly unusual for a team to travel 400 miles and still find themselves physically attacked.

Even the public debate about the club is nothing new. While working on this book, I studied countless issues of *Kicker* magazine, the venerable bible of German football. It's amazing how often I encountered a heated back and forth between the club's supporters and detractors on the letters pages, long before Bayern began to dominate the German game.

When I opened the issue dated 20 May 1974, I expected to read at least one or two notes that lauded the club for having become the first German team to win the European Cup a few days earlier. Instead I found three readers' letters, all sent from Bavaria, which bitterly complained how everybody was always carping about Bayern. One Mr Eduard Weidler, resident in Passau, wrote: 'There are people who will use every little thing to denounce the whole team and even the complete board as unsporting, stuck-up and mean.'

I guess it proves that the old German football mantra is true: you either love Bayern or you loathe them, there's no middle ground. Or maybe that's not entirely true, because there's at least one person in this country who has tried to locate this middle ground. That's because it's the best place from which to tell a story. And since this is a heck of a story, I've done my very best to neither love nor loathe.

PROLOGUE

He was walking. He did this partly because he wasn't a great natural runner. He wasn't fast, he wasn't agile, he didn't have much acceleration over the crucial first yards. He wasn't elegant, either. Some people felt he looked awkward when running.

However, that wasn't the main reason he was walking. In this game, you have to do some running now and again, even if you aren't fast or agile. And he didn't worry about how he looked while he ran. Unlike some of the others on the team, he was born without a trace of vanity.

The reason he was walking with the uncertain gait of a man who's turned the wrong corner and suddenly finds himself in a dark alley was that he was ten steps or so into the opposition's half. Many years later, people would claim that there was a rule at the club that said he must never, ever cross the halfway line. That was rubbish, of course. He had scored seven league goals this season and you can't do that by staying in your own half for ninety minutes.

So there was no rule. But there was a guideline. It said that if the sweeper moved upfield, he had to stay back and cover for him. And this sweeper moved forward all the time.

He understood the reasoning behind the guideline. After all, apart from not being a fine runner, he also wasn't a good dribbler. He wasn't a renowned passer of the ball. His shooting technique was decent but not great. And although he was more comfortable on the ball than he was given credit for, impeccable technique was not his strong point.

Come to think of it, what was his strong point? Why was he an undisputed member and integral part of a team that at this very moment was either the best or the second best on the entire continent?

Perhaps it was because he understood and followed guidelines. This wasn't exactly a widespread quality in the team. There was at the very least one certified genius in the side – said sweeper, who did as he pleased (on the pitch and sometimes off the pitch) without having to answer to anyone. Then there was this gifted winger who was so fast he would often just take off and not worry about what happened behind him. There was the off-kilter left-back with the piercing eyes who enjoyed being contrary so much that he said things he didn't believe, just to prove he was his own man. There was also the greatest striker who ever lived, of course. One of the things that made him great was that you never knew where he would pop up, except that it would be the right place. Even the team's goalkeeper was unpredictable – a jester on a good day, a nutter on a bad one.

He was in this team because he wasn't like them. He was reliable, he knew his place, he played by the rules. No wonder many of the others would one day be wealthy, famous and powerful beyond imagination, while he would quietly open his shop every morning at six o'clock to sell newspapers and stationery.

He looked over his left shoulder at the sweeper. As always, the man had the ball at his feet. Even though time was running out, the sweeper couldn't be rushed. His pass was, as always, elegant, unhurried and precise. However, there were two unusual things about it. The first was that the sweeper passed the ball almost sideways. Whenever someone else played a square pass like that, the sweeper would mutter under his breath that the goal stood at the end of the pitch, not over on the side. The pass seemed to indicate that, after two hours of football, even the sweeper had run out of ideas.

The second unusual thing about this pass was that the sweeper was giving the ball to him. Normally it was the other way around. Who knows, maybe the sweeper was so surprised to see him here that the pass was just an involuntary reflex.

He controlled the ball with his right foot, surprisingly deftly, and broke into a trot. About thirty yards in front of goal, he looked up. There was some space in front of him, probably because the opposition knew how rarely he crossed the halfway line and wasn't sure whether to attack him or not. He noticed the greatest striker who ever lived standing in the penalty area with his right arm raised, calling for the ball.

He wondered how much time there was left. He could see the stadium clock, but it just showed the time of day, not the minutes gone in the game. He reckoned it would be over in a few seconds. A blink or two of the eye, then this miserable match would finally be done with. In a way, he was almost grateful. The opposing centre-forward was one of those quick, nimble guys who sometimes made him look bad. And he had looked very bad tonight. The game had been one of his worst all season.

Suddenly a thought flashed through his mind. The referee was not going to blow his whistle while he was moving through midfield, moving forward. But what if he stopped? What if he passed the ball? That would give the referee a good excuse to end the game. He looked down and gave the ball another nudge with his right foot. He was no longer walking or trotting. Now he was running. For reasons he would never be able to properly explain, he turned his strong, muscular upper body and swung his right leg backwards, like a man who is about to deliver a powerful long-range shot.

He heard the screams of horror. He heard the greatest striker who ever lived yell, begging him not to shoot, not from this distance, not with eleven pairs of legs between him and the goal, not in this moment, not, for Chrissakes, in the biggest game of their lives. He hesitated for only a fraction of a second. Then he ignored the guidelines, the rules and the screams, and kicked the ball as hard as he could.

He heard a strange noise, a rumble. Then he saw the sweeper coming towards him, jumping into his arms. That's strange, he thought, the sweeper's never done that before. Later he would say that at first he didn't really know what had happened, what he had done.

Of course he didn't. Nobody, not even the certified genius, had a way of knowing that the most unlikely of men had just created a global superclub.

1. RENEGADES AND CAVALIERS

The twentieth century was barely eight weeks old when eleven young men stepped out of a public house and onto a narrow alleyway in the heart of Munich. Like many of the lanes in this part of town, the old quarter, it was named for an ancient profession. Germans called it the *Schäfflergasse*, which told you that coopers once traded here.

We don't know if the men turned left or right. But it was getting late and cold on this February evening and they had no time to waste, so it seems safe to assume that they took the shorter route to their destination. In which case they turned left and then, after only a few steps, left again.

Many years later, people would say it was very fitting that exactly eleven men walked past the imposing Field Marshals' Hall and then the equestrian statue of the former Bavarian king Maximilian I in order to form Bayern Munich FC. People would also say it was typical that all of them either came from a middle-class background or even from affluent families . . . and that none of them was actually from Munich or even Bavarian.

Yes, in a way this would have been typical – but it wasn't quite like that. Otto Naegele, at twenty years of age one of the youngest men present, was a local boy. The same went for 24-year-old Arthur Ringler and the Wamsler boys, Fritz and Karl. The 28-year-old Franz

John, meanwhile, was the son of a simple mail clerk and worked as a photographer.

But it's true that the eleven men who walked side by side on this dark, cold day – 27 February 1900 – with the express purpose of forming a football club were an unusually colourful group of people. Two of them, Kuno Friedrich and Wilhelm Focke, came from as far away as Bremen, 470 miles to the north. Focke, his friends joked, had more talents and interests than da Vinci. Among other things, he was a painter, sculptor, poet and inventor and would one day be recognised as a pioneer of German aviation. We can assume he got along very well with Naegele, who was studying at the Academy of Fine Arts and would soon become a celebrated graphic designer.

Amazingly, there was an even more famous artist among the club's founding fathers, although he wasn't present on this February night. A few weeks earlier, in January 1900, seventeen men had signed a document that declared their willingness to join a new football club if and when certain events made its formation necessary. One of these men was Benno Elkan, a 22-year-old sculptor from Dortmund who is today best known as the man who built the Knesset Menorah, the large bronze candelabra that stands in front of the Israeli parliament in Jerusalem, as well as the life-sized cock statue that adorns White Hart Lane.

The existence of this document tells you that the formation of Bayern Munich was not a spur-of-the-moment decision. Franz John – as the oldest of the group, he was something like a leader by default – and the others had known for quite some time that they might have to take drastic measures if they wanted to keep the one thing alive that united this motley crew: their love of football.

It may seem strange in retrospect that these educated, creative, liberal, cosmopolitan and rather sophisticated young men were crazy about a simple, crude game that we have come to think of as the classic workingman's sport. However, in *fin-de-siècle* Germany, things were very different. While football was already enjoying its first golden age in England, where people paid money to watch games involving professional teams, German sport was dominated by *Turnen*.

The term is normally translated as 'gymnastics', but this is a bit simplistic. The mass movement, which *Turnen* became in Germany during the nineteenth century, went back to an educator named Friedrich Ludwig Jahn, to this day widely known as *Turnvater*, the father of *Turnen*. Jahn was a fervent nationalist. During the years of French occupation (most German-speaking regions were under French rule between 1794 and 1815), he became convinced that Germans had to seek more power and influence in Europe. On a political level, he felt, this meant the various German kingdoms, such as Prussia and Bavaria, needed to be united. On a more basic level, Jahn argued, Germans had to become more disciplined, organised and physically fit. He developed a system of exercises he called *Turnen*, after an ancient Germanic word for moving about.

At Jahn's first public exhibition – which he staged in June 1811 in Berlin – many activities indeed looked like modern gymnastics. But his followers also engaged in exercises we would today associate with track and field (such as running, throwing and jumping) or combat sports like wrestling and fencing. Jahn referred to it all as *Turnen* and he made no qualms about the fact he considered it not harmless, carefree sport but 'patriotic education to prepare for the war of liberation [from French rule]'.

During the ensuing decades, Jahn's fortunes and reputation – and those of his brainchild *Turnen* – would ebb and flow. In 1848, a group of men led by a Viennese actor formed a *Turnverein* in Munich, a gymnastics club. Two years later, the Bavarian authorities disbanded this club, because they suspected the gymnasts to be republican revolutionaries. But, over the following years, the idea of a unified German empire gained wide currency (and would become reality in 1871). Gradually, the gymnasts were rehabilitated. As early as 1860, the Munich *Turnverein* – or simply: TV – was re-formed.

Like all German clubs, this Munich TV, which would one day become known as 1860 Munich, was a non-profit organisation owned by its members and serving a local community, in this case a working-class area of Munich known as Giesing. Every citizen of good repute could join the club – and anyone could leave it. A few years later, in June 1879, four disgruntled gymnasts did just that and formed their own club: MTV 1879 (for *Männer-Turn-Verein*, men's gymnastics club).

MTV may have carried the T for *Turnen* prominently in its name, but that didn't mean the club prohibited other activities. In 1880, a few members suggested opening a fencing division and later in the same year, the club added a singing division and set up a choir. If you think a singing division is a strange thing for a club to have, imagine how surprised the MTV members must have been when, in 1897, someone put forward the motion to create a football division.

Football! The word alone was enough to drain all colour from the faces of Jahn's disciples. A teacher from Stuttgart, Karl Planck, had just published a book about this new sport in which he referred to the game as 'the English disease' and the players as 'foot louts'. The well-known pedagogue Otto Jaeger had written: 'I loathe the game, also because of the pitiful, crouching stance in which the players chase the ball.' The general consensus was that football was depraved because it was about competition rather than communion. As such, it was un-German. Playing the game amounted to an unpatriotic act.

This explains why those Germans who took to football despite all the raised eyebrows and warning words during these formative years were very often precisely the sort of freethinking, progressive young men with a rebellious streak who would follow Franz John into the night on a Tuesday in February 1900.

Otto Naegele, for instance, had been a member of what is generally considered the very first football team ever formed in Munich. It carried the unusual Latin name Terra Pila (*pila* means ball) and was set up by students and schoolboys in September 1896. When Terra Pila (whose members were so adventurous they also played baseball!) was dissolved only two years later, some players formed a new club. Others, like Naegele, went for a more obvious solution and joined an existing one: MTV 1879, or more precisely that club's still young football division.

Initially, everything was fine. MTV had a good football team, built around a young English goalkeeper called Dr Cushing and the noted all-round athlete Julius Keyl. But in 1899, players with some experience joined the club. One was Josef Pollack, the son of a Jewish merchant. Back in his native Freiburg, Pollack had founded one of the best clubs in southern Germany, Freiburg FC. The other was Franz John, who had played for one of the oldest clubs in Berlin before he relocated to Munich.

They weren't experienced simply because they had played football before. Rather, they had played regularly – and competitively. While MTV only played friendlies, just five or six per year, the game was more advanced and organised in other parts of the country. There were regional associations and even championships. As early as 1894, a match between the best team from Berlin (Viktoria 1889) and the strongest side in southern Germany (Hanau 1893) was supposed to produce a national champion. In the end, the match didn't happen, because Hanau couldn't afford to send the team to the capital, more than 300 miles away.

Still, German football was rapidly becoming more regimented during the last decade of the nineteenth century. In 1897, the Southern German Football Association was set up and began to schedule games for the large region between Frankfurt and Munich. Or rather, that was the plan. But not a single club from Bavaria joined the association. Although Munich had grown to become the third largest city in the entire country, after Berlin and Hamburg, it was lagging behind with regard to football.

Franz John was unhappy with this situation. He felt MTV had to join the association and began lobbying the club's members. 'I started my work,' he recalled a quarter of a century later. 'First isolated, private conversations with one or another member. Ideas and hints about how we would be in a totally different situation if MTV would be part of the Southern German Association. Just look at organised sports in cities that are nowhere near as big as Munich and you must realise that we need sporting development to make progress.'

He swayed some, but not many. John was told in no uncertain terms that the gymnasts at the club were vehemently opposed to joining an association that staged competitive games. In fact, there was already some unrest because Dr Cushing, the goalkeeper, had imported track spikes from England and suddenly many of the footballers had begun to do track and field as well. What's worse, they were having success. In the eyes of the gymnasts, racing against each other and the clock in order to win silverware or set records was English. In other words: morally corrupt.

That's when Franz John realised there might be only one way to resolve the conflict: forming his own club. Of course, he and like-minded members like Pollack could have simply left MTV and joined another club – for instance 1860 Munich, which had started its own football division just a few months earlier, in March 1899. But this club centred around *Turnen* as well. John feared he would always clash with reactionary, nationalist gymnasts. What was needed was a club only for football. (Half a century would pass before the club that Franz John eventually founded became a true multi-sports club by gradually adding various non-football divisions. More than twenty years after his death, in 1974, Bayern Munich even opened a division for – gymnastics.)

These considerations explain the existence of the document with seventeen signatures. As early as January 1900, John was testing the waters to see if he could find enough supporters to set up a new team. 'MTV's leaders got wind of these plans,' he later wrote, 'and a general meeting of the club's football division was convened for 27 February 1900, at the Bäckerhöfl restaurant.'

Almost immediately after the meeting had begun, John was taken to task and accused of dividing the club. A heated debate ensued. Many of the footballers were perfectly happy at MTV, among them the influential Julius Keyl, an outstanding player. They assured John that there was still a chance they would join the Southern German Association. John, however, replied the gymnasts would always boss the footballers around. At this point, a mutual friend of John and Keyl spoke up. 'It is obvious,' he said, 'that what these gentlemen want is to go and form their own club. So why don't we end the debate here and now and part in peace and as friends so that we'll have a good understanding in the future?'

John and his ten disciples grabbed their coats and left the room. He later said that one prominent club member yelled after them: 'Let them go, they will be back soon!' Then they stepped out into the darkness and made for Café Gisela on Fürstenstrasse, a restaurant some ten minutes away, not far from the Odeonsplatz, one of the two most famous and important squares in Munich. (The other is the Marienplatz, where Bayern traditionally celebrate their title wins.)

At 8.30 p.m., John opened what would turn out to be the foundation meeting of one of the biggest and most famous football clubs in the world. Quite a few formalities had to be followed, but it seems that the eleven men knew exactly what they wanted, because only three of them gave fairly brief speeches: John, Pollack and Paul Francke, a young man from Leipzig who went on to become the new club's first captain and player-manager. The only extended discussion, according to the minutes of the meeting, concerned the matter of money. (Characteristically, one is tempted to add.) Eventually, the men agreed on a monthly membership fee of one mark.

Surprisingly, the crucial matter of the club's name was settled swiftly and without much ado. As was common at the time, the men decided to name the club for the region it was based in. Such patriotic flourishes were popular, not least because they signalled footballers, always viewed with suspicion, were faithful subjects of the kaiser. A famous club from Berlin was called Preussen (Prussia) and soon a team based in Augsburg would be named Schwaben (Swabia).

It was all the latest rage to use Latin names. Clubs in Westphalia, Hesse or the Rhineland loved to call themselves Westfalia, Hassia or Rhenania, and there were countless clubs named Alemannia, Germania or Teutonia. So you would have expected John and the others to call their new club Bavaria (which is both English and Latin). However, that name was already taken by a team set up only a few months earlier. Maybe that's why they used the German word – Bayern.

Despite – or maybe because of – the fact that most of the eleven men who were now Bayern FC had come to Munich from places far away, the traditional Bavarian white and blue were chosen as club colours. Then, as if final proof was needed that a lot of behind-the-scenes planning had already gone into the creation of this new club, John informed the others that the municipal authorities would allow the team to play on a public field at Schyrenstrasse, just south of the river Isar. At 11.15 p.m., everybody went home.

If you feel like retracing the historic steps taken by the eleven club founders on that Tuesday all those years ago, you will run into a few problems. Neither Schäfflergasse nor Fürstenstrasse still carry these names. The house where the Bäckerhöfl restaurant used to be is long gone, not least because large parts of central Munich were completely destroyed by British bombs. Café Gisela, too, has disappeared almost without trace.

Amazingly, though, the club's very first pitch is still there – and it is still a municipal football field. These days it is used by local schools. Almost 115 years to the day after Bayern were formed, I visited. Since it was February, the trees lining the pitch were still without leaves. Under a bright but chilly sun, I was able to stand there and imagine it was 18 March 1900, the day Bayern played their first-ever game – against Munich FC, a club that traced its origins back to Terra Pila.

I allowed myself to imagine a group of young men, all with short hair, most sporting a moustache. They are wearing white knee-length trousers. Otto Naegele is in goal. Bayern are awarded a corner and

Paul Francke walks over to the flag to take it. He kicks the ball hard, hoping it will find one of his teammates in the penalty area. Somehow, either because Francke has powerful legs or because it's a very windy day, the ball carries and carries and suddenly ends up in the goal. Bayern win 5-2.

Clubs can be strange things. On the face of it, they are just a coalition of people whose names and faces change over the years. (Not to mention that in Germany, where nearly all clubs are member-owned, the number of people linked to a club can be huge. Today, Bayern Munich has more than 270,000 members and is thus the largest sports club in the world, ahead of Benfica from Lisbon.) And yet some clubs seem to lead a life of their own. They possess an identity – to avoid the esoteric term collective soul – that never really changes, no matter whom the members elect to be in charge or who those members are in the first place.

Paradoxically, the two men who had worked the hardest to form their own club both left Bayern Munich in 1903, after less than three years. Franz John returned to Berlin and his old club, VfB Pankow, while Josef Pollack emigrated to the United States. And yet the circumstances of Bayern's formation and the identities of the eleven founding fathers would resonate down the decades and shape the future of the club to an astonishing degree.

Bayern Munich would never cease being progressive, freethinking and independent – qualities for which the club paid a heavy price during the Nazi dictatorship. Bayern Munich would also remain a club that somehow attracted and united people from all sorts of places, not necessarily only from the city whose name it carried. (To this day, there is a widespread preconception that people from Munich support 1860 rather than Bayern. This may have been true once, but it no longer is, partly because of 1860's long and seemingly terminal decline.) And Bayern would never stop being open-minded and cosmopolitan – when John went back to Berlin in 1903, a Dutchman by the name of Willem Hesselink became the new club president.

While serving in this post, Hesselink obtained a doctorate in both philosophy and chemistry. This piece of trivia underlines another Bayern characteristic that hasn't really changed since day one: the club which was formed by artists and white-collar workers would forever tend to be more cultivated, educated and sophisticated than most of its rivals. No surprise that during the club's early years, only members who had completed secondary education were eligible for the first team. And this team was so well-dressed that Bayern quickly gained the first of many nicknames: the Cavaliers' Club.

Needless to say, Bayern's detractors have always tended to replace 'cultivated' with 'arrogant'. (Not necessarily a far-fetched term once you have heard Bayern's fans sing a popular terrace song which refers to 1860 supporters as 'peasants from Giesing'.) And indeed, another nickname the club garnered during its first decade was *Protzenklub* – the flaunters' club.

Finally, the team that came into being when a ragtag group of renegades walked out on another club would for more than one hundred years remain homeless – in more than one sense. The 5-2 win over Munich FC was the only official game the club played on the Schyrenstrasse pitch. The next five home matches were staged on Theresienwiese, the open space where the annual Oktoberfest is held. Then, in 1901, Fritz and Karl Wamsler's father, a rich factory owner, allowed Bayern to use a piece of land on Clemensstrasse, in the bohemian borough of Schwabing. For a handful of years, the club called this place their own ground, then began an odyssey around town that saw Bayern use eight different stadiums, none of which they owned. It wasn't until the Allianz Arena opened in 2005 that this situation finally changed.

This shiny arena, built for the 2006 World Cup, is so far on the outskirts of town, seven miles north of where Café Gisela used to be, that some people say it's not even in Munich any more. (That's not true, but it's undoubtedly quite a trek to get there.) It may be inconvenient, but somehow it's fitting, because Bayern also lack what other clubs like to call a spiritual home.

Since the late 1940s, Bayern's training pitches have been on Säbener Strasse in Giesing, right in the middle of a residential area. Later the club's headquarters moved there, too. The low, red-and-white main building – which looks like one of those functional state schools they used to build in the late 1960s – has almost become a Munich landmark and is dearly loved by all club employees, despite the fact it's long since become much too small for one of the world's biggest clubs. But although Franz Beckenbauer grew up just a twenty-minute walk from here, Giesing is traditional 1860 territory. Bayern only ended up here because, well, you need a roof over your head, don't you?

Oh, and there is another thing that Bayern have been right from the start: very, very good. Less than two months after its formation, the team demolished one of the oldest football clubs in town, Nordstern FC, by a score of 15-0. In September 1902, Bayern easily won their first-ever derby against 1860: 3-0. In fact, during those early years, the true Munich derby was the match between Bayern and MTV 1879, because 1860 didn't really stand a chance. (Between 1907 and 1912, Bayern won fourteen out of fifteen games against 1860.)

But there was one thing the fledgling club was not: rich. There were a few wealthy patrons such as Wamsler or Alfred Walter Heymel, a publisher who had inherited a fortune from his adoptive father and bestowed the first kit (sky-blue shirts and white shorts) upon the club. But, like everyone else, Bayern was an amateur club that generated revenue only through membership fees and gate money. Since the club didn't boast a particularly large number of members, not least because it only offered football, and didn't have its own ground, finances continued to be a problem.

That's why Bayern joined forces with the Munich Sports Club (MSC), then also based in Schwabing, in early 1906. MSC is now primarily known as a field hockey club, but back then it dabbled in next to everything that wasn't *Turnen*, from boxing to tennis. At one point, MSC boasted twenty-two individual divisions and could call itself the biggest sports club in Europe. MSC was so large that the club had enough money to lease a spacious area of land from the city. There was a nice football ground on it that would soon have the first covered grandstand in Munich. This ground could hold 1,000 spectators and there was even talk of floodlights so that teams could train in the evenings.

The ground was so enticing that Bayern approached MSC and suggested becoming that club's football division. MSC agreed to the deal, mainly because Bayern's first team was already regarded as a powerhouse around town. MSC even allowed Bayern to play under their own name. There was only one condition which wasn't negotiable: Bayern had to play in MSC's colours – white shirts and red shorts.

The alliance between the two clubs would last only about a dozen years, partly because football – and Bayern Munich – became so popular so quickly that the ground which at first had seemed huge would soon be too small. However, the colour change would prove to be permanent. People began to refer to Bayern's players as *die Rothosen*, the Red Shorts. It was eventually shortened to *die Roten* – the Reds. It is still the club's most widely-used nickname. (1860 are known as the Lions, after their club badge, or *die Sechziger*, after their year of foundation. However, in Munich itself people tend to simply distinguish between Reds and Blues.)

Bayern severed ties with MSC in 1919 and it was during the following years that the club acquired yet another nickname, this one darker, uglier and more ominous, because it hinted at things to come. Some people began to call Bayern *der Judenklub* – the Jews' club.

In the wake of World War One, anti-semitism was dramatically on the rise in Germany. In his award-winning book about Bayern's Jewish heritage, the writer Dietrich Schulze-Marmeling says that some clubs were 'denounced as Jews' clubs although the number of Jewish members is usually small. What counts is not their number but whether or not they hold down official functions at the club and wield influence.' At Bayern, this was certainly the case – in the years just before the Nazis came to power, three Jewish men in a row coached the team, with great success.

Then there was the president. In January 1919, a 35-year-old accountant by the name of Kurt Landauer was elected to this post. It was his second stint as president. Landauer had already run the club in 1913–14, when Bayern quickly needed someone to take over from the well-liked Angelo Knorr, who had been arrested for homosexuality (a criminal offence under German law at the time).

Landauer, who had joined Bayern as early as 1901 and used to keep goal for the reserve team, was a larger-than-life character. Born near Munich, he loved women, beer and roast pork. If he had been Catholic he would have made a picture-book Bavarian. But he wasn't, he was Jewish. And although he wasn't a religious man and didn't observe the practices of his faith, it was enough for Bayern to be termed a Jews' club.

The same was said of Eintracht Frankfurt, because three Jewish businessmen, owners of a large shoe factory, were that club's main benefactors and sponsors. This is noteworthy due to a twist of fate you could call absurd, ironic or even tragic, as you prefer. Thanks in no small part to Landauer's skills as a club leader, on 12 June 1932 Bayern played in the final for the national championship. Bayern's opponents were Eintracht Frankfurt. Barely seven months before the Nazis seized power in Germany, two Jews' clubs were the best football sides in the country.

As the example of the Dutch president (and star player and coach) Willem Hesselink shows, Bayern were never afraid to look abroad for help. This was not unusual for a German football club in the early years of the twentieth century, because everyone was aware they were playing an English sport and thus looked for British expertise to learn the finer points of the game. However, the extent to which Bayern Munich opened up to outside influences from very early on was astonishing – and would remain another constant.

In Nuremberg, by comparison, 100 miles north of Munich, another club formed in the year 1900 was about to become the biggest and best team in the land. But Nuremberg almost prided themselves on the fact that they didn't have a proper coach until the 1920s, arguing their players were so good that they didn't need to be told what to do. Bayern handled matters markedly differently. Under the aforementioned president Angelo Knorr, the club signed an English coach as early as August 1911.

The key word here is 'signed'. It's worth remembering that German football was completely amateur at this time and would remain so for decades to come. In fact, everything to do with money was considered taboo in German sport for so long that even today, when clubs make hundreds of millions and pay their players accordingly, being considered commercial is still the worst possible insult.

Although, as we shall see later, the number of exceptions is growing, German clubs as a rule are not individually owned, either by persons or by corporations, and since they are not companies they cannot be bought or sold. In Germany, sport is not part of the entertainment industry – or, for that matter, any other industry. It is a communal experience.

This is also one of the numerous reasons why there was no nationwide league in Germany until the 1960s. Only professional clubs could have shouldered the costs that came with sending squads across such a large country and only professional players would have been able to criss-cross the land on a regular basis. And so the question of what came to be known as the Bundesliga was forever intrinsically linked to the concept of professionalism. You couldn't have one without the other.

That's why the German game remained regional long after everyone else had started thinking big. Over the years, the rules, the scheduling, the number of teams involved and the names of divisions changed, but the basic concept remained the same from 1903, when the first official national champions were crowned, to 1963, when the Bundesliga at long last came into being. Each of the country's regions was split into a few divisions, the rough equivalent of county leagues. At the end of the regular season, the best teams from each of the divisions went through to either a play-off or a small tournament to determine the regional champion. Then the various regional champions met each other in knock-out rounds which culminated in a one-legged final for the national title.

Bayern came close to reaching the later nationwide stages in both 1910 and 1911, when they finished the season as the second-best team in all of southern Germany, behind only a fiendishly strong Karlsruher FV side. One of the head-to-head games between the two teams attracted an unheard-of crowd of 4,000 to Bayern's cosy ground – and earned the club a pile of money.

Now the question was: how to invest those funds wisely? President Knorr suggested signing a full-time, salaried coach for a trial period of one season. Why the trial period? Well, some clubs in the south had learned the hard way that not every Briton was automatically a dedicated sportsman. Some coaches from the place that spawned the game had, as Bayern's club historian Andreas Wittner put it, 'distinguished themselves through regular trips to the pub and by consuming excessive amounts of alcohol rather than through teaching basic football tactics'.

In August, Bayern poached a man with some pedigree, Karlsruhe's Rugby-born manager Charles Griffith. He wasn't the first foreigner (not even the first Englishman) to coach the team, but he took things to a whole new level. Griffith introduced training sessions on every working day of the week and had the club rent a gym during the winter months to allow indoor practices. He improved the players' stamina with running exercises and their strength by having them work out with weights. Soon, Bayern's deputy chairman Hans Tusch would laud the team for 'playing well and also being worthy of a club like ours in terms of discipline and sportsmanship'.

There was just one problem: the results. An absurd fluke defeat on the last day of the regular season cost Bayern first place in their county league. Without the prospect of lucrative knock-out games against well-known teams, Griffiths could no longer be paid and was let go as early as April 1912. However, a seed had been sown. Griffith taught Bayern that it was possible to remain an amateur club and still be professional about how you approached the game. The following year, Knorr's successor Kurt Landauer signed a coach even more famous than Griffith – the former Blackburn Rovers forward and English international William Townley, the first man to score a hat-trick in an FA Cup final.

Townley had already coached three different German clubs with great success and Landauer had high hopes for him. Bayern were the best team in Munich, one of the two or three best in Bavaria and among the seven or eight best in southern Germany. The next step, Landauer felt, was to be among the country's elite. It was by no means an unrealistic vision, as the club had already produced three internationals – the fleet-footed right-winger Max Gablonsky, centre-forward Fritz Fürst and goalkeeper Ludwig Hofmeister.

True, the German national team was still in its infancy, having played its first-ever game only in 1908, and amateurish in the least flattering sense of the word. (When Gablonsky made his debut against Belgium in May 1910 in Duisburg, only seven German players arrived in time for the kick-off. Four local players were culled from the crowd to make up the numbers. Germany lost 3-0.) But Bayern were definitely up and coming. Hofmeister, for instance, may have been good enough to play for Germany, but he wasn't good enough to play for his club. In 1910, the Austrian goalkeeper Karl Pekarna had joined Bayern. He was so talented that he had played professionally – not for any old continental team, but for Rangers in Glasgow. On the continent, where professionalism was illegal, he was forced to become an amateur again, but it was well known that a not insignificant amount of money changed hands before Pekarna donned Bayern's colours.

The club as a whole was healthy, too. In the 1913–14 season, Bayern had some 900 members (400 of them being juniors). Twelve senior teams and twenty youth teams were playing at various levels of organised football. The future seemed rosy. But whether or not Townley would have been able to deliver nationwide success with his fine first team, we'll never know. In the summer of 1914, the Great War broke out. Townley, suddenly an enemy, hurried home and Landauer, along with almost two-thirds of Bayern's members and players, went to fight for what he believed to be his country.

More than sixty members did not survive the four-year carnage, but Landauer did. He returned from the front in France having been made an officer and with two military decorations dangling from his broad chest. The war was lost and the kaiser forced to abdicate; the German Empire had collapsed. But, along with many other German Jews who had risked life and limb for a nation that grudgingly tolerated rather than accepted them, Landauer felt he had proved himself to be a proper German citizen. Little did he know that right-wing groups would soon blame defeat in the war on the Social Democrats and the Jews – with gruesome consequences. Or that his beloved Munich would gradually change from a liberal, artistic and pleasantly provincial city into a hotbed of fascism. Or that the entire country would become more and more dangerously hostile until there was only one retreat for him, only one place where he was respected, loved and protected: his club, Bayern Munich.

In January 1919, the members elected Landauer president again – and thus began Bayern's first golden age. Under his guidance, Bayern temporarily merged with another club (named after, of all people, that dreaded *Turnvater* – Jahn), once again in the misguided hope that this would lead to getting a ground of their own. In the summer, Landauer brought William Townley back to Munich, a daring move, considering the war had ended only a few months earlier. A year later, in another typically progressive and far-sighted move, the president took out accident insurance for all first-team players.

It was a good time to move forward, because something very strange had happened during the war: Germans lost interest in *Turnen* and went crazy for football. The last final in peacetime (Fürth vs Leipzig in Magdeburg) had attracted 6,000 spectators. The first final after the war (Nuremberg vs Fürth, played on 13 June 1920, in Frankfurt) was watched by a sell-out crowd of 35,000. When the match began, throngs of people were still queueing in front of the gates and touts were demanding 200 marks for a single ticket. Nobody had ever seen anything like it. Social reforms after the war, for instance the introduction of the eight-hour day, had made football the workingman's game.

And the workingman didn't merely watch it. The DFB (the German FA) – only one month older than Bayern, having been founded in January 1900 – was growing rapidly. In 1919, the association represented 3,100 clubs and 460,000 members. Only one year later, the numbers had risen to 4,400 and 760,000, respectively. The clubs organised under the DFB's umbrella fielded more than 20,000 individual teams in all age groups and at all levels.

One of those teams was Bayern's first XI. It would be too much to say the side struggled after the war, but it certainly stalled – the coveted Southern German title remained elusive. Where once Karlsruhe had dominated this part of the country, it was now Nuremberg that would acquire truly mythic status. How mythic, you ask? Well, the club was so much better than anyone else that people nicknamed it . . . The Club. (In 1925, the club – or rather: The Club – became *Rekordmeister*, an honorary title conferred on the team which has more championships to its name than any other. Nuremberg would proudly carry the epithet for more than six decades until you-know-who overtook them for good. Today, *Rekordmeister* is a widely used synonym for Bayern.)

What's more, a pesky little Munich club was challenging Bayern's local dominance. A team called Wacker Munich gave Landauer headaches for a few years. There were no two ways about it, he needed help from abroad again. In 1924, Bayern signed a Scottish-born coach by the name of James McPherson, about whom little seems to be known, except that he was fanatical about conditioning. (Some sources say he used to play for Newcastle United, but that isn't the case. There was a trainer called James McPherson at Newcastle, but it's not the same person. I suspect Bayern's McPherson must be the same coach who was in charge of Norway during the 1920 Olympics in Antwerp.) Under his stewardship, the first-team players began to resemble semi-pros. They were now paid expense money for games and even training sessions. Although the sums were modest, Munich's municipal archivist Anton Löffelmeier calculates that a first-team regular might have made as much as 150 marks per month through what was essentially his hobby, at a time when a worker's monthly wage came to 200 marks.

It was a typical Bayern Munich move – and, of course, a logical development – but the timing wasn't good. The DFB was run by an increasing number of stout conservatives and was about to vigorously clamp down on the budding professionalism. In fact, the governing body's stance was so strict it even sought to prohibit clubs from playing friendlies against professional teams. In Bayern's club magazine, Landauer ranted: 'Where will the German game end up if German teams are barred from competing with sides from England, Austria, Czechoslovakia and Hungary?' (All these countries had legalised professionalism or were about to.)

At the end of McPherson's first season as Bayern coach, the club celebrated its twenty-fifth birthday with a spectacular party held at the German Theatre, a location so posh that *Kicker* magazine marvelled: 'Never before has a football club become the talk of town with such a brilliant event.' Bayern's anniversary publication said of Landauer: 'We owe the esteem in which we are held at home and abroad to his enormous workrate.'

The club's members and supporters were also treated to a spectacular, almost exotic, event on the football pitch – a game against a club side from South America. In early May, Bayern hosted Argentine champions Boca Juniors, based in Buenos Aires, the first team from the country to set foot on European soil. Manuel Seoane put the visitors ahead, but Georg Hutsteiner equalised before the break for a final score of 1-1. During their three months in Europe, Boca Juniors played seven games in Germany. This was the only one they failed to win.

Bayern's most eagerly awaited anniversary present, however, arrived one year late. In 1926, the team broke Nuremberg's stranglehold on German football, winning the regional Bavarian league two points ahead of the reigning champions. McPherson's team then also went on to win the Southern German championship in a small round-robin tournament ahead of Fürth. For the first time, Bayern would be playing on the really big stage – the final rounds for the national title. However, the joy was short-lived. In the round of 16, Bayern were beaten by a small club few people in Munich had ever heard of, Fortuna Leipzig. It was such a shock that many Bayern members called the radio station after hearing the result to make sure it hadn't been a mistake.

The next coach who tried to take the club all the way was another foreigner: Leo Weisz. The Hungarian was signed from local rivals Wacker Munich and guided Bayern to their second Southern German championship in 1928. In May, seven weeks before the nationwide knock-out rounds began, Bayern played a high-profile friendly against West Ham. The Hammers weren't one of England's best teams at that time, but they did play in the first division (and were, of course, fully professional), so Bayern's 3-2 win amounted to a shock result.

Unfortunately, it wasn't the last stunning scoreline of the season. Bayern progressed to the semi-finals of the national championship, where they met Hamburg. The game was staged at a neutral ground, in Duisburg, and was tied at 1-1 after forty-five minutes. In the second half, though, the roof fell in on Bayern. The team's 31-year-old goalkeeper Alfred Bernstein broke his fingers and, since it was the days before substitutions were allowed, defender Emil Kutterer went between the sticks. Bayern lost 8-2.

As his name suggests, Bernstein was the son of a Viennese Jew. His mother, though, was German. This probably saved his life, because while he would suffer considerable harassment during the dark times ahead, Bernstein would avoid deportation, agony and a near-certain death in one of the concentration camps. In contrast to almost everyone named Landauer.

2. THE MAN WHO INVENTED BAYERN

When non-Germans, particularly those raised on the British game, become interested in German football and ask a few questions, there are a number of things that rarely fail to amaze or confuse them. We have already mentioned some of them, such as the absence of owners, the amateur ethos or the fact that the Bundesliga is of comparatively recent origin. Which, on a related note, also means you must not substitute 'national championship' with the more common English 'league title'. Schalke, for instance, are seven-time German champions but haven't won a single league title, as their glory years predate the formation of the Bundesliga.

Another surprising fact is that when this nationwide league, the Bundesliga, at last came into being, Bayern Munich were not admitted to it. Finally, non-German fans usually wonder why there was a 37-year gap between the club's first national championship and the second – rather unusual for a member of the small group of really, really big European clubs.

It has given rise to the popular misconception that Bayern weren't an important club until they somehow got lucky and were gifted the golden generation around whom the great team of the 1970s was built. In fact, even many Germans were – and maybe are – not fully aware of the true story. When I grew up, in the 1970s and 1980s, we all took it for granted that 1860 were the big, tradition-laden club in Munich, while Bayern were just nouveau-riche Johnny-come-latelies.

Nobody told us that this was nonsense. Nobody told us there was a reason for Bayern's long, lean years in the wilderness. Nobody told us the Nazis had almost destroyed the best club in the land.

Landauer signed the first of the truly legendary coaches in Bayern's club history in 1930. Giving the reader his name is not as easy as it should be, because he went by many. He was born in Austria as Richard Kohn. In Barcelona, where he had a brief and disastrous stint as a coach, they knew him as Jack Domby. Most Bayern fans refer to him as Richard Dombi or Little Dombi. The confusion stems from the numerous nicknames the man picked up during his playing days. 'Little' on account of his lack of height and 'Dombi' came during his time in Budapest.

Nearly all sources claim this epithet stands for 'eminence', but it actually stems from the Hungarian word *domb*, meaning hill. *Dombi* is simply an affectionate term for a short, chubby person. Regardless of its meaning, he presumably preferred to be known as Dombi, because the name Kohn marked him out as a Jew.

Reading contemporary accounts, it often strikes you how modern many of the things Dombi did and said still sound. In 1932, he told a reporter: 'My main concern is that we always train with the ball and as match-like as possible. When we practise heading or trapping the ball, it's always done under pressure, because that's how it will be during a game.' When Bayern landed Dombi, they didn't just get a coach. Many years later, a club publication said: 'Never had there been a coach who dedicated his time to the club as completely as Dombi. He was coach, physio, masseur, general manager and organiser – all in one person.' He was also a good judge of talent. From one of his former clubs, VfR Mannheim, he lured an immensely talented kid to Munich – Oskar Rohr, who had barely turned eighteen.

In Dombi's second season, Bayern reached the final for the 1932 championship of southern Germany in Stuttgart. The opponents were Eintracht Frankfurt. At half-time, a strangely unfocused Bayern team were trailing 2-0. During the interval, Dombi gave his players a mouthful. Then captain Conrad 'Conny' Heidkamp stood up and said he couldn't wait to see their opponents' faces when Bayern equalised and then added a few more goals to win it.

It was indeed a different Bayern team that came out for the second half. Now Dombi's men dominated the game – but failed to score. The referee denied them what the players felt to be not one but two obvious penalties. Then, ten minutes from time, Frankfurt's defender Franz Schütz blocked an Oskar Rohr shot with his hand. Again the referee waved play-on. A group of incensed Bayern fans invaded the pitch – and hundreds of neutrals followed them. Bayern's right-back Sigmund Haringer later remembered how the fans lifted him and his teammates up and carried them around the pitch on their shoulders, as if to say they were the moral winners of this game. 'From up there I could see how the referee was knocked over the head with a chair,' he said. 'Then we found ourselves back in the dressing room.'

The match was abandoned and Frankfurt were awarded the title. However, that wasn't the end of the story. Both teams had qualified for the nationwide knock-out rounds and both did Southern Germany proud. In the semi-finals, Bayern defeated Nuremberg while Frankfurt prevailed over Schalke. 'So it was going to be a restaging of the battle of Stuttgart,' Haringer wrote. 'We didn't mind, while Eintracht let it be known from Frankfurt they wouldn't have wanted any other opponent. Like us, they felt the aborted Stuttgart fight should be finished.' Only now there was a much bigger prize at stake – the national championship.

The final was played in Nuremberg, roughly halfway between Munich and Frankfurt. It tells you a lot about how massive football had become in the fourteen years since the end of the war – and how popular Bayern were – that Dombi tried to shield the squad from journalists and fans alike by keeping the name of the team's hotel a secret. When the players were told to get off the train to Nuremberg in Fürth, a couple of stations early, they scratched their heads. 'We looked like right charlies,' Haringer recalled, 'when we were put into taxis that were waiting for us and eventually, after a great detour, stopped in front of a hotel right next to Nuremberg main station. It was a shrewd ploy and it took the fanatics and the press a long time to find us.'

Thousands of those fanatics travelled from Munich to Nuremberg on special trains or in private cars. But not everyone could afford the trip. The Great Depression was already in its third year (and driving more and more desperate voters into the arms of a fascist party called the NSDAP). Many Bayern supporters had lost their jobs, which is why the club gave away 500 tickets and organised accommodation for the unemployed. But there was still the question of transportation. It was solved in a spectacular manner. On the day before the game, at six o'clock in the morning, 421 Bayern fans straddled their bicycles, while a club representative held a brief speech, reminding them to behave well in Nuremberg. Then they took off on a 105-mile journey under a hot summer sun – and without any gears.

The final was played on a Sunday, 12 June. Barely one year later, the Nazis would hold the first of their huge annual Nuremberg Rallies just 700 yards away and use the stadium where the two Jews' clubs faced each other for Hitler Youth parades. But when the 1932 final kicked off at 4 p.m., nobody saw any of this coming.

Technically, Nuremberg's ground held 50,000 people, but contemporary accounts say close to 60,000 were on hand. One of them was Kurt Landauer, who watched from the sidelines, hoping the players would finally prove what he had been saying all along – that his club was the best in the country.

It was a tense, close game. But after only ten minutes, Bayern captain Heidkamp turned towards Haringer and said: 'Berge will win this alone.' He was referring to right-winger Josef Bergmaier, a 27-year-old Munich lad who was playing the game of his life. On thirty-five minutes, Bayern won a corner. The ball came to Bergmaier and his shot whistled past Frankfurt's goalkeeper Ludwig Schmitt. Defender Hans Stubb, standing on the line, instinctively raised his arms and punched the ball clear with both fists. This time not even the most myopic of referees could deny Bayern a penalty for handball. Young Oskar Rohr stepped up. Schmitt guessed the right corner, but Rohr put the ball just inside the right-hand post, out of the diving goalkeeper's reach.

Now the going got rough. Bayern's veteran left-half Ernst Nagelschmitz came off with an injury before the interval, seemingly unable to continue. In those days, it would have forced Bayern to finish the game with ten men. Nagelschmitz had joined the club in 1915, when he was thirteen. This match was his 378th game for Bayern. He would be damned if he watched the rest of it from the bench. Nagelschmitz gritted his teeth and came out with the rest of the team for the second half.

With fifteen minutes left, Bergmaier played the ball into the box and into the path of Franz Krumm. The forward feinted a cross, then cut inside, which wrong-footed Stubb. From ten yards out, Krumm curled the ball into the far corner with his left foot to make it 2-0 and put the match beyond doubt.

When the final whistle sounded, hundreds of delirious fans invaded the pitch and again carried the Bayern players on their shoulders. Even the neutrals cheered the new champions, leading *Kicker* magazine to remark that rarely before 'has a non-partisan crowd showered a German champion with such applause'. One of the Frankfurt supporters who had followed Eintracht to the final later complained that 'the game wasn't played at a neutral ground. There were Munich supporters from all parts of Bavaria and the majority of Nuremberg folk sided with Bayern, too. At the ground and on our way back home, we were greeted by taunts all the time. I think if we had won, those hotheads would've beaten us to a pulp.'

Munich, meanwhile, went bonkers. Tens of thousands welcomed the players home, who travelled around the town on open, horse-drawn carriages. The mayor received the team and lauded them not only for their sporting success but also for 'exemplary fairness'. Haringer was exaggerating only slightly when he later said that the celebrations lasted for two full weeks. The city loved this club.

Or did it? It's only with the benefit of hindsight that we know there must have been many, many people in Munich who clenched their fists at the sight of a Jewish president and a Jewish coach being cheered by the masses. One of those was a failed Austrian painter who lived on Prinzregentenplatz, less than three miles east of Landauer's home. His name was Adolf Hitler.

In the general election in November 1932, Hitler's party, the NSDAP, won a third of the votes. Even though the Nazis themselves considered the result a disappointment (Joseph Goebbels, the future minister of propaganda, used the word 'hiding' in his diaries), it led to Hitler being appointed chancellor in January 1933. While most people still believed the popularity of the openly anti-semitic and violent NSDAP was just a brief episode that would be corrected in one of the next elections, the Nazis had no intention of keeping even a pretence of democracy alive once this system had got them into power. Within weeks, the country was run by a dictatorial, brutal and racist regime.

In March 1933, Landauer stepped down as Bayern president. Otto Beer, a Jewish draper and the head of Bayern's famous youth set-up, followed suit. Both were trying to act before the party ordered the club to remove all Jews from official posts. It gave Bayern a little bit of breathing space to find out how to deal with the new situation. (Five weeks later, Landauer also lost his job at a Munich publishing house.) Dombi, meanwhile, left the country and joined Grasshoppers in Zurich, Switzerland.

At the end of the season, Oskar Rohr followed him. By all accounts, he didn't have political reasons for doing so, it's just that he held Dombi in high esteem – and dreamed of playing professional football. Over the previous years, there had always been talk about a professional league in Germany, but Rohr knew that now – with the Nazis in power – it would never happen. Felix Linnemann had been made head of the DFB and he was a fervent advocate of amateurism.

Today we know that Landauer and the others should have followed Dombi's example and left the country. But only one of Landauer's five siblings did so. His sister Henny went to Palestine with her husband

and two kids as early as 1934. The rest of the family stayed. Like many other German Jews, the Landauers genuinely loved the country and considered it their home. What's more, they truly believed their fellow countrymen would come to their senses soon and knock this madman Hitler off his pedestal. Finally, their lives had been made unpleasant, even dangerous, but they didn't feel they had to fear for them.

Little did they know that the only reason they were still fairly safe, for a few years, was that the Nazis had grandiose plans for the 1936 Olympics and didn't want to risk boycotts by being portrayed abroad as the monsters they were. But the mask soon fell. Otto Beer, his wife and his children were murdered in 1941. All of Kurt Landauer's siblings who had decided not to leave Europe – three brothers and a sister – lost their lives in concentration camps or on the way there.

Even Oskar Rohr was persecuted. He was called 'a traitor to his country' and 'a gladiator who sells himself abroad' in print. Having won the Swiss cup with Grasshoppers, he moved to France and signed for Racing Strasbourg. In 1937, Rohr won the Golden Boot and took his side to the cup final. But three years later, German troops invaded France and soon there was nowhere left for Rohr to go. He spent a month in prison and two more in a concentration camp, then he was sent to the Eastern Front to die for his *Führer*. (He didn't. A pilot from Munich recognised the former Bayern player and helped him get home during the last weeks of the war.)

In November 1938, Kurt Landauer was arrested and brought to the concentration camp in Dachau, ten miles north of Munich. He was let go after one terrible, degrading month, presumably because he was a decorated World War I veteran. In any case, Landauer now realised there was no future for him in his country. He tried to get a passage to the United States, but when that didn't work out he went to Geneva in Switzerland in May 1939, less than four months before Germany invaded Poland and started World War II.

By that time, the club Landauer had built and turned into the best in the land was no longer the best team in Munich, let alone in Bavaria. A few of the 1932 heroes were still wearing Bayern's colours, such as the great Ludwig Goldbrunner, perhaps the most famous player of the club's early history. There was the incredibly fast left-winger Wilhelm Simetsreiter. There was even a young, budding star – the future club legend Jakob Streitle. But they all knew that the heart had been ripped out of their club. Seven years after winning the national championship, Bayern Munich finished the last season before another war, 1938–39, in a lowly seventh place in the Bavarian league, six points behind table-topping Schweinfurt, five points behind 1860.

The club itself never questioned the reason behind this downfall. When Bayern celebrated their next jubilee, in 1950, the official publication looked back upon the years following 1933 and said: 'The club has always held the opinion that any respectable person, regardless of race or religion, could find a place in sport. Suddenly, this basic principle was stripped of its justification by government orders. Now there were race laws and the Aryan paragraph. Many old and loyal members left.' (The so-called Aryan paragraph was a clause that excluded minority groups such as the Jews – 'non-Aryans' in the vocabulary of the times – from membership of most organisations or societies.) Many young members left, too. Under a new rule, boys under the age of fourteen could only play football in the Hitler Youth, not in clubs. At the stroke of a pen, Bayern lost a sizeable part of the famous youth set-up carefully built by Otto Beer.

Meanwhile, 1860 Munich were on the up. In 1941, the Lions won the Bavarian league and reached the nationwide final rounds. In 1942, they lifted the precursor of the German FA cup against Schalke, the club's first real piece of silverware. In 1943, 1860 reached the quarter-finals of the national championship.

Perhaps it's a bit too simple to say that 1860 collaborated and were rewarded for being run by stout Nazis, while Bayern, always suspect due to the club's long history of Jewish and foreign influences, were punished for trying to stay independent for as long as possible. But it's certainly not far from the truth. The journalist Frank Linkesch has pointed out that 'a lot more players from Bayern were sent to the front line than from their local rivals'. Josef Bergmeier and Franz Krumm, the good friends who had linked up for the second goal in the 1932 final, both died in the same Russian city in March 1943, just four days apart.

In his study of football during the so-called Third Reich (*Fussball unterm Hakenkreuz* – football under the swastika), the historian Nils Havemann quotes statements from Emil Ketterer that send shivers down your spine. Ketterer, who had joined the NSDAP as early as 1923, served as 1860's chairman from 1936 until the end of the war. In February 1941, he reminded Munich's mayor Karl Fiehler (an even more committed Nazi than Ketterer, if that was at all possible) that many 1860 members had been amongst Hitler's original followers. He proudly added: 'And in contrast to other clubs, Jews never rose to the surface.' No prize for guessing which other club he meant.

If Bayern's drawn-out struggle with the Nazis had been a boxing match, you would have to say the club ducked and weaved until it was leaning on the ropes. In May 2016, the German magazine *Der Spiegel* would publish a piece that argued Bayern's opposition to the regime has been vastly exaggerated, citing as an example the fact that the club introduced an Aryan paragraph as early as 1935. While it's true that Bayern had their share of fascists like every other institution, this interpretation ignores what happened behind the scenes of the club.

The adoption of the Aryan paragraph and the fact that Landauer stepped down quickly bought Bayern valuable time. It meant, for instance, that the club could appoint a new president without party interference. The members elected Siegfried Herrmann. He was not only a good friend of Landauer's but also the man who – ten years earlier and in his role as a high-ranking member of the police force – had enforced the ban on public speaking which the Bavarian government had slapped Hitler with. So Herrmann was certainly not a person the Nazis would trust; and he was followed by a few other men about whom the party was not totally convinced. Amazingly, and in contrast to the majority of German teams, Bayern managed to avoid having a truly tried-and-trusted Nazi in charge until 1943, when the dissenting voices in the club were finally silenced.

But even then Bayern did not forget the man who had taken them to the top. In November 1943, the team played a friendly in Zurich against a Swiss select XI (needless to say, German sides could only play in occupied or in neutral countries). Kurt Landauer watched the game from the stands. According to Conny Heidkamp, the captain of the 1932 team and at that time Bayern's player-manager, the German secret police instructed the team to not acknowledge Landauer's presence in any shape or form. But the players ignored those thinly-veiled threats. After the final whistle, they walked over to the grandstand and applauded their former president.

In a German made-for-television film which premiered in late 2014, the Landauer character says at one point that 'Bayern saved my life yet again' through this moving – and bold! – gesture. It might be true. Landauer was living in constant fear of being deported back to Germany by the Swiss. Maybe the events of the day, the players showing their reverence despite the overt presence of none-too-pleased secret German police, did indeed help Landauer's cause. He was allowed to stay in Geneva indefinitely.

Seventeen months later, Hitler put a bullet through his own head and another stupid, bloody war was over and lost.

We don't know what Kurt Landauer thought and felt when he stepped off the train in Munich in the summer of 1947. But it seems safe to assume his heart sank. Half of the city he loved so much lay in tatters. The old town, where Franz John and his stalwarts had decided to form FC Bayern all those years ago, was even worse off. Nine out of every ten buildings had been destroyed.

We also don't know why Landauer came back at all. He possessed papers that allowed him to move to the United States, so he must have made preparations to leave Europe. It would have been the natural thing to do. Very few of the Jews who had survived the Holocaust through emigration moved back to Germany. In contrast to political dissidents who were now returning to help build democratic foundations, most

Jews just couldn't go back to a place where they would never be able to look anyone in the face without wondering if this person might have tortured or killed friends and family members.

But Landauer, who had lost three brothers and a sister, went back to Munich. Charlotte Knobloch, president of the city's Jewish community since 1985, believes there were two reasons.

'His love for his home won the upper hand,' she says. 'And his love for sport, for Bayern.' She adds: 'As it turned out, he made the right choice and he helped the club a lot.'

All clubs were in bad shape. There was no money, no equipment, little food and few places to play. Bayern and 1860 had shared the Grünwalder Stadion ground (named after the street that runs along the East Stand) since 1926. It was not an ideal solution for Bayern. Everyone in town referred to the ground as the *Sechzgerstadion*, 60's stadium, because it was built and owned by 1860 before the club was forced to sell it to the city for financial reasons in the late 1930s. Still, the Grünwalder Stadion was the only ground in town large enough for a big club, so it had gradually become Bayern's home. Now it was a ruin. In 1943, Royal Air Force attacks had destroyed the main stand and a terrace. The pitch was littered with bomb craters.

However, all these things could be overcome with determination and hard work. A bigger problem was the US military forces occupying southern Germany. They were suspicious of sports or gymnastics clubs and considered them to have been breeding grounds for militaristic, anti-democratic leanings (an idea not wholly unfounded). They were reluctant to grant the clubs access to public fields or allow them to organise games.

Thus Landauer's unexpected return was a stroke of luck for Bayern. Having a man with his background at the helm greatly helped the club in its dealings with the authorities. It wasn't just the fact that he, as a Jew, represented the Nazi regime's victims and enemies that made him so valuable. He was also still a force of nature – a man who made things happen.

In August 1947, he was elected Bayern's president once more and immediately wrote a letter to the municipality in which he assured the administration that 'in accordance with the club's traditions' Bayern would gladly assist the authorities. Put differently, Landauer promised his club would help spread democracy, tolerance and open-mindedness. Surely the city would support such a noble endeavour rather than hamper it? In 1948, he got what he wanted – the training ground on Säbener Strasse in Giesing, where Bayern reside to this day, a short walk from the Grünwalder Stadion.

But there were some things Landauer didn't achieve. When organised football slowly got back on its feet in Germany, the game remained regional and not fully professional. Yes, players were finally allowed to receive money for their services, but a maximum-wage system was put into place: clubs could pay a footballer no more than 320 marks per month. (In 1950, the average monthly wage in West Germany was 263 marks.)

Maybe it was a good thing that Landauer's lobbying for unrestricted professionalism came to nothing. Because something else that didn't work out as planned was the football. During the 1949–50 season, Bayern celebrated the 1,000th win in the club's history (a 3-1 victory against FSV Frankfurt in April), but this was a rare high. The team finished in a dismal thirteenth place in the Oberliga Süd, one of the five regional leagues that now formed the top level of the pyramid.

Even the old tricks didn't work any more. In the summer, Bayern became one of the first German teams after the war to sign an English coach. His name was David Davison. Just a few months later, in November 1950 and with the team again hovering only two points above the drop zone, Davison downed a few pints too many, became involved in a pub brawl and was fired.

It was also becoming obvious that Jakob Streitle, as great a defender as he was, couldn't carry the team alone. It would take some time before the once-fabled Bayern youth set-up could churn out talent again. Until then, the club's fans had to display two character traits that didn't come naturally to them – patience and humility.

And they had to bide their time without the man who – to quote the tagline for the film about his life – 'invented Bayern Munich'. In April 1951, at the club's annual general meeting, Landauer ran for president again. And lost. There are numerous theories why and how it happened. In the film, there is a moment when the Conny Heidkamp character tells Landauer: 'In the best case, you'll be the club's eternal bad conscience. And in the worst case, too. Now they cheer you because they need you. But one day they will hate you for it.' Maybe there's some truth to this, maybe Landauer's larger-than-life presence at the club had become awkward, an unbearable reminder of the Nazi years.

However, this is not too likely. Landauer had already announced he would step down for good in 1952. If he was no longer wanted at the club, seeing out this one year would have been a very elegant solution for everyone involved. So maybe he had quite simply stepped on too many toes. Landauer wasn't a born diplomat. He could be gruff and pig-headed. He was sixty-six years old and had been running the club for sixteen of these in three stints. Many members active in the handball division that Bayern had set up a few months after the end of the war attended the meeting and voted for their own candidate, who was younger and more popular.

Still, the defeat hit Landauer hard. He went into a huff – until the club honoured him a few months later for fifty years of membership. For the remaining ten years of his life, Landauer did what he'd always done: in one capacity or another he worked for the club he loved so dearly. He died four days before Christmas 1961, in Schwabing, two miles north of Café Gisela, where Bayern had been founded.

Maybe he died safe in the knowledge there were finally some promising kids in the club's youth teams again. Bayern had eventually managed to find a worthy successor to Otto Beer. Running the youth set-up now was a man called Rudi Weiss, a former player whose career had been cut short by a torn cruciate ligament. While his day job was working as a lawyer, his true gift was an unerring eye for talent. Perhaps Weiss had told Landauer about a Giesing boy called Beckenbauer. Or about the goofy kid from crazy town.

3. BARRED FROM THE BUNDESLIGA

The place has gone by many names. Sanatorium is a nice one. Hospital sounds good, too. Mental asylum less so. After the war, people didn't tend to be squeamish and had never heard of political correctness. So they simply called it the madhouse.

The madhouse stood in Haar, a small town less than ten miles east of Munich. It was a large institution – almost 3,000 patients could be treated there. Consequently, it was one of the biggest employers in the area. Many people moved to Haar because they found work in the sanatorium. Two of them were Josef and Maria Maier. She was a nurse, he worked as an office administrator.

The place was so big it had its own butchery. Sometimes the kids of the employees would be given a pig's bladder to play with. You could inflate the bladder using lung power and then tie it up with a string. It bounced like crazy and, depending on how many kids kicked it, rarely lasted longer than an hour. But for this one hour it felt almost like a real football.

That's why the Maiers' two young sons liked to go to the butchery – until 1950. That Christmas, the older of the two was given a proper football. The younger one received a shiny, expensive watch. He stared at it for a few seconds, then he broke into tears. He wanted a football, too.

Finally, his older brother agreed to a swap. Sepp Maier grinned and cradled the ball.

A year later, not long after Bayern's president Kurt Landauer was voted out of office, Sepp Maier stood on the meadow in front of his home, where he and his friends had their kickabouts. He looked at the clothes poles they had been using as goals and decided they would no longer do.

Maier and his friends broke into a nearby sawmill and made off with enough timber to build two goals. On their way back home they ran into Maier's father. He furrowed his brow but figured it was better not to ask any questions. Then he helped the small boys carry the building materials to the meadow. This was a mistake. A neighbour saw them and reported Maier's father to the police for wood theft. He lost his job at the sanatorium and was unemployed for four long years.

It was the first but certainly not the last time that goalposts played an important role in Sepp Maier's life.

Franz Beckenbauer's father didn't like football very much. You couldn't earn money playing it, so what was the point? Franz once called him 'a contrary, proud man'. In fact, he was so contrary that he went to work on 6 July 1954. Hardly anyone else in Munich did that. The shops were closed on this Tuesday, children didn't have to go to school. Two days earlier, West Germany had won the World Cup in Berne, Switzerland – a triumph so unexpected and momentous that the players who defeated favourites Hungary in the final remain the most famous and revered team in German football history.

More than 300,000 people filled the streets of downtown Munich to catch a glimpse of the players as they paraded the trophy around town. Traffic stopped completely. The coach carrying the players' wives got stuck on Marienplatz and couldn't move an inch either way, the square was so packed with people. Franz Beckenbauer, not yet nine years old, had walked with his mother Antonie all the way from

Giesing to the centre of town to see the men who would go down in history as the Heroes of Berne (Beckenbauer's mother always saved money by not taking the tram).

One of those heroes was a Bayern player. Left-back Hans Bauer had joined the club from local rivals Wacker in 1948, probably figuring his chances of enjoying success were better at Bayern. And didn't the World Cup prove him right? True, he'd made only two appearances at the tournament and wasn't in the side which overcame a two-goal deficit in the final against the best team in the world to lift the Coupe Jules Rimet. (Which, Beckenbauer thought while watching the team from the roof of a wooden shack, was a lot smaller than he had imagined.) But Bauer was still on top of the world. Standing on the balcony of the city hall, he waved and smiled at the masses below. He heard the mayor say how he was particularly proud 'that a Munich boy has been a member of the German expedition – Bayern player Hans Bauer'. Oh, how the people cheered!

Little did Hans Bauer know that the coming months would turn into a footballing nightmare – the worst season in Bayern Munich's history. Just ten months after being a Hero of Berne, Bauer would be a member of the only Bayern team ever to be relegated. Why and how this happened, nobody really knew.

After only three wins from the first fourteen games, the club fired their coach and the former players Bert Moll and Jakob Streitle took over the team. Initially, it seemed to steady the ship. By February, Bayern had climbed to within three points of safety. But suddenly they just couldn't win any more. Bauer, who ran a petrol station from early in the morning until late afternoon on every day of the week, was asked to play up front instead of at the back. It didn't make a difference. Nothing worked.

Things got so bad that Willi Knauer, who had joined Bayern from 1860 and was thus an easy target for disgruntled spectators, lost the plot and kicked a ball at the Bayern fans in the stands. But of course they weren't to blame. Quite the contrary. Although no Bayern team had ever endured such a terrible season (and none would ever again), the club still drew bigger crowds than everyone else in the Oberliga Süd. Over 15,600 fans came to every home game. Champions Offenbach attracted only 12,500 and runners-up Reutlingen a mere 8,900. But you don't get points for the loyalty of your support and so Bayern dropped to the second tier in May 1955.

The fans kept coming. In late February 1956, an amazing crowd of 30,000 filled the Grünwalder Stadion to watch Bayern take on Freiburg FC (not the club which later played in the Bundesliga but the team co-formed by Bayern's founding father Josef Pollack). At the end of the season, both teams won promotion to the Oberliga Süd. The Munich-based national newspaper *Süddeutsche Zeitung* said: 'With this sort of performance, gentlemen, you would have never been relegated in the first place.'

A cursory glance at the club's changing fortunes during the 1950s will inform the reader that Bayern were rarely more than just an average team in the Oberliga Süd during the next years, usually finishing somewhere in no man's land. And yet the club lifted its second major title during this period, winning the DFB-Pokal in the year after bouncing back from the second division. This needs some explaining.

In England, the domestic cup has a rich tradition and mystique. The trophy is coveted, the games hugely popular. However, this hasn't always been the case on the continent. In the mid-1950s, for example, countries like Italy, Sweden or Austria had stopped holding such a competition altogether. In Germany, there had been no domestic cup for club sides until 1935, when the leading Nazi sports official Hans von Tschammer und Osten set it up, mainly to have some action during the close season. That's why the cup bore his name – Tschammerpokal – until the DFB revived the competition seven years after the end of the war and renamed it DFB-Pokal.

So you have to say the cup simply lacked tradition in Germany and thus wasn't taken awfully seriously by a lot of people until the following decade. The scheduling could also be a problem. In what is normally referred to as the 1956–57 season, for instance, the competition began in January 1957 at the regional level and ended in December 1957. You can almost understand why Bayern's board considered not taking part, figuring the cup wasn't worth the travel expenses. However, the Austrian coach Willibald Hahn persuaded the club officials to give it a try and register the team. It turned out to be a very good move for the club – and for Hahn, who went on to win the only title of his entire coaching career.

It was hard work, though. In the first round, Bayern needed a replay to get past second-divison Neu-Isenburg, a town five miles south of Frankfurt. In the third round, against a very strong Offenbach team, Bayern won in extra time. The fourth round went to another replay and in the semi-final, it was extra time yet again.

But Bayern kept winning and the fans kept coming. Some 24,000 supporters saw the semi-final against Saarbrücken even though it was played on a depressing November day. Almost as many travelled to Augsburg, fifty miles west of Munich, for the final against Fortuna Düsseldorf on 29 December 1957.

Under ordinary circumstances, Fortuna would have gone into the game as favourites. At the time of the final, the team were in fourth place in the fiendishly strong Oberliga West, ahead of national champions Borussia Dortmund. Fortuna had also beaten a strong side in the semis, Hamburg. But these weren't ordinary circumstances. The evening before the game, the Fortuna players watched a Western, *Night Passage*, starring James Stewart. Then they went to bed. When they woke up the next morning, they couldn't believe their eyes. Heavy snowfall throughout the night had painted the city and the pitch white.

Bayern's midfielder Kurt Sommerlatt, who had just joined the club from his native Karlsruher SC and was hoping to win the cup for the third year running, predicted this would give his team an edge – and he was proved right. On a tricky surface, Bayern dominated the game and created many chances. But they all went begging.

With only ten minutes left on the clock, the game was still scoreless. Then the ball reached the young playmaker Rudi Jobst, whose day job was selling carpets in the same street where Kurt Landauer's parents used to have their shop for women's clothes. Jobst struck – but a Düsseldorf defender blocked the shot. The ball fell to Jobst again. His follow-up effort was parried by Fortuna's excellent goalkeeper Albert Görtz (who'd had an offer from Bayern before choosing Fortuna because they paid him a massive – and illegal – signing-on bonus of 10,000 marks), but the rebound reached Jobst once more and now he put the ball away for the only goal of the game.

Jobst, who was only twenty-two, was singled out for praise by national coach Sepp Herberger after the game and received, like all his teammates, a gold watch and 1,000 marks for winning the cup. But he never achieved the potential Herberger saw in him. Five years later, a dodgy knee ended his Bayern career.

Despite this unexpected cup triumph, the 1950s are often neglected, sometimes even bypassed altogether, when Bayern's history is told. You can see why. However, this doesn't mean that the decade was largely uneventful or insignificant. Quite the contrary. In fact, you could argue that the most important year in the club's entire history is 1958. If you did, I wouldn't object.

In 1958, Sepp Maier was playing for the Under-15 side of his local club TSV Haar, usually on the right wing. At home, when nobody was looking, he sometimes pretended to be Lev Yashin, the great and impossibly cool Russian goalkeeper. Maier says he saw him on television, perhaps during the World Cup in Sweden, and was fascinated by Yashin's elegance. He also says that everyone who might have watched him roll around in the mud, doing a Yashin without any other players nearby, will have said to himself: Ah, the poor boy must be from the madhouse.

In 1958, Franz Beckenbauer was following in the footsteps of his older brother Walter and playing up front for SC Munich 1906. The club was based just a stone's throw away from the family's home, so SC was the logical choice. However, there was one thing Franz wanted to do differently from his brother. Six years earlier, Walter had joined Bayern's youth set-up. But Franz's dream was to play for 1860

Munich – just like his great idol, the inside-right Kurt Mondschein. It's not that he had anything against the Reds, they were just a tad too posh. 'They came from Schwabing,' he once said, 'where most of us rarely went. But 1860 were a part of Giesing.' (At the time, Bayern's teams were training at Säbener Strasse in Giesing, but the club's offices were at Sonnenstrasse, in the centre of town.)

It seemed Beckenbauer's move to the Blues would happen a bit earlier than he had planned. There was talk that SC Munich would shut down its youth division. This was not unlikely, because the club's facilities just weren't up to scratch. A couple of years earlier, the field had been turned into a clay pitch, as that was easier and cheaper to maintain. Visiting teams shook their heads when they saw the surface. And so Beckenbauer and some of his teammates decided to join 1860 Munich in the summer, after the end of the season.

One Sunday, Sepp Maier's TSV Haar played a youth cup game against Bayern. Haar's regular goalkeeper was sidelined with a broken hand. The coach looked at Maier and said: 'You're playing in goal.' The kid's protestations and complaints were to no avail. He went between the sticks and was on the receiving end of the inevitable hammering. Depending on who you ask, young Maier conceded between nine and twelve goals. As he stormed off the pitch steaming with righteous anger, Bayern's 28-year-old youth coach approached him. He introduced himself as Rudi Weiss and said: 'You were really good. What's your name?'

One Sunday, Franz Beckenbauer's SC Munich played 1860 Munich in Neubiberg, some five miles southeast of Giesing. It was the deciding game of an Under-14 tournament, essentially the city championship. In the semis, SC Munich had defeated Bayern (with Beckenbauer scoring), while 1860 beat hosts Neubiberg. In the final, Beckenbauer played as a centre forward. He scored a goal from the penalty spot, but his team lost 4-1.

However, that's not why it was a memorable game. The reason was Beckenbauer's marker, an 1860 player whose identity is a bit of a mystery. For almost a quarter of a century, nobody had the courage to step forward and say he was the boy who changed football history. But, since then, no fewer than three men have accepted the blame. The most recent is a former restaurant owner called Gerhard König. He says he was 1860's reserve goalkeeper at the time, but since the team didn't have enough outfield players on this particular day, he was asked to play in defence and contain Beckenbauer. This would explain why one of his tackles was awfully late. When young Beckenbauer complained about the foul, the 1860 player slapped him in the face.

Later that year, Sepp Maier's father told his son there was a letter for him, from the Bavarian Football Association. Nonplussed, the boy opened the envelope and studied the letter. Even fifty-six years after the event, Maier can close his eyes and still see it. 'It was an invitation to a game between a select XI representing Upper Bavaria and a select XI from Salzburg,' he says. 'It came from Rudi Weiss, who was also working for the Bavarian FA.' The letter asked Maier to meet the rest of the team on the following Sunday morning at a square in Munich, where a coach would be waiting to take them to Salzburg, two hours away across the Austrian border. However, none of that really blew Maier's mind. What *did* blow his mind was the line that said he would be one of the two goalkeepers.

Maier watched the first half of the game from the bench. During the interval, Weiss came up to him and told him to go between the sticks. Maier replied he was a forward, not a goalkeeper. Weiss wouldn't listen. Maier saved two penalties. 'For the first and only time in my life,' he says with a grin, adding: 'I never saved one again.' (That's not true, but he would indeed finish his career as one of the worst penalty stoppers in Bundesliga history.)

Sitting in the dressing room after the Neubiberg final, Beckenbauer was fuming. Not because of the defeat. It was the slap in the face that hurt. 'I'm not going to join that club,' he announced. 'I will play for Bayern, like my brother.'

Sitting on the coach after the Salzburg game, Maier didn't know what to say. The Upper Bavarian select XI had won the game 3-1. The Bayern players in the team were making his ears ring. He was a natural in goal, they said. He should leave that small club from crazy town, TSV Haar, they said. He should come and join them at Bayern Munich, they said. Finally, Maier replied he would give it some thought.

That same year, West Germany reached the World Cup semi-finals in Sweden, losing to the hosts under contentious circumstances. For many people, this constituted proof that German football could hold its own – even without going professional. National coach Sepp Herberger begged to differ. He felt it would be impossible to compete with professionals for very much longer. He also feared he would be losing more and more players to money.

The strict German stance on professionalism meant that the national coach couldn't call-up players who were being paid to play abroad. This tacit agreement was why Manchester City's great goalkeeper Bernd 'Bert' Trautmann never played for his country. When I talked to Trautmann in 1998, on the occasion of his seventy-fifth birthday, he said he always understood and respected the unwritten rule and never held it against Herberger that he wasn't capped.

During the 1950s, this problem was becoming more pressing. In late 1949, an 1860 Munich striker by the name of Ludwig Janda signed for Fiorentina in Italy's Serie A. Three years later, a player called Horst Buhtz moved from a club based in Karlsruhe to Torino. Both were veterans Herberger didn't really need, but he knew it was only a question of time before a foreign team would make a move for one of his key players.

This moment arrived in April 1961. On a Wednesday evening, Hamburg played Barcelona in the European Cup. Herberger was sitting in the stands, but he wasn't really watching the game.

He was watching the man sat next to him: Internazionale coach Helenio Herrera. The legendary manager was in town to offer Hamburg's 24-year-old striker Uwe Seeler an annual salary of 155,000 marks (at a time when the average annual wage in West Germany came to less than 7,000 marks) and a signing-on bonus of 500,000 marks – all after taxes. For a man whose wages and bonuses came to 6,000 marks per year before taxes, Inter's offer was astronomical. Uwe Seeler declined.

Herberger sighed with relief, but now he intensified his efforts to make the DFB reconsider the question of a nationwide league and, consequently, professionalism. His case, if not his team, was helped by the fact that the international Horst Szymaniak entered into talks with Calcio Catania a few months later. Herberger convinced the DFB to lift the ban on professionals and allow him to pick Szymaniak no matter where he played.

Two months before Szymaniak ran out for his country as a professional, German champions Nuremberg were beaten 6-0 by Benfica in the European Cup. And, not long after this debacle, in the summer of 1962, Herberger's team disappointed at the World Cup in Chile, going out in the quarter-finals against Yugoslavia. All these events together prepared the ground for the most dramatic change in the history of the German game. In late July 1962, during the DFB's annual general meeting, the majority of delegates voted in favour of going professional and creating a nationwide league comprising sixteen teams. It would be called Bundesliga – federal league – and begin play on 24 August 1963.

At the time of the historic ballot, no fewer than seventy-four West German clubs were technically playing top-flight football in one of the five regional *Oberligen*. Now the DFB had to come up with a system that would determine which of those teams were worthy of being admitted to the new league. There were not only sporting matters that had to be considered. In 1962, many people still felt that professionalism would ruin the clubs financially. Others argued that football fans loved local derbies more than seeing some team from the

other end of the country. They predicted the Bundesliga would suffer
from low attendances. So the DFB not only needed good teams in the
new league, it also needed attractive, tradition-laden clubs from big
cities.

The selection process was complicated and controversial. In
October, the DFB's advisory board decided that five clubs from the
Oberliga West, five from the south, three from the north, two from
the southwest and one from Berlin should make up the new league. It
also revealed an intricate points system would be used to account for
a team's sporting achievements over the last dozen years in the league,
the nationwide championship rounds and the cup.

Crucially, and in contrast to what you sometimes read, the board
members did not disclose how what came to be known as the Twelve-
Year Rankings were going to be compiled in detail. Possibly with good
reason. They knew this whole procedure was a dream come true for
conspiracy theorists and that the DFB would catch flak from various
corners no matter the outcome.

A few months later, in January 1963, a special DFB committee
announced that nine clubs had been found: Cologne, Borussia
Dortmund and Schalke (from the Oberliga West), Nuremberg and
Frankfurt (south), Hamburg and Werder Bremen (north), Hertha
(Berlin) and Saarbrücken (southwest). The committee members also
let it be known that a few clubs that had had high hopes (including
Oberhausen and Borussia Mönchengladbach from the Oberliga West)
would not be admitted.

This was a mistake. Oberhausen went through the roof. Their
indignation led to another mistake. The committee explained
Oberhausen hadn't done well enough in the Twelve-Year Rankings
and told the club how many points it had collected. These figures were
leaked to the press, whereupon the DFB's secret formula was deduced
and the rankings were published. This led to wild celebrations in
Karlsruhe, Stuttgart and Offenbach. These teams were placed behind
Nuremberg and Frankfurt in the rankings of the southern teams

and were thus first in the running for the remaining three spots the Oberliga Süd had been allocated.

The mood among Bayern's supporters was not quite so ecstatic but still cautiously optimistic. Although Offenbach had never actually won anything, they were certainly Bundesliga material, having twice reached the championship final during the 1950s. But Offenbach was a rather small city. Wouldn't the DFB want a team from Munich, almost ten times the size of Offenbach, in the new league? And if that was the case, this team could only be Bayern, comfortably ahead of 1860 Munich in the Twelve-Year Rankings.

On 3 February 1963, the two local rivals met at Grünwalder Stadion, which they still shared, to contest the 144th Munich derby. (Bayern had won seventy derbies up to that point, thirty-eight matches were drawn, 1860 had won thirty-five.) It was a big game, because 1860 were in first place, Bayern in second. It was also almost a final for a place in the Bundesliga – but nobody on the pitch or in the stands knew this.

It was a terribly cold day in Munich, which explains why only 35,000 attended the match. The pitch was covered in snow. Peter Grosser, a talented local boy who had joined Bayern's youth set-up in the mid-1950s, put the Reds ahead, but the young striker Rudi Brunnenmeier, destined to be an 1860 legend, made it 1-1 with five minutes left in the first half. After the restart, Brunnemeier found the target again and 1860's winger Alfred Heiss, who'd just made his debut for West Germany, added an insurance goal for a 3-1 win. In late April, 1860 were crowned champions of the last-ever Oberliga Süd season, three points ahead of Nuremberg, four points ahead of Bayern.

Ten days later, on 6 May, the DFB published the names of the remaining seven Bundesliga teams. They were: Münster, Brunswick, Kaiserslautern, Meiderich (today MSV Duisburg) and, from the Oberliga Süd, VfB Stuttgart, Karlsruher SC – and 1860 Munich. There was uproar all over the country. Offenbach were livid and suspected powerful local rivals Frankfurt didn't want them in the league. Aachen said the same thing about Cologne. Bayern, meanwhile, announced they would file a protest.

The *Süddeutsche Zeitung* said: 'The case of Bayern seems particularly harsh. This Munich club can certainly point to tradition and quality. For the last four years, the club has been among the best teams in the south and has finished third twice in a row.' The newspaper also accused the governing body of 'arbitrariness' and quoted an 'important' but unnamed DFB official as having cynically said: 'We have kept numerous rankings in reserve for the selection of the Bundesliga clubs. We'll always find one that suits us.'

Five days later, the DFB explained its decision in a letter to the club. The governing body said 1860 had been chosen because they were the reigning champions of the Oberliga Süd. This made some sense – but it had never before been mentioned as a criterion. The DFB also argued that 'it didn't seem to be in the best interests of football in general to have two teams from the same city' during the new league's inaugural season.

The fact that Bayern were left out in the cold when the Bundesliga came into being has often been called a blessing in disguise. 'With hindsight, it was a stroke of luck,' said Dietrich Schulze-Marmeling in his ground-breaking club history in 1997. 'If the club had been admitted to the new league, it would have been forced to radically change the face of the team. This would have put a substantial financial strain on the club and also sabotaged the coming of age of a young team which would soon make German and European football history.'

That is certainly true. Yet Bayern were very unhappy about the fact that 1860 had been chosen ahead of them, for the simple reason that their rivals had now become far more attractive for local talent and established players alike. Peter Grosser, who had scored against the Blues in that derby in February, which suddenly seemed a lot more important than it had at the time, left Bayern in the summer and joined 1860 (he went on to have a very fine career, winning the

DFB-Pokal and the Bundesliga and reaching the 1965 Cup Winners' Cup final against West Ham).

And as Franz Beckenbauer disclosed a few years ago, Bayern came close to losing him as well. 'There was a critical period in 1964, when I came close to joining 1860,' he told Bayern's club magazine. 'We were still playing in the second division, but they were in the Bundesliga and courting me.'

That would have been a shame, because Schulze-Marmeling is right that the Bayern team that was slowly coming together during those years was very promising and fascinating indeed. Even some of the members that you only rarely hear about nowadays were interesting: take goalkeeper Fritz Kosar.

Today it's all the rage for goalkeepers to be comfortable with the ball at their feet. Bayern's Manuel Neuer is rightfully lauded for being an excellent footballer and few reports fail to mention that he often trains with the outfield players rather than with the other goalkeepers. Kosar, however, went a step further half a century ago. He didn't just train with outfield players – he sometimes became one himself.

At a time when the other famous goalkeeper in town, 1860's Petar Radenković, was making a name for himself by dribbling deep into the opposition's half, Kosar was used up front from time to time. In early December 1962, when Bayern met Drumcondra FC from Dublin in the Fairs Cup, star striker Rainer Ohlhauser suffered an injury and couldn't continue in the outfield. Normally, this would have meant that Bayern had to finish with ten men. But since Kosar was such a good footballer, the two players switched roles – the goalkeeper played up front and Ohlhauser tended goal. (Kosar scored Bayern's second goal from the penalty spot.)

Kosar's impressive skills as a footballer led to an important moment in club history. A few weeks after the Fairs Cup game, on 30 December 1962, Bayern played away at Eintracht Frankfurt. The team was plagued by injury problems and came up with an unusual solution: Kosar played as an inside-forward – and the eighteen-year-old

Sepp Maier was given his first-team debut. It looked an inspired change. Kosar was his side's most agile attacker on a snowy surface: he set up Bayern's opening goal and almost made it 2-0 himself, being denied in a one-on-one with Eintracht's goalkeeper. At the other end, Maier saved everything that came his way, tipping a dangerous free kick over the bar shortly before half-time.

However, Bayern were effectively a man down after the break when an ankle injury reduced midfielder Willi Giesemann to a passenger. He was put on the right wing, where he could hurt his team the least. Bayern eventually lost 2-1, but Maier had done well and went on to make three more league appearances that season.

It was not the last time that Kosar played for Bayern in the outfield. However, the next time it happened he was no longer considered the team's regular goalkeeper. A new coach had given the number-one shirt to Maier, still a teenager.

4. THE GOLDEN GENERATION

It's not just sweeper-keepers who are old hat at Bayern; the same goes for controversial agents pulling strings behind the scenes and journalists telling the club what to do. Sometimes, though, neither has to be a bad thing.

Less than three weeks after Bayern had been denied admission to the Bundesliga, the phone rang in a Nuremberg hotel room. It was late and it was the night before a crucial game, so Zlatko Čajkovski was none too happy when he picked up the receiver.

'Mr Čajkovski,' the concierge said, 'there's someone on the line for you from Munich.'

Čajkovski, born in Zagreb, was thirty-nine years old. He was small and chubby, which is why he had acquired the nickname *Čik* in his native Yugoslavia, meaning cigarette stub. (Pronounced 'cheek' with a short e-sound. In Hungary they would have probably called him *dombi*.) He was also a very successful football coach. Čajkovski had won the German championship with Cologne the previous year and now his team had reached the final rounds again, which would begin on the next day with a game against Nuremberg.

'Who is it?' Čajkovski wanted to know.

'He said his name is Dr Ratz,' the concierge answered.

Georg-Otto Ratz, a Budapest-born lawyer, was based in Switzerland but had an office in Munich. He was known across the continent as 'Mister Ten Per Cent', after his non-negotiable share in the many deals he brokered between clubs and clubs or between clubs and players, and sometimes between clubs and coaches.

'Okay, put him through.'

'Čik,' Ratz said, 'I have a team for you.'

During the winter, Cologne had urged Čajkovski to extend his contract, but the coach had stalled. He was in loose talks with the Rotterdam club Feyenoord, who were offering a lucrative deal. Finally, Cologne could wait no longer and signed a new man for the summer. Then the Feyenoord deal became increasingly protracted. Suddenly it seemed Čajkovski was only a few weeks away from unemployment.

'Bayern Munich are unhappy with their coach,' Ratz added. 'It's a good job. Give it a go, Čik.'

Čajkovski hesitated. Ratz sensed what the problem was and explained that even though the team were in the second division, the club had many good, young players. This sounded like Čajkovski's cup of tea. Three years later, he would entitle his autobiography *I Build Teams* because, well, that's what he did best. Čajkovski told Ratz he would meet Bayern's officials to see what they were like.

At about the same time, a journalist with the *Süddeutsche Zeitung* by the name of Hans Schiefele approached Bayern's new president. Schiefele wasn't a normal journalist. He had joined Bayern Munich's youth set-up a few weeks before his ninth birthday in 1928. Few people knew the club, the game and the business as well as he did.

'Mr Neudecker,' Schiefele said, 'if Čik Čajkovski is available, you have to make him an offer.'

Wilhelm Neudecker, a 49-year-old general contractor, was Bayern's seventh president since Landauer had been voted out of office. One day he would be recognised as perhaps the most important president in the club's history. The first signs of why and how he managed to take Bayern to unprecedented heights might have become apparent during this conversation with Schiefele in May 1963. Because, instead of wondering if such a famous coach would be at all interested in joining a team in the southern tier of the second division, Neudecker took it for granted that Bayern were an attractive option for Čik. He told the club's treasurer, an ambitious man called Willi O. Hoffmann, to prepare a contract – and make Čajkovski the sort of financial offer the man could hardly refuse.

Čajkovski started his job on 1 July 1963. Five days later, he saw his new team play for the first time. In the Intertoto Cup, an annual continental summer competition, Bayern met Sparta Rotterdam, who had just finished third in the Dutch Eredivisie, ahead of the club Čajkovski had come close to joining, Feyenoord. Bayern wiped the floor with Sparta, winning 6-0. Čajkovski, cheerful by nature to begin with, grinned like the Cheshire Cat. Ratz was right, this could be fun.

Čajkovski changed the team's formation to an attack-minded 4-2-4, which produced goals by the truckload. But more important than his tactical nous was his character. Maier once called him 'fanatical about football, crazy and loveable'. He added: 'We were all his children, his boys. It often happened that he suddenly stopped the afternoon training session when he noticed we weren't focused. "No good today," he said in his artfully broken German. "Let's go home to Rada. Drink coffee."' Rada was his wife. She must have loved him dearly, considering how regularly he brought the entire first team to their house unannounced.

Some years down the line, Čajkovski's good-naturedness would become a problem. But, during these first, formative years of a team destined to dominate Europe, he was the right man in the right place. He loved working with young players because their enthusiasm matched his own. And young players loved him back, not least because he treated them like a father would. In Čajkovski's eyes, his kids could do no wrong. According to his world view, placing trust in people was always rewarded. One of the first things he did was put Fritz Kosar – at barely twenty-four years of age still a fairly young player himself – on the bench and make nineteen-year-old Sepp Maier the new regular goalkeeper.

However, as funny and chummy as Čajkovski was, he wanted to win. And he wasn't above a little gamesmanship. Bayern tore through the season in the Regionalliga Süd, the southern division of the five-tiered level below the Bundesliga. As early as the first week of April, the team reached the milestone of 100 goals scored. The only club able to keep pace was Hessen Kassel.

Čajkovski took a long hard look at the table and the schedule. The two best teams from this league would qualify for the promotion tournament to reach the Bundesliga. Since the weather had been typically harsh in Bavaria and many matches were postponed, Bayern still had a couple of games left to play while the other regional divisions had already finished the regular season.

The coach calculated that if his team won the Regionalliga Süd, they would be put in a group with Hannover 96, Alemannia Aachen and a third club to be determined through a one-game playoff. If they finished second behind Kassel, their opponents would be Borussia Neunkirchen, Tasmania Berlin and FC St. Pauli. Čajkovski preferred the sound of the latter group. He decided to finish second.

In the penultimate game, at home against TSG Ulm, the coach started five reserve-team players. Two of them were called Otto Jaworski and Georg Bogeschdorfer. Writer Schulze-Marmeling says that Čajkovski only informed 'captain Adolf Kunstwadl and two other players about his plan'. We can assume that one of the two others was Rainer Ohlhauser, because Čajkovski must have explained to the team's best striker why he was playing him as a centre-half. Of course the visitors 'went past him at will', as Čajkovski dryly noted in his memoirs.

However, nobody had told the second-stringers about the secret plan. With twenty minutes left on the clock, Bayern were leading 4-3, with all the goals coming from Jaworski and Bogeschdorfer. Now Čajkovski had to be a little less discreet. He gave a few instructions from the sidelines and finally news of the directive spread through the team. Ulm scored three goals in the final quarter of an hour to win 6-4. Bayern finished the season in second place.

Ultimately, the question as to whether this was merely cheeky or unsporting behaviour became a moot one – because Čik Čajkovski's fine plan backfired badly. After a good start to the promotion tournament, Bayern suffered an unexpected setback, losing 2-0 at home to Neunkirchen. Four days later, the team travelled to Berlin. Čajkovski started Fritz Kosar on the right wing and for one hour the game hung in the balance. Then a rare Maier mistake allowed the hosts to take the lead. Bayern eventually lost 3-0 and were to all intents and purposes out of the race.

All in all, it was a disappointing end to the season for Bayern. And yet something positive did emerge from those final weeks of the club's campaign.

President Neudecker is primarily remembered, and revered, for taking Bayern to a whole new level in terms of professionalism. He was the man who hired German football's first full-time business manager. He also knew that you had to spend money to make money and wasn't afraid of spending big. But he knew football, too, and had an instinctive understanding of what made a player special. It was Neudecker who promoted two of the greatest talents in the club's – and the game's – whole history, pretty much against Čajkovski's will.

The first was Beckenbauer. In early April 1964, the young man returned to Munich after having starred for West Germany at the annual International Youth Tournament. Neudecker called him in and told the youngster he would be sending him to the senior side. Then the two went over to the training pitch to break the news to Čajkovski.

In his autobiography, Čajkovski claims that he had been 'fighting' for Beckenbauer for quite some time. However, the man who would one day be called *der Kaiser* remembers it differently. 'Our president introduced me,' he recalled. 'And Čajkovski said: "Have heard you're not a fighter."' Beckenbauer added that despite this 'unpleasant reception' the coach later always stood up for him.

Looking back, it seems bizarre that a coach as experienced and as enamoured of youth as Čajkovski had to be sold on a unique talent like Beckenbauer. However, perhaps he knew that even though the rosy-cheeked youngster from Giesing had the innocent look of a choir boy, he was a handful.

Rudi Weiss, his coach at the youth level, had even demoted Beckenbauer to the second team for a few months, because he felt the player could be a disruptive influence and was undermining the squad's discipline. The coach also disliked the boy's habit of making a dismissive gesture with his hand when a teammate committed a technical or tactical error. Weiss understood that Beckenbauer was impatient with lesser players because he had such immense God-given talent that everything came easily to him. But, Weiss told the kid, it made him look arrogant and aloof. He had to cut down on it.

During the International Youth Tournament in Holland, Beckenbauer had shared a room not with a teammate but with national coach Dettmar Cramer, who wanted to keep an eye on him. Even though Beckenbauer was not yet nineteen, he had already fathered a son (and, even more shockingly, not married the mother). So when Čajkovski gave him the once-over and said, 'Have heard you're not a fighter,' what he really meant – but of course couldn't say in Neudecker's presence – was probably more like: I have been told you're trouble.

If so, the kid dispelled all doubts in record time. On 6 June, Čajkovski gave him his debut in the opening game of the promotion rounds, away at St. Pauli. Beckenbauer played on the left-wing, scored Bayern's third goal in a 4-0 rout of the team from Hamburg and became an instant regular. A few days later, in the home leg against Tasmania Berlin, he started up front again but moved into midfield after the break. From then on, he was often, though not always, used as what we would now call a creative midfielder.

While Beckenbauer was convincing Čajkovski he could help the team without being a fighter, two Bayern officials were sitting in a flat in Nördlingen, a town between Nuremberg and Munich. When the doorbell rang, the lady of the house excused herself from their presence. She came back a moment later and told her visitors she was sorry but they had to leave quickly and through the back door. She explained that two 1860 Munich representatives were standing in front of the building.

All these strange people were here because of her son, eighteen-year-old Gerd Müller. Legend has it that the Reds delegation, headed by board member Walter Fembeck, beat the Blues to Müller's signature only because Ludwig Maierböck, his counterpart at 1860, had misread the railway timetable and arrived late. Another account tells how Müller at first didn't realise that Fembeck was representing Bayern; he thought he was talking to someone from 1860. Müller himself, though, has always said he preferred Bayern because the team was young and only in the second division, where there was going to be less pressure on him to repeat the otherworldy goalscoring records he was racking up at his lowly hometown club.

It was a part-time Bayern scout, the hairdresser Alexander Kotter, who had spotted Müller and it was Fembeck who signed him – not Čajkovski. When Müller reported for duty at Säbener Strasse, the coach was underwhelmed. You can understand why. Müller was small, stocky, heavy. He had massive thighs. He was shy. He just didn't look and act like an athlete. Or at least not like a footballer. 'I don't need a weightlifter,' Čajkovski supposedly sneered.

Müller didn't help his cause by breaking his arm in a friendly match in early August. It was a good excuse for Čajkovski to ignore the man he would soon – famously and ungrammatically – christen *kleines, dickes Müller*: shorty, fatty Müller.

Things got so bad that Gerd Müller, without match and win bonuses, had to earn something on the side as a removal man. He carried a cupboard up three flights of stairs for Hans Schiefele, the journalist who had urged Neudecker to make Čajkovski an offer. Schiefele gave him five marks as a tip.

Finally, in October, Neudecker had had enough. Müller's arm had healed more than a month ago, still he wasn't playing. The president confronted his coach and said: 'If you don't field the guy with the heavy legs I'm not going to watch another football game in my life.' Müller scored on his debut, against Freiburg FC. That wasn't particularly impressive, as pretty much everyone scored on that day – Bayern won 11-2. But he also scored in his second game, a week later. He scored four goals in his third. He scored two goals in his fourth. Actually, it was only on his thirteenth appearance for Bayern that he failed to find the target. It was just a blip. He started scoring again a week later. And, you could say, he never stopped.

Many, many years later, when Gerd Müller celebrated his fiftieth birthday, Franz Beckenbauer gave a speech during which he said: 'Without Gerd Müller, we'd probably still be in the wooden hut that was once our clubhouse.' (This wooden hut was not a figure of speech. It was Neudecker, the building contractor, who put it up at Säbener Strasse in the early 1960s.) Truer words have rarely been spoken. There would have been no money without Neudecker, no class without Beckenbauer, no fun without Maier. But there have been clubs who made it to the top without money, class or fun. The one thing a football club can't do without is goals. And from the moment shorty, fatty Müller was let loose, goals would never again be a problem for Bayern Munich.

When Beckenbauer made that remark about the wooden hut, in November 1995, Gerd Müller squinted through his spectacles and mumbled something nobody could understand into his salt-and-pepper beard. Life after football hadn't been kind to him – he battled alcoholism until the Bayern Munich family picked him up. Looking at him on this day, you realised he had always been a reluctant and very unlikely hero, one of those men who cherish the relative anonymity of supporting roles and then suddenly find themselves at centre stage.

*

With Müller up front and Beckenbauer pulling the strings, Bayern became even more dominant. This time they scored their 100th goal in the Regionalliga Süd as early as January. However, again there was one team that put up a fight – Reutlingen. With three games left in the season, they were breathing down Bayern's necks.

On Sunday, 24 April 1965, the Reds were scheduled to play against Schweinfurt at home. It was raining heavily. A few hours before the game, 1860's president Adalbert Wetzel approached Neudecker and asked him to move the game from the Grünwalder Stadion to another ground – the Dantestadion, six miles to the north. He explained that 1860 would be playing against Torino on Tuesday, in the Cup Winners' Cup, and were afraid that Bayern's game could ruin the pitch. Neudecker refused.

Over the following hours, the fans slowly began to arrive at the ground. Sixty minutes before the scheduled kick-off, about 1,500 of them filled the stands. Then came a call from the municipality. The city, as the ground's owner, prohibited Bayern to play the game at Grünwalder Stadion. A fuming Neudecker quickly organised coaches to transport the fans to the Dantestadion. Bayern won 2-0 and held on to first place in the league.

Čajkovski, it seems, had been cured of trying to play it smart. Two weeks later, on the final day of the regular season and with Bayern topping the table only one point ahead of Reutlingen, the coach sent out his best team against Pforzheim. Bayern won 6-1. After the final whistle, defender Werner Olk and striker Dieter Brenninger lifted the coach onto their shoulders. Čik raised his arms. Neudecker squinted through his glasses at the photographers' cameras and smiled. It was almost as if they all knew this day – 9 May 1965 – would be the club's last-ever in the second division.

Before the promotion rounds began, Neudecker said: 'If we go up, I'll walk around the Tegernsee.' He was referring to a lake near his home, thirty miles southeast of Munich. The Tegernsee is quite big, so the length of the hiking trail came to more than seventeen miles.

It was probably on 13 June, after the third game of the promotion tournament, that Neudecker took out a map and began to study the various routes.

On this day, Bayern hosted Alemannia Aachen, the team Čajkovski had tried to avoid the year before. Beckenbauer, the best player on the pitch, was used in a defensive role and yet set up Müller for the opening goal. But Aachen tied things on the hour. It was a close, tense game that could have gone either way. Seven minutes from time, Ohlhauser volleyed home the winner and a near sell-out crowd of 42,000 cheered so loudly that Grünwalder Stadion was shaken to its very foundations.

Two weeks later, Bayern sealed promotion with a stunning 8-0 away at Tennis Borussia Berlin. The young team – the squad's average age was only 21.8 years – had scored 146 goals during the league season and then another eighteen during the six promotion games. When the team landed at Munich airport later that day, more than 6,000 fans greeted them, many of whom jumped the barricades and darted across the runway.

1860's president Wetzel sent his best wishes and announced: 'Munich is big enough for two top-class sides, we wish FC Bayern a lot of success!' Neudecker's reply is unrecorded; maybe he just thought back to the day of the Schweinfurt game and gritted his teeth. Two weeks later, on 10 July, he circled the Tegernsee. But he wasn't alone. Almost 520 Bayern supporters walked with him.

One month later, Neudecker met Wetzel again. Bayern's first-ever game in the Bundesliga pitted them against, of all teams, 1860. And in less than sixty seconds, it became obvious for anyone to see there was no love lost between the two local rivals. A thundering volley from 1860's Timo Konietzka hit Bayern's centre-half Dieter Danzberg, just signed from Meiderich, in the head and knocked him out cold. While Danzberg was lying on the ground (and, some accounts say, Maier went over to see how badly he was hurt), Konietzka collected the ball and slotted it into the net.

After that, the game turned ugly. Beckenbauer later recalled he'd 'never heard such a barrage of catcalls and boos before', as people who had come to see a thrilling derby were instead treated to the sight of players kicking lumps out of each other. After all of ten minutes, Kunstwadl was so badly hurt that he could do little more than limp around. Finally, he had to come off and none other than Gerd Müller replaced him at the back. It later turned out the 25-year-old Kunstwadl had sustained a meniscus injury that would ultimately end his career.

Five minutes from time, Danzberg was sent off for getting even with Konietzka. New national coach Helmut Schön, watching from the stands, rose in disgust, shook his head, told a reporter he'd seen way more than enough and left. The local press later called the match 'a barroom free-for-all'.

As depressing as the game was, it had quite a few important repercussions. Ten months later, when the season ended, 1860 were in first place, three points ahead of Dortmund – and newly promoted Bayern. It was the first, and so far only, championship for the Blues. Who knows what would have happened if Bayern had won the derby on opening day?

Then there was Dieter Danzberg. Because of his dismissal, Čajkovski needed a new centre-half for the next game. He decided to pull his best player back, Beckenbauer. Over the next couple of years, the two men – Čajkovski and Beckenbauer – would gradually reinvent this role until they arrived at a new position: *libero*, or sweeper.

It was not necessarily the position as such that was new. The Romanian Alexandru Apolzan is sometimes credited with playing sweeper for Steaua Bucureşti in the 1950s and the Italian Ivano Blason was a kind of *libero* under the legendary Nereo Rocco at Triestina even earlier. But these men had been freed of man-marking duties in order to defend more flexibly and thus effectively. Beckenbauer, though, wasn't really a defender. He was too elegant, too smart and just too plain good to be wasted at the back. Čajkovski gave him the freedom – *libero* is Italian for 'free' – to move upfield if and when he felt like it.

A rarely mentioned knock-on effect of this innovation was that the other central defender had to take on a slightly new role as well. He became what Germans called the *Vorstopper*. It's not quite what the English call a centre-back – but it's not completely different, either. In contrast to the two centre-backs in a flat back-four, the *Vorstopper* did not just have to man-mark a striker, usually the centre-forward, he also had to cover for the sweeper if he surged forward. So the sweeper system not only stood and fell with the quality of the *libero*, it also relied on a good *Vorstopper*. For Bayern, this would never become a major problem, because there was a teenager in their youth set-up who soon turned out to be perfect for this position.

Franz Beckenbauer quickly blossomed in his new role. After a game against Karlsruher SC in September, his coach was unable to contain himself. 'I have played football for twenty-five years and met the best in the world,' he told reporters. 'But I have never seen a better player. Let me tell you, Franz Beckenbauer is in a class of his own.' Yes he was. And he knew it. And some people found that hard to take. A newspaper from Essen, a city in the industrial region in the western part of Germany known as the Ruhr valley, said: 'You have to be a very devoted Bayern fan not to shake your head at his airs and graces and his arrogance.'

Then again, you could understand why the young man was a bit full of himself during these months. In September, he won his first full cap – at barely twenty years of age and in a crucial World Cup qualifier, no less. In April 1966, his hometown Munich was awarded the 1972 Summer Olympics. (He had no way of knowing this, but it would turn out to be an important moment for Bayern, too.) In May, his old flame 1860 won the league. And in June, Beckenbauer lifted the first trophy of his young career. That's because once again Bayern had done quite well in the DFB-Pokal.

The competition that was almost an afterthought when Bayern had first won it, nine years earlier, had become very popular in Germany. The main reason was the introduction of the European Cup Winners'

Cup in 1960. A triumph in the DFB-Pokal now meant not only prestige and a title for the letterhead but also a payday since the winner got to play in Europe.

The fans had finally embraced the cup, too. In the semi-finals, almost 60,000 people filled Nuremberg's ground to see Bayern, the cocky promoted team that seemed to find it so easy to adapt to the Bundesliga. Čajkovski later said his team's performance on this day was one of the best since he had taken over the side. Beaming with pride and joy, he saw Bayern win 2-1 after extra time to book a date with Meiderich in a final that would be staged in Frankfurt.

Meiderich (still seven months away from being renamed MSV Duisburg) may not have been the most glamorous of clubs, far from it, but they had a good, experienced team that was hard to break down. Still, Bayern went into the game as favourites. Yes, they were very young and had only been promoted the previous summer, but they had finished the season more than twenty points ahead of Meiderich.

But on 4 June 1966, league form counted for little. In stifling heat, Meiderich took the lead on twenty-eight minutes. An Ohlhauser header from close range and a ferocious Brenninger strike turned the game around. Two dubious penalties, one at either end, resulted in a 3-2 scoreline with eight minutes left. Then sweeper Beckenbauer went on one of his soon to be famous forays deep into the opponents' half. He ran into space, received the ball from Ohlhauser and scored Bayern's fourth with a powerful shot into the far corner.

'Now 1860 can't become too big in Munich,' Čajkovski said after the game. He was smiling but not joking. While Bayern went with homegrown or regional talent, their local rivals had assembled a strong team largely through spending lots of money. (Even their coach, the Austrian Max Merkel, earned more than twice as much as Čajkovski did.) For the time being, the Blues were still the star-studded, more established team, the Reds the loveable upstarts. When Bayern presented the trophy to their fans, few of the 20,000 supporters who filled the Marienplatz could have imagined how quickly – and completely – these roles would change.

While everybody was celebrating Bayern becoming a force to be reckoned with in Germany again, Neudecker was already plotting the next step. The cup win against Meiderich meant that his club would now be competing on the European stage, where clubs were far more professional than their German counterparts. Some were even proper companies. The Scottish giants Rangers, Neudecker marvelled, were trading shares on the stock market! There was no doubt in his mind that Bayern had to be run more efficiently.

In the summer, while West Germany did well at the World Cup in England and Beckenbauer blossomed into an international star, Neudecker approached a sharp and ambitious man called Robert Schwan. He had been a Bayern member for eight years, held an administrative post at the club and was, like everyone else not directly connected to the first team, working in an honorary capacity, meaning: unpaid. Neudecker offered Schwan a full-time, salaried job at Bayern Munich. He became the first technical director in Germany, for a monthly wage of 5,000 marks (then £450), about the same amount Čajkovski was making.

Over the years, his official title would change now and again. The most commonly used was business manager. In England, football coaches not only worked with the team, they also negotiated contracts, made deals and signed players, which is why they were usually referred to as 'managers'. In Germany, these two roles were and are strictly separate. The coach only does what his title suggests, while money and contractual matters are handled by someone else.

When Beckenbauer returned from the World Cup, Neudecker told him: 'I've put Schwan on the payroll to have someone who is close to the team from early in the morning until late at night.' Schwan would take this assignment so seriously that he even sat on the bench during games, puffing on his pipe. This, too, set a precedent. Later, the greatest business manager in Bayern's history, Uli Hoeness, would sit on the bench next to the coach for more than thirty years, until he signed Louis van Gaal – who was neither accustomed to this nor keen on it.

But Schwan not only managed the club. He quickly realised that a lot of money could be made from Beckenbauer's popularity. And so the man who – with a characteristic lack of modesty – once said 'There are only two smart people, Schwan before noon and Schwan after noon' also became German football's first personal agent. For the next four decades, he would manage Bayern's biggest star. In the mid-1960s, there were many people who couldn't quite understand why an athlete needed someone like that. Schwan told them: 'First, we have to avoid that people shed a bad, or even a false, light on Beckenbauer, the sporting idol. Second, we have to look out for a good price. We won't take advantage of anyone, we ask for reasonable fees. But nobody should assume that footballers are stupid.' When Schwan died, in July 2002, Beckenbauer said: 'He was my best friend. And he was one of the architects who built the foundation on which Bayern today rests.'

And so, in the summer of 1966, Bayern were poised to take on the world. Almost all the pieces of the puzzle were now in place. From the brilliant spine of the team – goalkeeper Maier, sweeper Beckenbauer, centre-forward Müller – to a no less talented alliance of movers and shakers in the boardroom, Neudecker and Schwan. The only thing that was missing was the guy who would score when no one else did.

'To be honest, I thought he was taking the piss,' Franz Roth recalls. Then he roars with laughter. He has just recounted the story of how he came to join Bayern in 1966. Merely two years earlier, he had played at the very bottom of the league pyramid; now somebody by the name of Robert Schwan was on the telephone offering him a two-year contract at Bayern Munich.

Alexander Kotter, the hairdresser who spotted Gerd Müller, had seen Roth play amateur football for Kaufbeuren, fifty miles west of Munich. On his recommendation, Walter Fembeck, the man who had literally beaten 1860 to Müller's door, went to watch the fast, powerful forward on two different occasions. He told Schwan to give him a call. 'I didn't cost any money, so it was no risk at all for them,' Roth says.

His hair is white as snow now, but he still oozes vitality. Although he is now seventy, you can see why everybody used to call him *Bulle* – the bull. 'When we began the pre-season training camp, Beckenbauer and Maier were still on holidays, because they had been at the World Cup with the national team,' he remembers. 'They joined us ten days later. On the first evening, Čik told Maier about all the new signings. Finally, he said: "And this is Roth, has strength like moo-moo."

'Sepp replied: "No, no, Čik. We don't say someone has the strength of a cow. We say: He is strong like a bull." And that was that.'

The twenty-year-old quickly became a regular. In his first game, he was played as a winger, but then Čajkovski had another inspired idea. He pulled Roth back into what we would now call defensive midfield. His main job was taking the opposing playmaker out of the game. Roth was made for the role because he never shied away from a tackle. And although they called him the Bull, he had the lungs of a horse and could run all day. 'It's true, I never got tired,' he grins.

Roth's legendary stamina would soon come handy, because Bayern played around eighty games, including friendlies, over the course of 1966–67, his first season as a professional. There were the league matches, of course (the Bundesliga having grown to eighteen teams), but once more the team truly shone in the cup competitions. Čajkovski's side became the first since Karlsruher SC in the 1950s to defend the DFB-Pokal, beating Hamburg in the final. The 4-0 scoreline doesn't quite reflect how close the game was until the final stages. One reason for the outcome was that Hamburg's greatest star, national icon Uwe Seeler, was closely marked by Werner Olk. Seeler's striking partner Bernd Dörfel, meanwhile, couldn't get past a nineteen-year-old defender who had been at Bayern since the Under-14 level: Hans-Georg Schwarzenbeck.

However, although Bayern's domestic cup campaign offered many such highlights – there was also a prestigious derby win against local rivals 1860 in the semi-finals – it was overshadowed by the team's triumphant season in the Cup Winners' Cup.

Bayern Munich have always been a cosmopolitan club that tried to learn from playing foreign opposition, not least because of Munich's geographical location in the south of Germany. Austria is only fifty-five miles away, Switzerland and what is now the Czech Republic barely 140 miles. Even a French city like Strasbourg, 220 miles to the west, can be reached fairly comfortably. Many people from Munich regularly cross the Alps to travel south but only rarely venture north of the so-called *Weißwurstäquator*, literally: white sausage equator (a humorous term to describe the invisible border between southern Germany, where this dish is common, and the rest of the country, where it's considered mildly nauseating). You can almost understand why some Bavarians feel a closer affinity to their neighbouring countries than to the northern part of Germany. After all, Munich is actually closer to Milan than to Hamburg or Berlin.

Bayern first travelled across one of those borders to play a game of football as early as December 1900, when they were invited to Prague by a club that had been formed by German Jews, DFC Prag. (At the time, Bohemia was a part of the Austro-Hungarian Empire.) The hosts won the match 8-0, but the visitors from Munich were unfazed. In fact, Bayern would never fear the prospect of being on the receiving end of a hiding if they could glean inspiration from it.

In the summer of 1919, MTK Budapest, an excellent and widely admired team, came to Munich. They played the hosts off the park, winning 7-1, but nobody was dispirited. A local newspaper said that 'the entire population of Munich expresses gratitude to Bayern for having made this exhibition possible.' The game broke all local attendance records for a football match and the Hungarians' combination game, based on short passes as opposed to the classic English long-ball approach, left a lasting impression on Bayern, who would attempt to copy it.

Despite such a long history of playing foreign opposition, Bayern were left on the outside looking in when official competitions between continental club sides at long last became a reality in the 1950s with the introduction of the European Cup. Bayern just weren't good enough to play at such an exalted level. Maybe that's why the club decided to take part in the Fairs Cup in 1962, a competition not everyone was very keen on. Bayern went out in the quarter-finals, to eventual winners Dinamo Zagreb. (Initially, the Fairs Cup was supposed to be contested by city representative teams instead of club sides, but this rule was quickly changed as it proved impractical.)

Only a few years later, everything had changed. By 1966, Bayern were a professional club playing in a professional league. Their avuncular coach had done what he promised – he had built a strong team. And German clubs had become increasingly competitive at elite level, especially in the Cup Winners' Cup, which seemed to have become a British-German speciality. In 1965, 1860 Munich reached the final against West Ham. A year later, Borussia Dortmund played Liverpool. So when Bayern finally entered the European arena, in which they would one day lay the foundation for their greatness, the club approached the task with optimism and confidence. Walter Fembeck, sent to scout first-round opponents Tatran Prešov from Slovakia, reported back home: 'A strong team. But not so strong as to knock us out.'

This set a precedent. Fembeck was ultimately proved right, yet the games were a lot closer than he could have imagined. In the last five minutes of the second leg, Tatran hit the post and then Gerd Müller, of all people, blocked a shot on his own goal-line. If either attempt had gone in, Bayern would have been out. The team was then drawn against Shamrock Rovers and came away from Dublin with a 1-1 draw. Čajkovski said: 'We didn't play well, but I'm happy with the result. It means we should go through.' He, too, was right, but aged a few years during the second leg. With four minutes left, Rovers were through on the fairly new away-goals rule, then Müller scored the winner.

In the quarter-finals, Bayern met Rapid Vienna. This time it was Robert Schwan whom the press asked for comment. 'Not an easy draw,' he said, 'but we should make the semis.' You guessed it – he turned out to be right, but only after a major scare. In the second leg, staged in Munich, an Ohlhauser goal took the game to extra time. It was a controversial goal, as the linesman signalled for offside while referee Tom Wharton waved play-on. The deciding moment, though, came seven minutes later, when another disputed decision led to a melee during which Rapid's August Starek pushed the referee away. Wharton then dismissed Walter Seitl, who refused to leave the pitch for many minutes, arguing justly but futilely that he had done nothing wrong. Against ten men, another Ohlhauser goal finally saw Bayern through.

The only easy ride was the semi-final against Standard Liège. The Belgian fans sported a banner that read: 'They have Beckenbauer, we have Claessen.' It referred to prolific striker Roger Claessen, but ignored the fact that 'they' also had Gerd Müller. He scored four goals, Bayern won 5-1 on aggregate and reached the final against, of course, a British team – Rangers.

'They were the overwhelming favourites,' says Franz Roth. 'They had been playing in Europe for years and years, whereas it was all new for us.' That was true, but Bayern's lack of experience was probably offset by the fact that the final was played in Nuremberg, less than a two-hour drive away and the very place where the Reds had won their first-ever title more than forty years earlier. Also, but probably unbeknownst to the Germans, there was some pressure on Rangers. Six days earlier, Celtic had lifted the European Cup in Lisbon against Inter. As Keir Murray wrote in a retrospective piece for the BBC: 'Their great rivals had won the European Cup at their first attempt and had made a clean sweep of the domestic honours. After the shocking exit to Berwick Rangers in the Scottish Cup at the start of the year, Rangers captain John Greig and his teammates knew their season rested on one match.'

Bayern's big worry, meanwhile, was Gerd Müller. He had broken his forearm in an international less than four weeks before the final. On 31 May 1967, he took to the field against Rangers with a support brace made of leather. Still, he had the first chance of the game. With fewer than five minutes gone, a Rudi Nafziger cross found the striker near the penalty spot. He trapped the ball with his first touch, turned and struck with his second. The ball whistled inches past the post. Just a minute earlier, Beckenbauer had made one of his spectacular runs, intercepting a pass deep in his own half and then moving upfield, exchanging one-twos until appearing near the opponents' penalty area. The partisan crowd in Nuremberg cheered wildly – Bayern were on top of their game.

Only not for long. Dave Smith had a great opportunity in the twelfth minute, also with a strike on the turn from inside the box. And on thirty-four minutes, Smith pulled the ball back from the touchline for Roger Hynd, who struck from six yards out – Maier made a great save, couldn't hold onto the ball but grabbed it before it rolled across the line. Now Rangers dominated the game and Beckenbauer was forced to cut down on his solo runs. Deep into the second half, the German television commentator would remark: 'He is condemned to playing as a no-frills stopper today.'

The game was broadcast into twenty-four countries. Photos taken that night in the streets of Munich remind you of scenes from post-apocalyptic movies: the city was totally deserted, as everybody sat at home, glued to their television sets. People were rewarded with a thrilling game, much better than the previous year's final, in which Dortmund had become the first German club to win a European trophy by beating Liverpool.

The second half was more open. There were chances at either end and with three minutes left, Bayern came close to winning it. John Greig slipped and Ohlhauser would have been clear through to goal if the Scottish midfielder hadn't grabbed the ball with both hands while lying on the pitch. Less than a minute later, Müller and

Dieter Brenninger exposed Rangers' backline with a simple but nicely executed one-two. Brenninger had only goalkeeper Norrie Martin to beat, but the Scot brilliantly parried the left-footed shot from an angle.

Those final stages already suggested that Rangers might be fading physically. It had been raining all day in Nuremberg and the waterlogged pitch seemed to be sapping strength from Scottish legs first. However, extra time began with a moment of anxiety. Maier went up to collect a cross and was challenged by Hynd as he caught the ball. The goalkeeper crashed to the ground, the ball came loose and Hynd put it away. 'The linesman immediately waved his flag,' says Roth. 'There was never any question that the goal was illegal and none of the Scots protested the referee's decision when it was chalked off.'

So it was still scoreless – and a replay two days later was looming large – when Roth received the ball in the 109th minute at the halfway line. He played a pass to Ohlhauer and accelerated, starting a run that took everyone by surprise. 'Like I told you, I never got tired,' he says. 'Ohlhauser carried the ball and waited until I was near the box, then he played the long ball into my path.' The pass was perfectly timed, because it came down eight yards in front of goal, between goalkeeper Martin and Dave Smith, who was doing his best to stop Roth. 'He was grabbing me by the shoulder and pulling me down,' says the Bayern player. 'I lost my balance. I think if I had not made contact with the ball, we would have won a penalty.' But somehow he did make contact. 'People sometimes say I didn't have a first touch, I only did things with power,' Roth says. 'But you needed a lot of skill to score this goal, because Martin was right in front of me.' Roth lobbed him with a volley.

As the ball hit the back of the net, all hell broke loose. Flares and rockets went off, ecstatic fans invaded the pitch. The atmosphere had been electric all night and now the onlookers found an outlet for all that pent-up excitement. But they had to wait a few more minutes. The pitch was cleared and Rangers somehow mustered the strength for another onslaught. Maier dived left and right and flew through the air with the sort of utter disregard for personal safety you normally associate with, well, poor boys from the madhouse. He wasn't Yashin, he didn't elegantly catch balls and then calmly look around. Instead he brushed his way past friend and foe and punched them clear.

Then the final whistle rang. Maier raised his arms and tried to run towards a teammate. There was none. They were all making for the subs' benches, where the police were marking off space for the trophy presentation with a cordon. Maier looked around. The pitch was already black with people. He evaded two supporters and ran towards the police and the bench. Čajkovski was standing there, arms outstretched like a father waiting for his kids. He embraced each and every one of them, tears streaming down his rotund face. Once again the players lifted him onto their shoulders. (Him and Dr Erich Spannbauer, the club physio, who'd got Müller match-fit and who'd done so much work during this long, long season.)

On the following day, more than 100,000 in the centre of town celebrated what was so far the greatest day in Bayern Munich's history. Tellingly, the four men who led the parade, driving the trophy around in a Porsche 911 Cabriolet – red, of course! – were captain Olk, coach Čajkovski, president Neudecker and technical director Schwan. One wonders if Čajkovski already knew the schedule or whether Neudecker and Schwan were just about to tell him that the long, long season wasn't over yet. There would be four games in five days in June, all against small amateur teams. (One of which was the Munich club FT Gern, which would one day spawn Philipp Lahm.) And, unlike nowadays, Čajkovski was expected to play his stars, not second-stringers.

The reason was, naturally, money. Neudecker and Schwan may have been many things but they were no fools. They knew the hard part was not getting to the top but staying there. It was going to cost money. Although this great team had been assembled without spending any, it would be expensive to keep it together. Both men were convinced that you needed to pay key employees accordingly. Čajkovski, it was announced, would soon net as much money as Merkel used to get at 1860.

The problem was that in those days before television deals and merchandising, a club had only two sources of income. One was membership fees. Bayern made a concerted effort to increase their number, reaching 8,000 in 1967, which translated into fees of 400,000 marks. (One of the newly recruited members was Franz Josef Strauss, the conservative federal minister of finance and a very powerful presence in Bavaria.) The other source was gate money, hence the relentless schedule. Schwan had told a newspaper that the team 'would have to play about sixty games' per season, but now this figure was much closer to eighty or eighty-five. Not all of these were against the likes of Gern, of course. A year earlier, Bayern had netted 70,000 marks by agreeing to travel to Milan and play Inter.

The number-one reason why everyone wanted to host Bayern (and pay for the privilege) was that graceful, gifted kid from Giesing. Earlier in the season, Beckenbauer had been voted Germany's Footballer of the Year, the first Bayern player to win an honour that was destined to become a club preserve during the coming years.

Dieter Danzberg, the man who should have been Bayern's centre-half, until he was sent off in the club's first Bundesliga game, is in his mid-seventies now. He suffers from Alzheimer's. You can talk to him for as long as you want – if you come back the next day, he won't remember you.

However, his long-term memory is incredible. With absolute clarity, he recalls matches and incidents that happened half a century ago. 'I discovered him,' he says, jokingly. 'I discovered Beckenbauer, the *libero*.'

5. BEATLES OR STONES?

On 8 May 1968, a proud run ended with a whimper rather than a bang. It was a Wednesday night and almost 50,000 people, way above the legal capacity, had come out to Grünwalder Stadion to watch cupholders Bayern play Milan in the second leg of the Cup Winners' Cup semi-final.

The Italians had won the first game 2-0, a match marred by some controversy surrounding the opening goal. After a scoreless first half, Sepp Maier collected a back-pass from Franz Roth and then tried to kick the ball upfield. But Milan's Angelo Sormani blocked the kick with his outstretched leg and the ball rebounded into the net. When Maier realised the goal would be allowed to stand, two of his teammates had to physically restrain the goalkeeper from having more than just a word with the referee.

Now, in the return match, Bayern needed two clear goals of their own against one of the best defences in the world. It had been another immensely taxing season for the team, not least because of all those friendlies. Bayern thought nothing of jetting off to Brussels or Barcelona in-between two Bundesliga games to make money. The players didn't really mind this hectic schedule; they understood very well the money would go into their pockets, not the club's. (Bayern made almost no profit at all during these years; everything was reinvested back into the team. This approach would lead to problems some years later.) Still, money didn't make all that travelling less draining.

Against Milan, the machine finally broke down. Gerd Müller didn't score, Dieter Brenninger didn't score and even Franz Roth didn't score. When the final whistle rang, it was still 0-0. Bayern had been eliminated from the competition. This happens to the best teams in football, but it hadn't happened to this team in a very long time. Amazingly, Bayern had survived nineteen knock-out rounds in a row in the domestic cup and in Europe! At the twentieth hurdle, they finally fell. A week later, the Reds were knocked out of the DFB-Pokal, also in the semis, and then stumbled across the finishing line in the Bundesliga in fifth place, having been unable to win any of the last five games of the league season.

Was this Čajkovski's fault? Not directly, of course. He had worked wonders and everyone at the club knew they were indebted to the little man for a thrilling, daringly offensive team everyone loved to watch. But more and more people wondered if Čajkovski's style was too frenetic. Yes, it often won cup games, because the players fed off his energy and ran themselves into a frenzy. But would it ever win the league? The Bundesliga was a marathon, as the saying went, not a sprint.

And so Bayern decided to not extend Čajkovski's contract. The fact that the decision was made even before the winter break, when the team was still in contention in all competitions, tells you how convinced the board were that the club needed a change. In November 1967, Čajkovski announced he would be looking for a new job at the end of the season. There's little doubt that he had no choice and that this method was chosen to allow the well-liked coach to save face.

Bayern received quite a few applications from potential successors, but it took only one conversation to find the right man. In February 1968, president Wilhelm Neudecker and technical director Robert Schwan travelled to Salzburg, Austria, to meet the 38-year-old Branko Zebec. Like Čajkovski, he was Croatian – but nationality was the only thing he had in common with Čik.

Zebec was a stickler for discipline. He was stern, taciturn, distant. (A magazine profile later that year bore the headline: 'The Man Who Rarely Laughs!') He knew Germany well, having played for Alemannia Aachen, and he could point to some success as a coach. Zebec had guided Dinamo Zagreb to the Fairs Cup final in 1967, before he fell out with the club and was replaced by Ivica Horvat. But what made him really attractive in the eyes of Neudecker and Schwan were his ideas about the game. Zebec said the key to success was fitness. Fitness and tactics. Neudecker and Schwan signed him on the spot.

Bayern's players quickly learned that the days of going to Čik and Rada's home for some coffee were over. In June, before he was officially their new coach, Zebec accompanied the team on a tour of Peru, Chile and Colombia. While the players had hoped for a nice holiday, he made sure they kept in shape. Later, during the pre-season preparations, the squad was woken up at seven o'clock in the morning and told to go to the gym (before breakfast and, as Sepp Maier noted, 'before washing yourself'). Müller, always prone to being overweight, had to wear a tracksuit over not one but two kits and then run lap upon lap – after the normal training session. He quickly lost sixteen pounds. 'There are no improvisations during training,' skipper Werner Olk told the press. 'It's all pre-planned and tailor-made to address our deficiencies.' Hans Schiefele, the journalist and long-time Bayern member, couldn't resist a friendly dig and noted: 'Even Franz Beckenbauer, sometimes prone to conserving energy, participates in the full schedule.'

When the season began, Bayern were the fittest team in the league. This was a crucial asset, because the club's squad wasn't very big. In Zebec's first season, 1968–69, the team went more than twelve games without making a single substitution. Eight players started every game, five of them also went the distance every time. Neudecker and Schwan weren't opposed to making big transfers to bolster the squad – they had just signed two Austrian internationals. But they hoped Rudi Weiss, the head of the youth set-up, would continue churning out great players for the first team. The club even paid him a little bit of money now – a modest 2,000 marks per month to compensate for all the days he stood on football pitches instead of sitting in his law office. It was money well spent. The most recent of Weiss's discoveries was Hans-Georg Schwarzenbeck. Until Zebec came in, he had often been used as a full-back, but now he was Franz Beckenbauer's partner in the centre, his trusted and indispensable *Vorstopper*.

But Bayern were more than just the fittest team, they were also the most modern. Zebec, who would pioneer zonal marking and the pressing game in Germany during the 1970s, was not only fanatical about conditioning and discipline. He wanted his players to understand the game. 'If you have the ball,' he told Müller, 'the other team doesn't have it. And this means you have to do less running.' Long before Louis van Gaal and Pep Guardiola extolled the virtues of possession football in Munich, Zebec taught Bayern how to dominate the game and wait for the right moment to strike. For Čajkovski's young rascals, this was a radical change. But then again, they weren't really rascals any more. They were men in their early twenties who'd had their fun – now they craved success.

Zebec repaid Neudecker's and Schwan's faith in his capabilities not just with the club's first Bundesliga title but also with the first league-and-cup double. For all practical purposes, the title race was over by mid-April, when Bayern won away at Dortmund. The only goal of the game was scored by a young midfielder called Helmut Schmidt, another Rudi Weiss protégé, after a goalmouth melee and with only one minute left on the clock. The hosts loudly complained Schmidt had handled the ball, but the goal was allowed to stand. Zebec said: 'I was not one hundred per cent satisfied, but our lead in the standings now allows me to sleep more peacefully.' This lead had grown to five points over VfB Stuttgart and six over Hamburg (who had two games in hand).

The reference to his sleep reveals that Branko Zebec felt the pressure and wasn't quite as cool and controlled as he often appeared to be. When Bayern defended a narrow lead away at Alemannia Aachen, his old club, he even left the bench during the final stages and went into the dressing room, unable to stand the tension any more. He missed Gerd Müller's 88th-minute goal, which put the result beyond doubt.

Bayern finished the league season a whopping eight points ahead of surprise runners-up Aachen, to finally claim their first Bundesliga title. A week later, on 14 June 1969, the Reds met Schalke in the cup final in Frankfurt. Müller put the newly-crowned league champions ahead with a great left-footed volley from ten yards. But then something unusual happened. Schalke striker Manfred Pohlschmidt equalised with a tremendous shot from distance that flew into the top corner. It was unusual because it was the first goal Bayern had conceded in the entire cup campaign. It was also the last. Ten minutes before the break, Roth chipped a ball into Müller's path and the forward scored the winning goal with a powerful shot from a difficult angle.

Schalke couldn't come back after the restart because the game was played in stifling heat. Pohlschmidt later admitted: 'We were knackered.' Thanks to Zebec's relentless conditioning, Bayern ran down the clock without running into major problems. Then Müller could lift his third trophy of the day. Before the match he'd been presented with the small wooden cannon that goes out to the Bundesliga's top goalscorer and also the mounted golden ball that is the award for Germany's Footballer of the Year.

Yet even this glorious season wasn't without some low points. In December 1968, Bayern Munich travelled to Hannover to meet Čik Čajkovski's new team. There's little doubt that Bayern's August Starek, one of the two Austrian internationals who'd joined the club in the summer, used what in another code of football would be termed 'unnecessary roughness'. But the hosts responded in kind. Why there was so much bad blood is hard to tell, considering Čajkovski was still on excellent terms with the Bayern players and used to be Zebec's teammate at Partizan and Yugoslavia's national team. But rough it was. Hannover had to make a substitution after less than ten minutes;

on the half-hour Roth was badly fouled and hobbled off with an ankle injury.

This was the game briefly alluded to in the introduction to this book. Sepp Maier floored an assailant, who later sued him for assault. Franz Beckenbauer was so annoyed by the hostile atmosphere that he pretended to urinate in the direction of the crowd, which earned him a hefty fine from the DFB. Even Gerd Müller lost his cool, got into an argument with a Hannover player and gave him a slap under the chin. The coach of West Germany's youth teams, from the schoolboys to the Under-23s, had been watching the game from the stands. He later criticised the Hannover player for 'going down spectacularly'. Still, Müller was sent off and Bayern lost the game 1-0. (Both the national youth coach and the Hannover player would go on to play important roles in Bayern's history. The former was called Udo Lattek, the latter Jupp Heynckes.)

Maybe, just maybe, this day was the first indication that a sea change was about to take place with regard to Bayern's image and popularity. The contrast between the austere Zebec – whose motto was: 'Success is all that counts' – and the charming Čajkovski, who exuded joy and carefreeness, was as striking as it was symbolic. Under Zebec, Bayern had become more businesslike and clinical, they were no longer the youthful swashbucklers everyone had loved and admired. And what was worse – they had been replaced in people's hearts by a team that was almost the mirror image of Čajkovski's Bayern and the opposite of Zebec's Bayern: Borussia Mönchengladbach.

The club, which Germans tend to call just 'Gladbach' for the sake of brevity, had been promoted to the Bundesliga in the same year as Bayern, 1965, but needed a little bit longer to adapt. Now they were not only competitive, having finished third two years on the trot, but had developed a cavalier style that centred around counter-attacks which could resemble smash-and-grab raids. During the following decade, the question 'Bayern or Gladbach?' would become German football's version of the 'Beatles or Rolling Stones?' debate.

Bayern would often be typecast as the Beatles in this controversy: a global brand, elegant and smart, not to mention rich, but maybe a bit too rational and too much part of the Establishment. Gladbach, on the other hand, were often described in the terms you also heard used about the Stones: wild, visceral, rebellious – successful, yes, but always and only on their own terms. Underdogs made good.

Politics played a role, too. Famously and boldly, the writer Helmut Böttiger said the long passes that were a speciality of Gladbach's playmaker Günter Netzer 'were football's equivalent of the extra-parliamentary opposition', at the time a left-of-centre outlet for student dissent. Meanwhile, Beckenbauer made an oft-quoted disparaging remark about the Social Democrats – referring to Chancellor Willy Brandt as a 'national misfortune' – and his club was on good terms with ultra-conservatives like Franz Josef Strauss or Alfons Goppel, the long-time prime minister of Bavaria. (Goppel began one of his first speeches after taking office in 1962 by declaring: *'Mia san mia'* – we are who we are. But more about those weighty words later.)

Although countless articles have been written about this supposed battle between the forces of good and evil, it was largely nonsense and not only because it was Bayern left-back Paul Breitner, rather than one of the Gladbach stars, who toyed with radical Maoist chic and loved the Rolling Stones. Gladbach simply never were the gung-ho revolutionaries who won 6-5 or lost 7-6 every time they stepped onto a football pitch; Bayern never were the calculating conservatives who tried to keep a clean sheet and cynically ran down the clock when they held a lead. Life is more complicated than that. Even football is. But the juxtaposition made for good copy because, in sports, nothing beats a good rivalry.

And as the 1960s became the 1970s, there was none in German football on a national level. The first six seasons of the Bundesliga had been won by six different teams – and the seventh, 1969–70 – would be won by a seventh: Gladbach. Nobody seemed to be able to stay at or near the top for more than a few seasons. The most absurd example for this trend were Bayern's old Bavarian rivals Nuremberg: having won the Bundesliga in 1968, they fell out of the top flight a year later. Or take 1860 Munich: the Blues had been champions as recently as 1965, but in 1970 they, too, were relegated.

These roller-coaster rides made the league exciting, because you never knew who would end up where, but it also made it confusing. All the other big footballing countries either had a version of the Rangers–Celtic duopoly or an equivalent of England's 'Big Five'. So perhaps the German fans secretly longed for two big teams who forced – or allowed – them to take sides even when their own, local club was going nowhere.

That one of these two teams would turn out to be Bayern was not totally improbable. After all, Munich is a big, wealthy city and Bayern had a lot of pedigree and tradition. But it may have been Bayern's misfortune that the other consistently strong team to evolve during this period was not one of the most likely candidates – Cologne or Hamburg – but a poor club from a city of barely 150,000 inhabitants. No matter who competed with Gladbach, they would always be cast in the role of the bad guys.

There was another thing that made Borussia Mönchengladbach more attractive for many football fans during the 1970s. Although the club was, contrary to popular opinion, domestically more successful than Bayern, terrible mishaps tended to befall them in Europe. While Bayern often won when they should have lost, Gladbach regularly lost when they should have won. (Once they even lost when they won. In October 1971, Gladbach demolished Inter 7-1: the game was later annulled, because a can thrown from the stands might or might not have hit an Italian player. The match was replayed and Gladbach went out.) In other words, Borussia were tragic heroes, which is always very sexy.

Bayern, of course, preferred to be proper heroes. They didn't even seem to mind playing the role of bad guys. Sometimes they gave the impression of relishing it.

*

There are many theories that try to explain why the relationship between Zebec and Bayern deteriorated rapidly only months after he had delivered the biggest triumph in the club's history.

In his 2006 book about the club, the noted journalist Thomas Hüetlin says the coach became a 'liability' through his drinking. It might have played a role. Sepp Maier used to say that when the players saw Zebec 'standing in the showers, wearing sunglasses, a cigarette dangling from his lips', they knew he had been having a few the night before. Then again, blaming it all on drink is a bit of a knee-jerk reaction whenever talk turns to Zebec, because alcohol did ruin his career and, ultimately, ended his life. But most of the people who knew him very well maintain that Zebec didn't have a serious drinking problem until a pancreas operation in 1970 vastly reduced his alcohol tolerance.

Hüetlin also says the pressure got to Zebec and that he knew the writing was on the wall when Bayern unexpectedly crashed out of the European Cup in the first round against a widely unknown opponent – and despite carrying a two-goal advantage into the second leg. This opponent was AS Saint-Étienne. The French club weren't an entirely unknown quantity, having won their league four times in the previous six years, but they weren't yet the great team they would become (indeed, after eliminating Bayern, they went out to Legia Warsaw in the next round).

In the home leg, Brenninger put the hosts ahead on twenty-three minutes. Roth made it 2-0 seven minutes after the restart. But what everybody talked about after the game was the goal that never came. Local lad Günther Michl, yet another Rudi Weiss find, hit the crossbar; Beckenbauer dribbled past four defenders and then missed the target by inches; Müller's first touch let him down with only the goalkeeper to beat.

All observers agreed that Bayern should have won by a much bigger margin, but the disappointment was short-lived. Surely a two-goal lead would be enough to go through. Zebec said: 'We know it's going to be much harder in France and we have to be prepared for an opponent with a lot of fighting spirit. But the French have to come at us and my team is a good counter-attacking side.' The German defender Karl-Heinz Schnellinger, who'd won the European Cup with Milan a few months earlier, said: 'One day a Bundesliga club will go all the way in the European Cup. Maybe it'll be Bayern. This team has been carefully constructed over many years.'

But on 1 October 1969, in the industrial town of Saint-Étienne, the carefully constructed team came apart. With sixty-one seconds gone, the Bayern defence lost the first of many aerial duels on a night none of them would forget. Robert Herbin flicked the ball on for Hervé Revelli, who scored from close range. Spurred on by their fanatical crowd, Saint-Étienne looked like a different team. Time and again, Sepp Maier had to come to the rescue, but even his heroics weren't enough. Revelli and the outstanding Salif Keïta scored two more in the second half – with headers.

An enraged Maier later complained: 'Only Beckenbauer went up for those balls.' And Wilhelm Neudecker said: 'I'm not surprised that we lost the game. I'm surprised we never had a chance.' When a club employee told him he didn't know how to transport Saint-Étienne's gift – a vase – safely back to Munich, Neudecker hissed: 'I don't care if it gets smashed. We don't need anything that reminds us of this game.' Zebec, meanwhile, walked over to the press pack that was travelling with the team. 'Please, let's all stay up and play cards,' he begged, dreading a sleepless night in his hotel bed.

A third, and very plausible, theory for Zebec's decline says that the players had grown tired of his slave-driving methods. Maier still refers to the coach as 'that sadist' and does it only half-jokingly. Under Neudecker, Bayern Munich had become a club where players had a lot of power and were regularly consulted about club matters, first and foremost Beckenbauer (ironically, this player power would dethrone Neudecker himself many years later).

But not only the players were heard. Many people wielded influence at Bayern and possessing a fine sense of the intricate balance of power remains one of the secrets of surviving the Munich jungle. Maybe it was all too much, too complicated, too stifling for Zebec. In November 1969 he announced he would leave the club at the end of the season. Asked for comment, Neudecker coolly and somewhat cryptically said: 'Zebec has signed a contract that says he has to report to Schwan.' This triggered speculation that Zebec had asked the club to spend more money on transfers and had been rebutted by Schwan.

In any case, Bayern now needed a new coach for the summer. While Zebec quickly reached an agreement with VfB Stuttgart, Schwan consulted the man he considered to know more about the game than anyone else – Beckenbauer. Bayern's sweeper drew up a mental list of names, then crossed them off one by one. Finally, he said: 'What about Udo Lattek?'

It was a baffling suggestion. Lattek was barely thirty-five years old. He had never played professional football, and had in fact worked as a PE teacher in two small towns near Cologne until accepting an offer to join the DFB in 1965. Now he was coaching the national youth teams. And, crucially, serving as an assistant to the national manager Helmut Schön. That's why Beckenbauer knew and rated him. All the players liked Lattek. He was the total opposite of Zebec.

Before November was over, Bayern dispatched Beckenbauer to Cologne to have a word with Lattek. 'I'm speaking on behalf of the board of Bayern Munich,' the player explained. 'They want to know if you'd be interested in coaching the team.'

Stunned, Lattek hesitated for a moment. He had been Schön's assistant coach for many years and, according to the unwritten rules under which the DFB operated, this meant he was being groomed for the main job and was set to become national coach as soon as Schön retired, either in four or in eight years. Still, Beckenbauer's offer was the chance of a lifetime. The highly ambitious Lattek knew he had to grab it with both hands even if that meant jumping in at the deep end. He told Beckenbauer that, yes, he would be interested in succeeding Zebec.

Then he packed his bags and travelled to a small town south of Hannover, where his national Under-19 team would be playing Denmark. On a frozen pitch, West Germany went ahead after thirteen minutes. The goalscorer represented TSG Ulm and his name was Uli Hoeness. In the second half, Lattek brought on a player from Freilassing, very close to the Austrian border, called Paul Breitner. The game ended 1-1.

After the match, Lattek approached Hoeness and asked him if he had signed a contract somewhere. Lattek knew that almost a dozen Bundesliga clubs were courting the fleet-footed seventeen-year-old midfielder, 1860 Munich among them. He also knew that the negotiations were complicated, because Hoeness was bright and strong-minded. The player was adamant about signing an amateur contract because it would allow him to play for West Germany at the 1972 Olympics (the Games were closed to professional athletes until the 1980s). He also said he wanted to study at university on the side – preferably business administration, or maybe English literature – and thus needed some sort of office job at the club to earn money until he signed professional forms. Such determination stumped many club officials, who were used to players being far more simple-minded. So the various talks dragged on, which is why Hoeness told Lattek that he was close to signing for VfB Stuttgart but hadn't yet done so.

'Do me a favour,' Lattek said. 'Wait just a little bit longer before you commit yourself.' Hoeness promised he would.

Less than three weeks later, Robert Schwan parked his car in front of the Hoeness family's butcher's shop in Ulm. Schwan made the young player a good but not great offer. There were soon rumours that Hoeness had been promised a new car and a huge signing-on bonus in return for pledging his allegiance to Bayern, but this has never been substantiated and seems unlikely. Hoeness later said he liked Schwan's no-nonsense manner and the idea that he was joining a club with a reputation for giving young players a chance. And, of course, the fact that Schwan told him Lattek would be the new coach. In January,

Hoeness announced he would become a Bayern player. His close friend Paul Breitner soon followed suit.

Ludwig Maierböck – yes, the same 1860 man who had missed out on Gerd Müller six years earlier – was boiling with indignation when the news spread. He claimed to have reached a verbal agreement with Breitner as early as August and with Hoeness back in October. 'Maierböck had been scouting me since I was fifteen,' Breitner recently admitted. 'He came to our house and said he wanted me to play for 1860. But he never hit upon the idea of presenting a contract to my parents or myself. 1860 simply missed the boat.'

While these momentous events were happening behind the scenes, Bayern dropped out of the title race. First they lost the derby with 1860, although the Blues were mired in the drop zone, then they couldn't protect a lead against Essen, another relegation candidate.

On Friday, 13 March 1970, the phone rang in Lattek's Cologne flat. He glanced at the bedside clock through drowsy eyes. It was 4.30 in the morning. He instinctively knew that this was the phone call he had secretly been expecting since the conversation with Beckenbauer. Lattek picked up the receiver and listened. Then he woke his wife. He told her that Bayern had fired Branko Zebec and that he had to be in Munich as quickly as possible.

At first there was very little to indicate that Bayern had entered their glory decade – and sowed the seeds for an unprecedented period of dominance – when the club signed Lattek, Hoeness and Breitner. Quite the contrary. Some of the established players resented the youngsters because of their cockiness. They also thought that the two pals were a bit too close to Lattek, the man who had coached them before and who had signed them. Even Schwan, who often made a point of putting the duo in their place, was obviously fond of them. Schwan, who could quickly lose his patience in the presence of stupidity, liked Hoeness and Breitner because they were smart. Some others felt there was a fine line between being smart and being a smart alec.

Hoeness had been a Bayern player for less than four weeks when the Reds played a warm-up match against his old club, Ulm. In the first half, he played on the right wing, while the international Erich Maas, who had been signed for this position from Brunswick for a considerable sum, sat on the bench. After the break, Maas came on and Hoeness moved into midfield. When a reporter later asked Hoeness about the switch, he replied: 'I was played on the wing, which is not my normal position, to teach Maas a lesson.'

Many teammates felt this was a bit much, coming from an eighteen-year-old. Hoeness was not only criticising the coach for playing him out of position (in contrast to Breitner, who quietly accepted that he was put at left-back), he was also showing up Maas, not to mention that he was making internal matters public. Next he rubbed Beckenbauer and Müller up the wrong way. Things got so bad, the journalist Peter Bizer wrote a few years later, 'that only an open debate moderated by Lattek and Schwan prevented a palace revolt against this Swabian greenhorn'. During the debate, Lattek was accused of giving Hoeness preferential treatment, which he vehemently denied.

The talk must have cleared the air. Bayern went into the seven-week winter break in first place in the Bundesliga, one point ahead of title-holders Gladbach. They had also reached the quarter-finals of the Fairs Cup (just about to be renamed the UEFA Cup) and the round of 16 in the DFB-Pokal. Finishing off a near-perfect first half of the season was the news that Gerd Müller had been voted European Footballer of the Year 1970, the first German to win this honour. Bobby Moore came second, Luigi Riva third and another Bayern player, Beckenbauer, fourth.

But the new year dampened the mood. First Bayern were played off the park by Liverpool in the Fairs Cup. Then they went into the last matchday of the Bundesliga season level on points with Gladbach. Both teams played away from home: Bayern at MSV Duisburg, safe in mid-table, and Gladbach at Eintracht Frankfurt, knee-deep in the relegation fight. With fifty-five minutes gone, the soon-to-be fierce rivals were still level, because Gladbach were drawing 1-1 in Frankfurt while the game in Duisburg was scoreless.

And yet the two games were very different. Calling the atmosphere in Duisburg hostile would be an understatement. Beckenbauer was booed whenever he touched the ball. In the very first minute, Duisburg's defender Hartmut Heidemann brutally fouled Roth, who was clear through on goal. By all accounts, Heidemann's teammate Đorđe Pavlić kicked everything that moved. The Duisburg players were just as fired up as their fans for a game that meant nothing to them.

Deep into the second half, Bayern were hit on the break and Rainer Budde gave Duisburg the lead. Spectators ran onto the pitch, waving blue-and-white flags. Fifteen minutes later, Budde scored again, probably from an offside position. There was another pitch invasion, Maier was hit in the head and had to come off (Duisburg's star player, Bernard Dietz, is still convinced that Maier was faking the injury in an attempt to get the match annulled, but eyewitnesses said that Maier was indeed knocked down by a fan). So chaotic was the game that the referee allowed Udo Lattek to make a third substitution before howls of protest from the crowd alerted him to the fact that this was against the rules. Gladbach, meanwhile, won 4-1 and claimed the title again.

Kicker magazine said: 'Bayern shouldn't hang their heads. Second place is something. It's even a lot for coach Udo Lattek. He has been accused of bringing in too many young players and some experts predicted failure. But the young players came through.' The coach had indeed put a lot of faith in youth. Besides Hoeness and Breitner, he had also made 22-year-old Rainer Zobel a regular and was often playing 21-year-old Edgar Schneider. But Lattek knew that second place would be forgotten soon. He needed a title, and it was one of his kids who helped him to it.

More than 15,000 Bayern fans travelled to Stuttgart to see their team play Cologne in the cup final on 19 June 1971. They were rewarded with a great game. Cologne went ahead early, but the best player on the pitch, Beckenbauer, equalised after the break. Bayern were then reduced to ten men when right-back Herwart Koppenhöfer retaliated against Hannes Löhr and was sent off. But they should have won the final in regular time, because in the last minute, Müller was blatantly wrestled to the ground in the penalty area. The referee shook his head and waved play-on. He did the same when Müller was brought down in the box again five minutes into extra time. Then Zobel hit the underside of the crossbar with a long-range shot. Nobody knew whether the ball crossed the line as it came down or not. The referee said no. Then Brenninger, in his 335th and last competitive game for Bayern, missed an open goal. In the 118th minute, Müller was unmarked five yards in front of the target, but Cologne's goalkeeper made an amazing save and turned the shot around the post.

Lattek stared at the running track. He must have wondered what he had to do to get a break. The ensuing corner was cleared and the ball reached Schneider. He rode a tackle and fired the ball into the top corner from twenty yards. Lattek jumped up, raced onto the pitch and hectically yelled instructions at Breitner. A minute later he was in the air again, this time to celebrate. As Čajkovski used to do, he embraced every single player. He knew how important this win was for the team. Few things weld a side together more thoroughly than winning a final, even more so when the team had been reduced to ten men.

But it was also important for him. Three decades later, when Bayern celebrated their 100th birthday with a big party, Lattek spotted Edgar Schneider. He walked over to the man who'd never really broken through at the club, pointed a finger at him and beamed: 'There's the man who won my first cup!'

The early 1970s were a critical period for German football, littered with tumultuous events. In June 1971, the big Bundesliga bribe scandal broke which kept writers and lawyers busy – and fans disgusted – for years. Eventually, two teams were demoted (Offenbach and Bielefeld) and more than fifty players and officials from ten different clubs were suspended, some for life, for agreeing to throw a large number of league games, most of them relating to the relegation fight.

Bayern Munich and Borussia Mönchengladbach were not involved, although the names of both clubs came up from time to time during the investigations. Duisburg's goalkeeper Volker Danner claimed to have been offered 12,000 marks (at the time the equivalent of £1,400) for letting in a few goals in the final game of the 1970–71 season when his club hosted Bayern. He didn't say who made him the offer, only that it came 'from Munich'. Danner said he refused to throw the match. Ironically, he was later convicted and suspended for having received 2,000 marks from an unknown and unnamed source for winning this game, which helped Gladbach claim the league title. (It was illegal to accept bonus payments from third parties.)

These few lines alone will illustrate how unsavoury and murky the whole affair was. Many players had accepted bribes because they didn't make much money. Many clubs had paid bribes because they feared nothing more than dropping from the Bundesliga to the semi-pro, multi-tiered lower flight. And so the most immediate effects of the scandal, on a technical level, were the abolishment of all caps on wages and transfers and the creation of a professional second division, the 2. Bundesliga.

But more dramatic were the psychological effects. Just a few years before the 1974 World Cup on home soil, football was suddenly a dirty business, populated by crooks. In the mid-1960s, more than 7.5 million fans per year attended Bundesliga games; in the early 1970s, this figure dropped to 5.3 million.

Not all was doom and gloom, though. Luckily for German football, just when many fans became disillusioned with the game, the best side in the country's history took to the field. In 1972, a universally admired West German team won the European Championships in great style. Beckenbauer had never been more graceful under pressure, a dashing Netzer was at the top of his game. Two years later, the national team – starring six Bayern players – won the World Cup. Although this side is not as fondly remembered, let alone as revered, as the 1972 team, those successes greatly helped restore football's reputation.

In-between these two sporting triumphs, something else happened. In 1973, the owner of Jägermeister, the company producing the digestif, took on the DFB – and won. The man's name was Günter Mast (his uncle had started the company) and he'd got it into his head that his local club, Brunswick, should endorse his product on their shirts. The DFB stopped him, whereupon Mast simply convinced the club's members to change the badge and use the Jägermeister logo instead. It was the beginning of a legal tug-of-war that ended when the DFB decided to legalise shirt sponsorship, four years ahead of the English FA.

However, for the team whose shirt would soon be the most coveted and lucrative, the most important event during these years was something else entirely – the 1972 Olympics in Munich.

For the Games, the city built a ground that even now, more than four decades later, is breathtakingly beautiful: the Olympic Stadium. Designed by the architect Günter Behnisch and the engineer Frei Otto and situated in Schwabing-West, five miles north of Grünwalder Stadion, the stadium quickly became a Munich landmark, not least because of the sweeping and transparent canopy that covers three of the four stands.

It's not, however, a perfect place for football. Due to the running track around the pitch, one is not as close to the action as a modern fan would like to be. The elegantly curved stands rise gently rather than steeply, impeding the view from the lower rows. The open, light construction means the wind can pass freely through the ground, so the Olympic Stadium tends to be a cold, wet place on inhospitable days. And yet it's still a brilliantly atmospheric ground as long as the conditions are right and enough people come out to watch.

Both Bayern and 1860 Munich decided to move into the Olympic Stadium as tenants, starting with the 1972–73 season. One reason was the capacity of around 80,000, twice what Gründwalder Stadion could hold. (Today, Bayern fans may sneer that the Olympic Stadium was too big for 1860, but in fact the ground's attendance record is held by the Blues. It was set in a second-division game against Augsburg in August 1973, when more than 90,000 were on hand, many without tickets.) The other reason was the deplorable state of Grünwalder Stadion. In January 1971, the main stand had burned to the ground, probably a case of arson, and soon a thunderstorm would destroy the roof of the terrace.

The new stadium was officially opened on 26 May 1972, three months before the Olympics, with an international between West Germany and the Soviet Union. (Coincidentally, these two teams would also meet in the European Championship final a few weeks later.) Six Bayern players saw action on that day: Maier, Beckenbauer, Schwarzenbeck, Hoeness, Breitner and Müller, who scored all the goals in a 4-1 rout. What they didn't know was that they would be playing at this very place with their club a lot sooner than planned.

For the first and so far only time in Bundesliga history, the last matchday of the 1971–72 season amounted to a final. Bayern were leading Schalke by one point and would be hosting them on the evening of 28 June 1972, a Wednesday. For a 2005 book on the history of the Olympic Stadium, Uli Hoeness looked back upon that magical summer and said: 'We were supposed to relocate in the new season. But Wilhelm Neudecker, our president at the time, knew how attractive the new stadium was – and how much bigger the revenue would be for Bayern if he moved the match.'

Even Neudecker was surprised by the response when he let it be known the Schalke match would be staged at the Olympic Stadium. The match sold out in just two hours; some people bought as many as 100 tickets; countless fans had to be turned away. Neudecker apologised, promised to limit the number of tickets a single person could purchase in the future and said: 'We just didn't expect such a rush.' He wasn't being coquettish. At Grünwalder Stadion, Bayern had sold barely 900 season tickets.

Neudecker knew how hard it would be to fill a ground as huge as the Olympic Stadium on a regular basis, which is why he reduced ticket prices – a smart but unusual decision, considering he was moving to a much more comfortable, modern location. (At Grünwalder Stadion, the best seats cost 25 marks. At the Olympic Stadium, a seat on the roofless East Stand was 10 marks for non-members, only 5 marks – less than 65 pence in early 1970s money – for members.)

But of course everyone wanted to watch the 1972 game. The eventual 5-1 scoreline seems to indicate a one-sided match, but it wasn't quite like that. Early on, Maier came out to collect a corner but missed the cross completely, whereupon Hoeness had to clear the ball off the line with a header. Bayern's two full-backs – the Dane Johnny Hansen and Breitner – made it 2-0 before the break, but Klaus Fischer, a former 1860 player, pulled one back for Schalke. So the title race wasn't decided until Bayern's left-winger Wilhelm Hoffmann converted a Müller through ball for the third goal midway through the second half. Ten minutes from time, Hoeness scored his team's 100th goal of the season, then Beckenbauer put the finishing touch on a glorious campaign when he converted a free kick from the edge of the penalty area with a nonchalance that was regal indeed.

It was the first and as yet only time that a Bundesliga team has recorded a century of goals. In the same season reigning champions Gladbach lagged far behind with an otherwise impressive eighty-two. In fact, there were only three years during the 1970s when Gladbach managed to rack up more goals than Bayern. Sometimes the Reds outscored their rivals even when the latter won the league (as in 1970, 1976 and 1977). So much for the supposedly attacking Gladbach and the allegedly calculating Bayern.

The Schalke game pocketed the club a cool 1.1 million marks. For the coming seasons, Neudecker hoped for an average attendance of 35,000 and calculated that a normal league match should earn the club at least 250,000 marks. The president would reach his goal, but not immediately. During Bayern's first full season in the Olympic

Stadium, 1972–73, the club drew 31,000 per game. It was by far the best figure in the league but still below Neudecker's target. Who knows, the reason may have been that his team was just too good.

In early October, Bayern met Schalke again and won easily, 5-0. After the game, Schalke's coach Ivica Horvat shook his head and said: 'What were we doing here in the first place?' Then he predicted Bayern would win the Bundesliga by twenty points. (Eventually, the lead was only eleven points – but since these were the days of the two-points-for-a-win rule, it was a heavy margin nonetheless and set a league record that would stand until 1999.) Horvat spoke for many opponents: Udo Lattek's team was just overpowering.

The Reds scored five or more goals on eight different occasions. They won the title with four games in hand following a 6-0 thrashing of Kaiserslautern. Müller scored five goals that day, the second but not the last time he'd pull off this feat in a league match. Actually, Müller finished the season with sixty-six goals in all competitions (including the short-lived League Cup). It was a European record that survived for almost four decades, until Lionel Messi finally broke it.

After the Kaiserslautern game, Beckenbauer said: 'Of our three league titles, this was certainly the one that came easiest to us.' A writer who was present in the dressing room reported: 'Bayern celebrated their trophy the way you celebrate a constantly recurring event. The champagne didn't flow freely, it was passed around in glasses.' He quoted Maier as saying: 'We're all creatures of habit.' An even more famous quote popped out of Breitner's mouth after the final matchday. Together with a couple of other players, he ran a few laps of honour, then he walked into the dressing room – and was stunned to see that the rest of the team had already left. Breitner undressed, grabbed a bottle of champagne, jumped into the pool and loudly yelled: 'Does nobody at this shitty club know how to party?'

When photos of the naked Breitner and reports of his rhetorical question appeared in newspapers, Neudecker was furious. He was annoyed by the player's antics, anyway. Breitner wore an afro. He was about to adopt a little girl from Vietnam (as much a political statement as a humanitarian one at a time when opinion about the war in Southeast Asia still divided the nation). A year earlier, he had been photographed reading Chairman Mao's Little Red Book and not long after the end of the season an even more famous image would make the rounds, showing him under a Mao poster, studying the *Beijing Review*. Neudecker threatened to sell Breitner, saying he demanded more discipline from someone 'who earns as much as ten workers put together'. Breitner told the press: 'As long as I play well, I can get away with anything. Even a political opinion.' As it turned out, he was right.

However, this blasé attitude – the aristocratic indifference with which Bayern seemed to take success for granted – fostered resentment even more. Six months after their second league title in a row, in December 1973, the players were sitting in their coach, ready to leave for Bremen airport, when about twenty yobs blocked the exit. Beckenbauer later said they were yelling: 'Maier-manure, Müller-shit, Beckenbauer-piss!' Maier said all he heard was: 'Kill those Bayern pigs!' When the Bremen fans started throwing rocks, a group of Bayern players left the coach and distributed a few punches until the loudmouths legged it, then the team left town. Needless to say, they had won the football match, too.

But no matter whether you liked Bayern or hated them, you had to admit that they delivered some mightily entertaining games during the 1973–74 season. Actually, these were the sort of games people normally attributed to Gladbach. At Schalke, in September, Bayern conceded five goals before the break, but came away with a 5-5 draw, with Müller scoring four goals. Six weeks later, Bayern raced into a 4-1 lead away at Kaiserslautern – and then conceded six goals in half an hour to lose 7-4.

In early May 1974, the title race was still completely open, because table-topping Bayern led Gladbach by only a single point. With two games left in the season, the mouth-watering prospect of another quasi-final seemed to become reality, as Gladbach would be playing against Bayern on the last day. But it was not to be. Gladbach were beaten on the penultimate weekend by Rhineland rivals Fortuna Düsseldorf and the Reds had won their third straight Bundesliga title. They could afford to stumble across the Gladbach pitch on the last matchday like drunken men and lose 5-0.

This isn't a turn of phrase – they were indeed drunk. Contrary to what Breitner had said about the club a year earlier, the Bayern players had partied so hard that the smell of alcohol on their breaths might have put off their opponents. But of course it was not the Bundesliga title they had been celebrating. It was a much bigger trophy.

6. SHINING UNDER FLOODLIGHTS

Many modern fans bemoan that the football boom of the 1990s and the subsequent remodelling of the European cup competitions has led to the situation whereby a small number of elite super-clubs – Bayern Munich among them – treat their domestic league almost like an afterthought and focus on the real prize, the Champions League.

This is not a recent phenomenon, though. The glittering European nights of the 1970s that allowed Bayern entry into the inner circle of clubs that transcend their own leagues were more than just the icing on the cake. They were almost a necessity.

In the build-up to the 1972 Bundesliga decider between Bayern and Schalke, Neudecker issued a thinly veiled threat to his players: 'We can only keep this expensive team together,' he said, 'if we earn additional money from European matches and exhibition games. If we lose these sources of income, we have to part ways with some of our star players.' In other words: win the league and get into the European Cup – or get out of here.

As the renowned sports journalist Ulfert Schröder said about Bayern's squad in a Beckenbauer biography in mid-1973: 'It costs more than four million marks per year. And those four million marks have to be earned. Four million or Bayern go bust. That's the minimum.' Hence the average attendance of 35,000 Neudecker was aiming at, because if they could secure that then seventeen home games per league season translated into guaranteed revenues of 4.25 million, which might just cover the operational costs. (In 1973, four million marks were £615,000.)

It was a dangerous gamble, the sort of vicious-circle approach to spending and earning that would almost ruin Borussia Dortmund three decades later. It also meant that homegrown players became increasingly marginalised, because the club needed success so badly that it seemed wiser to spend money on proven players than to try untested ones. But in the absence of a wealthy owner or investors, Neudecker's options were limited. While Uli Hoeness was already marketing his own wedding (offering magazines exclusive rights to photos and interviews for 25,000 marks), Neudecker was looking for similarly innovative ways to finance deals such as his big transfer coup in the summer of 1973: Bayern shattered all German records by signing Cologne's midfielder Hans-Josef Kapellmann for 800,000 marks (roughly £125,000).

In his search for extra earnings, Neudecker even suggested making the professional football division independent from the non-commercial parent club. One day, many years down the road, this revolutionary idea would indeed become reality, but for now Neudecker and his treasurer Willi O. Hoffmann had to make do with a few questionable tax-saving schemes. And, of course, those lucrative mid-week games under floodlights against prestigious foreign opposition. While the Fairs Cup or the Cup Winners' Cup had been appealing competitions only a few years earlier, now only the real deal would do – the European Cup.

However, Bayern's second foray into this competition was only marginally less disappointing than the defeat at the hands of AS Saint-Étienne back in 1969. In the 1972–73 season, the Germans survived the first two rounds but then suffered a painful setback against Ajax in the quarter-finals. The Dutch, as the title-holders, were widely favoured, yet Bayern felt an upset wasn't beyond them. But following a scoreless first half in Amsterdam, the team collapsed after the break and lost 4-0.

Or rather, Sepp Maier collapsed. He later said that on a good day he should have saved three of Ajax's goals, all four on a very good day. He was probably a bit too harsh on himself, as Gerrie Mühren's volley (2-0) and Johan Cruyff's header (4-0) were very hard to keep out. In any case, Maier shouldered the blame and, back at the hotel, threw his kit and his gloves into a canal before asking the German journalists if any of them had a day job for him so that he could give up goalkeeping. (Bayern would take drastic revenge for this heavy defeat some years later, when they were invited to meet Ajax for Cruyff's testimonial. Despite the festive occasion, they got stuck in and won the game 8-0.)

Ahead of the following season, 1973–74, Neudecker announced that Bayern 'would gladly forgo another Bundesliga title for winning the European Cup'. His team then came within a whisker of going out in the first round to a club nobody had ever heard of, Swedish champions Åtvidabergs FF. Bayern won the home leg 3-1, but the game in Sweden unexpectedly turned into a nerve-racking thriller. The 24-year-old Swedish striker Conny Torstensson scored a hat-trick and Bayern teetered on the brink of the abyss, until Hoeness knocked the ball in from six yards in the seventy-fifth minute to take the game to extra time and, eventually, to the first-ever penalty shoot-out in Bayern's history. Maier somehow saved a spot-kick and another one went wide. In the stands, Neudecker sighed a deep sigh of relief. Then, legend has it, he told Schwan: 'I want the guy with the red shoes.' The player whose name he didn't know was, of course, Torstensson. Bayern signed him for 580,000 marks (then about £90,000) during the winter break.

Although Bayern certainly hadn't covered themselves in glory, the games against the Swedish part-timers were forgotten less than two days later. On Friday, 5 October 1973, at the Hotel Atlantis in Zurich, UEFA held the draw for the second round. At 11.15 a.m., there were gasps all around the plush room. The very first tie that had been drawn was Bayern Munich vs Dynamo Dresden. Moments later, a wire-service announced: 'There it is – at last!'

Since the end of the war and the division of the country, there had never been a competitive game between club sides representing West Germany and the communist East Germany (GDR). Even though both countries had taken part in the various continental cup competitions since 1957 (when Karl-Marx-Stadt, now Chemnitz, entered the European Cup), the draw had kept them apart again and again, until a rumour started up that it had been fixed and that UEFA was trying to avoid such a politically charged encounter.

For Neudecker, though, the draw was a dream come true. Surely his highly-paid professionals would have no problems against those unknowns from behind the Iron Curtain. And yet everyone would want to watch the game, at the ground and on television. Barely 25,000 had been scattered around the spacious Olympic Stadium for the Åtvidaberg game, but the Dresden match was a surefire sell-out. The club announced that a ticket for the terraced area would cost 12 marks, the best seat 60 marks. In his weekly column for *Kicker* magazine, editor Karl-Heinz Heimann noted: 'The two games will be the matches of the year. What a pity that Bayern are determined to turn it into the business deal of the year as well.'

Putting it mildly, public relations weren't Bayern's strong suit during these months and years. Eight days after the draw, Lattek and Schwan crossed the heavily fortified and guarded border between West and East to scout their coming opponent. Away at Zwickau, Dresden lost 3-0 and sank to seventh place in the GDR's top flight. Schwan told a reporter: 'If Dresden knock us out of the European Cup, Lattek and I will stay in the GDR.' It almost seemed as if the only person who took Dynamo seriously was Bayern's coach. 'They have knocked out Juventus,' Lattek reminded people. 'And that takes some doing.' Few listened.

In his thirteen years as Bayern president, Neudecker had been right more often than not. But on the evening of 24 October, he was wrong on many counts. First, there were more than 20,000 unsold tickets, even though the first leg against Dresden was not shown live on West German television. Second, the communists were no pushovers. At half-time, the visitors were leading 3-2 and the hosts were mercilessly booed as they trotted off the pitch. After the interval, a deflected Franz Roth shot and an opportunist Müller goal gave Bayern a narrow 4-3 win that didn't bode well for the second leg.

Bayern did more damage to their image two weeks later, in the build-up to the away game. The team left Munich on 5 November, a Monday, travelling the 290 miles to Dresden by coach. They were booked into the Interhotel Newa (the term *Interhotel* denoted fairly posh places almost exclusively for guests from non-socialist states). Of course the East German football fans knew that the club would be staying there and a large number of them waited in front of the hotel to catch a glimpse of the famous stars from West Germany. There were at least 500 of them; some reports speak of as many as 1,000. What they didn't get to see was Bayern.

At 3.15 p.m., during a stopover, Neudecker told Schwan, Lattek, Beckenbauer and Müller that he wanted to have a word with them. The president announced the team would not travel to Dresden and would instead spend the night in Hof, a Bavarian town close to the border. Neudecker then informed the press about this change of plans. 'Dresden is situated 116 metres above sea level,' he explained. 'Munich is 567 metres above sea level. This difference might turn out to be detrimental to our performance and two days in Dresden do not suffice to acclimatise ourselves.'

Nobody knew better than Neudecker that this was nonsense. But he didn't care what people thought of him or the club, he was trying to protect an investment. At the time, not many West Germans had ever been in East Germany, but two Bayern players had: Breitner and Hoeness represented West Germany at the 1969 UEFA Youth Tournament, essentially the European Under-18 Championship, which was held in various East German cities. Hoeness told Neudecker that some Western teams had suffered from diarrhoea and that there were rumours their food had been tampered with. Neudecker himself had also heard stories about bugged hotel rooms and undercover agents spying on West German visitors. He decided to play it safe and spend only the hours directly before and after the game at the hotel in Dresden. This violated a UEFA rule which said visiting teams had to be at the site of the game on the evening before the match, but Neudecker was willing to risk a reprimand or even a fine.

His prudence garnered Bayern, often denounced as unapproachable and arrogant anyway, a lot of bad press. Many years later, Hoeness apologised for what he called 'an over-reaction'. It wasn't until the Berlin Wall came down in 1989 that information came to light that put a slightly new slant on the episode. As it turned out, the hotel had indeed been bugged. Shortly after Lattek had finished his pre-match talk, Dynamo's coach was informed about Bayern's line-up and tactics.

At first it seemed as if the man didn't know what to do with this inside information. The brilliant Hoeness ran rings round his marker and scored a brace in the first half. But Dresden got on the scoreboard shortly before the break and then added two more goals between the fifty-second and the fifty-sixth minutes. Suddenly, the hosts were going through on away goals! 'Things are not looking good for the German champions from Munich,' the West German television commentator said in a sombre voice, momentarily forgetting that the other team were German champions, too. Well, it was hard to hear him above the din at Dynamo's ground, anyway.

Bayern's entire season suddenly hung in the balance, but it did so for only ninety seconds, before Gerd Müller revealed why one of his numerous nicknames was the Ghost of the Penalty Area. He materialised at the edge of the six-yard box like an apparition, pounced on a loose ball and scored on the turn to see the Reds, no political meaning intended, through to the quarter-finals.

By comparison, the next two rounds – against CSKA Sofia and Újpest FC from Budapest – were much less dramatic, though it might be worth a mention that Torstensson, 'the guy with the red shoes', scored four goals for Bayern over the course of those ties, a few months after he'd scored three goals against them in the same competition. Today, he would be cup-tied and unable to play, but back then, the Swede who had almost knocked Bayern out helped them reach their first European Cup final, in Brussels against Atlético Madrid on 15 May 1974.

Were they ecstatic to become only the second German club (after Eintracht Frankfurt in 1960) to reach a final for the biggest prize in European club football? 'It's relief more than rapture,' Beckenbauer admitted. 'People expected this from us. Anything else would have been a surprise.' For football fans back home in Germany, this was further proof of Bayern's infuriating smugness. But of course Beckenbauer was right. After his team had eliminated Újpest FC, the Hungarian newspaper *Magyar Nemzet* said the German team's 'dream to finally win the European Cup will most certainly come true, because right now Bayern are the best side in the world.'

And yet – if it hadn't been for Katsche, Bayern would have blown it. Katsche was what everyone called the man who was the shield-bearer to Franz Beckenbauer's knight in shining armour: Georg Schwarzenbeck. His full first name was Hans-Georg and since every team he had ever joined already had two or three people called Hans, he was never able to shed this childhood moniker he slightly resented. The others had great names like Kaiser or Bomber (Gerd Müller again), the Bull or the Cat (Sepp Maier); he was just plain old Katsche (the word is a dialect expression for a dent or a bruise and the nickname seemed to indicate he was not the most refined of players).

Against Atlético, Katsche was having the same subpar game as all of his teammates except Maier and Beckenbauer. Torstensson and Roth missed very good chances in the first ten minutes, but then Atlético Madrid settled down and became increasingly comfortable. Schwarzenbeck had massive problems with José Gárate and needed the help of his sweeper Beckenbauer more than once.

Bayern were probably lucky there was still no score after the regular ninety minutes. Early into the second half of extra time, the Spanish right-back José Capón hit the side-netting with a first-time shot from ten yards. At the other end, Müller had a penalty appeal turned down. Six minutes from time, Atlético's substitute Heraldo Bezerra was brought down by Johnny Hansen just inches outside the box. Luis Aragonés curled the ball over the wall and raised his arms while it was still in the air. Maier hardly moved, he never had a chance. The Reds, playing all in white, probably weren't aware of this, but they were now a few minutes away from becoming the first-ever Bayern team to lose a final. The ground reverberated with Spanish chants and the 25,000 Atlético fans on hand waved their red-and-white flags.

With three minutes left, Gárate dribbled over to the corner flag to run down the clock. A frustrated Breitner sent him to the floor with a push in the back. With two minutes left, Schwarzenbeck gave away possession with a disastrous pass and allowed the Spanish to knock the ball around for another precious twenty seconds. Gárate had a feeble attempt at goal and when Maier calmly collected the ball, the exhausted striker sank to the ground.

With one minute left, Bayern won a throw-in and the ball reached Beckenbauer. Gárate was still lying on his back in Bayern's box. Beckenbauer looked up and saw Schwarzenbeck walking at a measured pace deeper and deeper into the Spanish half. Kapellmann signalled for Beckenbauer to hoof the ball into the penalty area, but for some reason the Kaiser passed the ball to Schwarzenbeck. Katsche picked up speed and then struck from almost thirty yards. The ball whistled past friend and foe in Atlético's box and crossed the line next to the left-hand post, just out of the diving goalkeeper's reach.

Fifteen seconds after the Spanish kicked off to restart play, the referee ended the final. Atlético's captain Adelardo Rodríguez, who had taken Hoeness out of the game, and sweeper Ramón Heredia, wept openly. In those days, before penalty shoot-outs were used to decide a title, Schwarzenbeck's last-gasp goal had done nothing more than necessitate

SHINING UNDER FLOODLIGHTS

a replay, but everybody who saw the game – at the ground or on television – knew that Katsche had beaten Atlético. Many of the Spanish players were over thirty. Quite apart from the mental damage inflicted by Schwarzenbeck's equaliser, the physical strain of having to play again just two days later would almost certainly be too much for them.

And that's exactly what happened. The replay was as one-sided as the first game had been tense. In the fourteenth minute, Hoeness went past goalkeeper Miguel Reina but then missed an open goal from a tight angle. Two minutes later, Müller headed a Roth cross from the left flank against the post. On twenty-eight minutes, Paul Breitner released Hoeness with a tremendous pass from deep in Bayern's half. Hoeness was younger, faster and fitter than any of the three players chasing him. He raced into Atlético's box and then clinically put the ball through the legs of Reina (whose son Pepe would, incidentally, briefly play for Bayern forty years later).

The goal played into Bayern's hands, because now the Reds could sit back and hit Atlético, who were fading fast, on the break. Ten minutes into the second half, Kapellmann ran down the left wing and then found Müller at the far post with his cross. From an almost impossible angle, the centre-forward made it 2-0. Seven minutes later, Müller scored again with an even more beautiful goal, a delicate chip from the edge of the box. With eight minutes left on the clock, Hoeness won the ball at the halfway line and had enough energy left for another solo run. He outpaced two defenders, rounded Reina and sidefooted the ball into the net.

After the award ceremony, the players celebrated exuberantly in their dressing room. This time, the champagne was not passed around in glasses but did flow freely. Laughing, Beckenbauer said: 'If Gladbach don't beat us tomorrow, they never will.'

Then the team left for Keerbergen, a small town twenty miles northeast of Brussels. At the Hotel Grand Veneur, Bayern partied all night until the staff began to fear for the famous art deco building. In the morning, everyone left for another hotel, this time in Mönchengladbach, and another game of football. Knackered but happy, the players lay down on a meadow next to the hotel and dozed off until they had to go to the stadium. They lost 5-0.

Bayern's European Cup triumph in 1974 was the greatest success for German club football up to that time. Yes, it was a lucky win considering how close Bayern had come to losing the first final. However, in their history of the European Cup, John Motson and John Rowlinson claim there was some justice to the outcome. The reason was Atlético's disgusting, shameful semi-final against Celtic. 'It was never a match,' Celtic's manager Jock Stein said about that ugly night. 'They used people to try and take players out of the game.' Motson and Rowlinson wrote: 'In the event their misdemeanours were punished in almost poetic fashion in the final, where . . . their hopes were dashed in the last seconds of the match.'

Interestingly, you could say the exact same thing happened again one year later. Again Bayern reached the final, again they needed luck to win it, again quite a few people felt the result was some sort of just punishment for the other team's often reckless, sometimes brutal football, not to mention the behaviour of their fans.

Bayern even met an East German team again along the way, this time Magdeburg. When Sándor Barcs, the Hungarian UEFA vice-president, drew the slips of paper bearing these two names, once more cries of surprise echoed around the room, this time because the draw was so ironic. Magdeburg had won the previous season's Cup Winners' Cup, and so they should have played Bayern in a fairly new competition, the UEFA Super Cup. However, the East German team declined the offer, probably on orders from above. Now they had to face the class enemy regardless.

Again Bayern dug a deep hole for themselves, falling behind 2-0 in the home leg before coming back to win 3-2. And again the club then scored an own goal in the popularity department. Neudecker had learned from all the bad press in the wake of the Dresden debacle (or maybe he was just careful not to break a UEFA rule twice).

Bayern Munich did travel to Magdeburg and stayed at their *Interhotel*. However, the club had brought their own cook along, the famous chef Gerd Käfer, and asked for use of the hotel kitchen to prepare their own food. It was not an uncommon practice, but their piqued hosts declined, whereupon Bayern had sandwiches and coffee – in the coach. Even Sepp Maier cringed. 'I was so sorry for the waiters,' he recalled. 'They had been looking forward to serving us, to talk to us. They almost cried when we stayed in the coach.' He said that news about the silly scene soon spread around town and people muttered: 'Fucking Bayern.' Maier added: 'But we'd got used to that.' Müller scored twice in Magdeburg, Bayern went through, business as usual.

Yet not everything was the same as Bayern marched towards their second European Cup in a row. For one, the team had changed. In mid-August 1974, just a week before the season began, Bayern sold Breitner to Real Madrid (where Günter Netzer was already plying his trade). Asked for comment, Neudecker coldly replied: '*Reisende soll man nicht aufhalten.*' The German saying translates as: don't stop those who wish to travel. Obviously, Neudecker was glad to see the back of Breitner and happy to pocket what was by German standards an almost absurd three million marks (£500,000 in 1974). A realistic Breitner said: 'For both sides, this is a farewell without melancholy. I don't shed a tear over leaving the club.' Of course not. He received a signing-on bonus of 1.5 million marks from Real, widely – if perhaps erroneously – considered General Franco's club. Maybe he wasn't such a Maoist after all.

Another different element was the coach. Bayern had a disastrous start to the 1974–75 league season and by Christmas the team was in fourteenth place. One reason was certainly mental fatigue, another was that the physical strain began to tell. When Bayern flew to Japan for two friendlies against its national team in early January 1975, five regulars – Hoeness, Kapellmann, Maier, Roth and Zobel – were so severely injured they couldn't make the journey. Lattek announced he would bolster the squad with four amateur players. As it turned out, the coach wouldn't be on the plane, either.

Much worse than the results on the pitch was the relationship between Lattek and Neudecker. Things had probably begun to turn sour in late 1973, when the president, as was his wont, made decisions without consulting his coach, such as the signing of Torstensson, or the manner in which he handled the Dresden trip. In December 1974, Lattek announced he would not extend his contract and would leave the club in the summer. A few weeks later, he explained: 'I don't want to play the prima donna, but my feelings have been hurt too much.' According to Lattek, the straw that broke the camel's back was the fact that Bayern's anniversary publication for the club's seventy-fifth birthday 'devotes not a single word of recognition to the coach'. If this sounds thin-skinned, one mustn't forget Neudecker's overbearing personality. One of the people who knew him well once said about Neudecker: 'He would be a nice guy if he didn't think he was God.'

On the day before the squad left for Japan, Lattek and Neudecker had a conversation. Lattek opened it by saying: 'Something has to change at this club.' Neudecker replied: 'You're right. Let's change something. You're sacked!' An hour later, Bayern announced the coach was 'released from his duties' with immediate effect. While Lattek left to go skiing in the mountains, Schwan again asked Beckenbauer for his opinion. The Kaiser said the best thing might be to get Branko Zebec back. This, however, was not an option, as Zebec was under contract at Brunswick. Then Beckenbauer, as he'd done five years earlier, mentioned the name of a coach who had made his name working for the DFB, Dettmar Cramer.

Since August, Cramer had been coaching the United States' national team. When Schwan called him in New York City, Cramer told him he was available 'from a legal point of view' because he didn't have a signed contract with the US Soccer Federation. That was true. As USSF president Gene Edwards admitted, the deal had been sealed with a handshake only. He added he didn't think Cramer would renege on his word. But Edwards had underrated the lure of Bayern Munich. On 19 January 1975, Cramer put his name on the dotted line.

The small, delicate man – Cramer stood just five foot three inches – seemed like a fish out of water in Munich. He was an intellectual (they didn't call him the Professor for nothing) and although the 49-year-old had a tremendous amount of coaching experience, he knew almost nothing about professional club football. He had worked on behalf of the DFB and FIFA in countless countries, from Japan to Egypt, yet rarely in his native country, which is why *Kicker* headlined: 'He knows the world – but he doesn't know the Bundesliga.' But he knew football. Or maybe it was enough that he had a group of players at his disposal who were still exceptionally good at playing this game.

In the quarter-finals of the European Cup, Bayern squeezed past Soviet champions Ararat Yerevan, coached by the legendary Victor Maslov, a hugely influential man credited with inventing the pressing game and a few other things besides. In Armenia, Bayern were often surrounded by supporters eager to see the celebrated players up close. On one occasion, a policeman over-reacted and hit a fan with a truncheon to drive him back, leaving the man with a gaping head wound. Kapellmann stepped forward and applied first aid expertly – he was studying medicine at the time (and would obtain his doctorate in 1988).

Bayern took revenge on Saint-Étienne in the semis, winning 2-0 on aggregate, and found themselves in their second European Cup final in as many years, even though they were still stuck in midtable mediocrity in the Bundesliga. It was the twentieth final, so UEFA staged it at the same ground that had seen the very first one, the Parc des Princes in Paris. Bayern's opponents on 28 May 1975 were Leeds United, only the second English side ever to reach the final.

Under manager Don Revie, the club had acquired a reputation for a very physical game during the 1960s – and the nickname 'Dirty Leeds'. In fact, Motson and Rowlinson say that when Leeds lost two finals in May 1973, some fans 'felt their failures no more than just reward for some uncompromising football in the 1960s'. But Revie had left the club in the summer of 1974 and there had been no major nasty incidents, either on the pitch or in the stands, during the team's excellent European Cup campaign. When Leeds knocked out Johan Cruyff's Barcelona in the semis, most neutral observers considered them the favourites to lift the trophy.

The game has entered the annals as the 'Shame of Paris', because Leeds fans rioted before, during and after the match (the *Yorkshire Evening Post* headlined: 'Blood-lusting bullies crucify the name of sport'). It has also gone down in British football lore as the night Leeds were robbed. While it's true that the team were given ample reason to feel hard done by, it must also be noted that Leeds should have been reduced to ten men after all of three minutes and fifteen seconds.

Frank Gray brought down Kapellmann five or six yards into Bayern's half. The French referee Michel Kitabdjian whistled for a foul. Bayern's Swedish right-back Björn Andersson ran over to the loose ball. Just as he was about to knock it over to Kapellmann for the free kick, Leeds United's Welsh midfielder Terry Yorath stamped on his right leg. Watching the slow-motion replay, it's inconceivable that Yorath didn't realise play was halted. Yet he brutally kicked Andersson behind the referee's back, breaking the Swede's leg in two places. The injury was so awful that Kapellmann – the medical expert, remember – covered his face with his hands. Andersson, who would be sidelined for nine months, was stretchered off and Sepp Weiss, a 23-year-old homegrown defender, replaced him.

Fifteen minutes later, Norman Hunter played a pass into the path of left-back Frank Gray, who was racing down the wing, Hoeness at his heels. When Gray was let down by his first touch, Hoeness made a stab at the ball and somehow Gray hit his right knee. It was not a nasty foul, maybe no foul at all, but Hoeness was clearly in pain. And the controversial moments just kept coming. In the twenty-third minute, Leeds had a penalty appeal for handball turned down. Ten minutes later, Allan Clarke went past Beckenbauer in the box and the sweeper missed the ball with his tackle, instead hitting the striker's right leg. It was an obvious penalty, but Kitabdjian gave a corner.

This wrong decision wasn't the only reason Bayern were lucky to not concede a goal in the first half, as Leeds were more active and dangerous. Yorath's strike from inside the box cleared the bar, then Peter Lorimer and Paul Madeley missed the target with long-distance shots and Maier saved from Joe Jordan. Müller and Hoeness, meanwhile, spent almost the entire first half defending rather than attacking.

After the restart, nothing much happened at either end for almost twenty minutes, apart from the fact that Jordan committed his team's twenty-first foul as early as the sixty-fifth minute. Then, abruptly, Maier was forced into a brilliant save by Billy Bremner's point-blank shot and only thirty-five seconds later, Lorimer fired home a volley from twelve yards. He raised his arms and raced away to celebrate, while the Bayern players hung their heads and Maier quietly picked the ball out of the net. Then Beckenbauer noticed something. The linesman was waving his flag. Calmly, the Kaiser raised his right arm, to indicate an opponent had obviously been offside.

However, it was anything but obvious. As Lorimer made contact with the ball, two players were standing in front of Maier – Beckenbauer and Bremner. The latter might have been in a passive offside position, but since he was moving away, out of Maier's line of vision, it was excessive to say he was interfering with play. Enraged English fans threw ripped-out plastic seats and bottles onto the running track and eventually Maier's penalty area. Their mood worsened dramatically five minutes later.

A few yards outside Leeds' penalty area, Torstensson trapped a Müller pass. With his back to goal and three defenders behind him, he looked up and saw Roth making a diagonal run. Torstensson laid the ball off for the man who had decided Bayern's very first European final eight years earlier. Roth ran into the box. Madeley, wrong-footed by Torstensson's fluent movement, had lost a half-step on him and Roth made the most of it. He struck from twelve yards and as soon as the ball left his left foot, he knew it would go in. With outstretched arms, he ran over to the bench and wrapped his arms around the tiny man, Dettmar Cramer.

It had been Bayern's first genuine scoring opportunity of the game. Ten minutes later, they had another one. Kapellmann, playing one of his best games for the club, dashed down the right wing, left Gray and Hunter in his wake and crossed into the goalmouth. For the first time this night, Gerd Müller was where a centre-forward should be and made it 2-0 on eighty-one minutes. A frustrated Hunter then kicked Kapellmann and accepted the booking with the scowl of a man who doesn't care if he's sent off or not.

After the final whistle, the television cameras were not on the jubilant Bayern players but followed referee Kitabdjian as he was escorted into the dressing room by almost two-dozen stewards, clad in blue tracksuits. After the victory ceremony, Bayern went on a lap of honour and were either courageous or foolish enough to approach the Leeds stand. A hail of missiles drove them back. Three weeks later, UEFA banned Leeds United for four years from its competitions.

The joy was great, yet the mood at the post-match banquet at the Hôtel de Crillon was subdued. The Leeds players refused to attend; it had been an ill-tempered, bad game; English supporters rioted in the streets of Paris. And there was something else. Dettmar Cramer, as always sensitive to a fault, stated: 'People tend to laugh when I say something like this, but it affects me very much that Björn Andersson and Uli Hoeness suffered such serious injuries.'

He had no way of knowing this, but in a way the most lasting legacy of this final was indeed the thirty-ninth minute. Hoeness tried to challenge Yorath near the touchline, but as he was moving in on the Leeds player, his right leg buckled under him. Clutching his knee, he lay on the ground. Cramer signalled for Klaus Wunder, signed from Duisburg before the season began, to warm up. Hoeness received treatment for a few minutes, but it was clear he couldn't continue.

His knee never properly healed and he was never again the same player. Less than four years later, shortly after his twenty-seventh birthday, Uli Hoeness would be forced to find a new job.

7. MIA SAN MIA

When you cover football for a number of years, you see some strange things. I have seen a player sing karaoke to the Red Hot Chili Peppers. I have seen players wield sledgehammers to batter a building to the ground. Once, in a very posh hotel in Spain, I called the elevator and when the doors opened I laid eyes on a rather well-known footballer standing there and fixing me with a stare while wearing not a single piece of clothing on his body.

But I don't think I have seen anything stranger than Pep Guardiola, the epitome of sartorial elegance on the sidelines, wearing a cardigan the colour of mustard, a check shirt only partly tucked into the belt and the sort of knee-length breeches that are also known by their German name, *Lederhosen*.

It was the last day of the Munich *Oktoberfest* in 2014 and I knew Pep would be there and wearing *Tracht*, the traditional Bavarian costume, because there was no alternative. When he became Bayern's coach in the summer of 2013, he was allowed to do a lot of things that are alien to German football culture. He could decline to do one-on-one interviews and he could close training sessions to the general public. But what he could not do was chicken out of this annual spectacle.

Once a year, Bayern Munich's star-studded squad, full of highly-paid players from all corners of the globe, change into local *Tracht*, climb onto the team coach, drive to the world's largest funfair, pile into a wooden shed, sit down on long benches and wait until they are served huge mugs of beer. They can't bow out of it. On the day I travelled to the site of the *Oktoberfest* to catch a glimpse of this tradition, goalkeeper Manuel Neuer was late for the squad's meeting and missed the coach's departure. Knowing how notorious the traffic is around the *Oktoberfest* area, he took the underground rather than a taxi to catch up with the rest of the team. Wearing, of course, *Lederhosen*.

At first it seems strange that a club as cosmopolitan as Bayern Munich should attach such great importance to what is essentially folklore. Rangers don't dress their foreign contingent in kilts and force them to drink Scotch in public. Real Madrid don't ask their expensive superstars to wear the close-fitting tights you see on bullfighters, while downing red wine for the photographers. But Bayern, the most global of German clubs, regularly indulge in an ethnic, regional activity that is considered bizarre even by many non-Bavarian Germans.

However, despite the club's international focus, and contrary to popular opinion, Bayern have always been stoutly, and proudly, Bavarian. Kurt Landauer used to say that the aim of his club was to spread both open-minded liberalism and the Bavarian way of life. And of course Bayern's members and players always went to the *Oktoberfest*. In the club's wonderful museum, situated in the Allianz Arena, you can find a telegram dated 29 September 1951. It was sent from Giesing to the 'Bayern Box at the *Oktoberfest*, in [innkeeper] Xaver Heilmannseder's Löwenbräu Lodge'. The telegram was posted at 5.49 p.m. It reached the club's board eleven minutes later and informed them that '1860's brief winning run has been stopped', as Bayern had held their rivals to a 2-2 draw.

This charming exhibit not only tells you that the players knew exactly where their fellow club members could be found on this early Saturday evening. It also tells you that at least some of Bayern's board members considered a visit to the *Oktoberfest* to be more important than attending the Munich derby less than three miles away.

And yet Bayern didn't make a big show of being Bavarian for many decades. When Čik Čajkovski attended his first *Oktoberfest*, in September 1963, he wore a plain sleeveless shirt while president Wilhelm Neudecker was dressed in his customary grey suit. In 1976, Sepp Maier attended the fair in normal, if dapper clothes. He was photographed while trying his hand at a strength tester, his tie perfectly in place despite the physical effort.

But gradually this changed; not least because of a chain of events that took place during the second half of the 1970s and which we will come to in a few moments. Today, Bayern Munich's players not only regularly don *Lederhosen*, they also play in shirts which – on the back, under the collar – bear the message *Mia san mia*. During recent years, this has become something like the unofficial club motto (in contrast to their English counterparts, German clubs do not have traditional, usually Latin, mottos).

In 2008, when Jürgen Klinsmann began his brief and rather unfortunate stint as Bayern coach, the club distilled its philosophy – its raison d'être, if you will – into sixteen guidelines. They were published in a small book given to the club's employees and players to tell them what Bayern is all about. The sixteen guidelines centred around terms such as tradition, innovation, confidence, respect, loyalty. But they all began with the words *Mia san*. A year later, when Uli Hoeness was elected president, he told the assembled members: 'We have to go back to living *Mia san mia!*'

Mia san mia is often translated as 'we are who we are', which is neither wrong nor completely right, because those three – just two, really – innocent dialect words have many connotations. Literally, they just mean 'we are we'. However, as Alfons Goppel, the former prime minister of Bavaria, a man who played a major role in popularising the expression, pointed out in the early 1960s: 'But we are not only we, we also carry weight.'

And so the term stands for pride and self-assurance, for the conviction that you are first and foremost a Bavarian, a German second. Consequently, when Goppel received foreign guests in Munich, the band played the German national anthem and then, afterwards, the song 'Gott mit dir, du Land der Bayern' – God be with thee, land of the Bavarians. Heinrich Lübke, then the president of West Germany, asked Goppel to stop doing this, but the prime minister refused (in fact, he later saw to it that the song became Bavaria's official anthem).

However, there is another, less positive connotation of *Mia san mia*. In the 1970s, the term was often used outside of Bavaria to denounce the brawny, brazen and brash approach to politics that characterised someone like the controversial conservative Franz Josef Strauss as reckless and not always above-board. His *Mia san mia* attitude, this darker definition said, meant having the chutzpah to bend the rules. Or, to use the words of Paul Breitner: 'As long as I play well, I can get away with anything.'

Bayern's *Mia san mia* approach to money came back to haunt the club in 1976. The German historian Nils Havemann says the conservative Bavarian government (traditionally headed by the Christian Social Union, CSU) had protected the club for many years, granting Bayern tax benefits and probably also turning a blind eye from time to time. But now the pressure was mounting. Many small sports clubs wondered why they had to pay amusement tax, while the much bigger and richer Bayern had been made exempt from it (a Bavarian tennis centre even filed a suit against the club).

'The growing opposition to the CSU-led state government's patronage of Bayern Munich,' Havemann wrote, 'increased the pressure on the social–liberal federal government to close another tax loophole.' And so, in early March 1976, a letter from the Munich tax office landed at Säbener Strasse. The long and the short of the legalese was that the local authorities, at the behest of the Federal Ministry of Finance, had to inform Bayern that considerable tax payments, which had previously been deferred, would become due. To this day, we don't know exactly how dramatic the club's situation was, but it must have been bad. Bayern's tax consultant sent a letter of response to the

Friedrich Ludwig Jahn.

op left: Friedrich Ludwig Jahn, the father of German gymnastics. His disciples would make life very ard for anyone who indulged in so-called un-German activities like football. Which is why eleven men alked out on their gymnastics club in 1900 to form their own team, Bayern Munich.

op right: Kurt Landauer spent eighteen years as Bayern's president and oversaw the team's rise to the op. In 2013, the club named him Honorary President, a title bestowed on only three people. (The other vo being Franz Beckenbauer and Wilhelm Neudecker.)

ottom: Bayern shared the Grünwalder Stadion ground with local rivals 1860 from 1926 (the year efore this photo was taken) until 1972, when the Olympic Stadium opened.

Top left: Pulling in the same direction: coach Zlatko Čajkovski (l) gave Franz Beckenbauer his first-team debut.

Top right: Crosstown rivals trading blows: Bayern's Sepp Maier (r) seems to get the better of 1860's goalkeeper Petar Radenković.

Bottom: Pre-season training in the 1960s: goalkeeper Fritz Kosar, striker Gerd Müller and midfielder Dieter Koulmann (l to r) use their teammates as vaulting horses.

Top: Gerd Müller in his – and Bayern's – first Bundesliga season, 1965–66. (The Gladbach player on the right is a young man by the name of Jupp Heynckes.)

Bottom left: May 1966: Franz Beckenbauer is voted Germany's Footballer of the Year for the first time. He would win the award again in 1968, 1974 and 1976 – by which time the trophy was less unwieldy.

Bottom right: Flying the flag: a large number of Bayern fans followed their team to Nuremberg for the cup semi-final in 1966.

Top left: Werner Olk (l) captained Bayern from 1965 to 1970. Here he is exchanging pennants with Meiderich (today: MSV Duisburg) skipper Werner Krämer ahead of the 1966 cup final.

Top right: When you get a lot of post, Germans say there are 'laundry baskets full of letters'. Franz Beckenbauer demonstrates how much fanmail he was being sent by 1966.

Bottom: The architects of Bayern's rise parade the cup in 1966. From left to right in the car: president Wilhelm Neudecker, Čajkovski, Olk and business manager Robert Schwan.

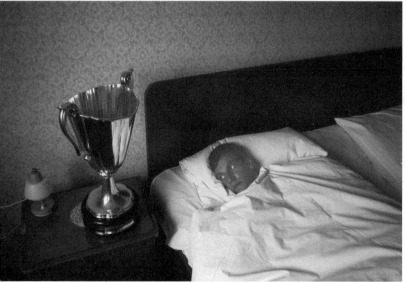

Top left: Franz Roth makes the difference in the 1967 Cup Winners' Cup final against Rangers.

Top right: Franz Beckenbauer presents Bayern's first European trophy to photographers. It wouldn't be the last.

Bottom: A dream come true: Franz Roth and the Cup Winners' Cup his goal won for Bayern in 1967.

Top: The Ghost of the Penalty Area: Gerd Müller materialises in Schalke's box to score the winning goal in the 1969 cup final.

Bottom left: In the summer of 1969, shortly after his teammate Franz Beckenbauer had been dubbed Kaiser by the press, Gerd Müller posed as the King of the Goalscorers.

Bottom right: Midfielder Paul Breitner joined Bayern in the summer of 1970. Nine months later, coach Udo Lattek turned him into a left back.

Top: Udo Lattek celebrates the first of many titles with Bayern, the 1971 DFB-Pokal. Robert Schwan (with his customary pipe and hat) joins in.

Bottom left: Gladbach striker Jupp Heynckes (l) and Uli Hoeness, were opponents during their playing days, but they would become good friends – and mastermind Bayern's greatest achievement, the 2013 treble.

Bottom right: Uli Hoeness (l) and Paul Breitner, were such close pals they always shared a room on away trips.

Top: A small man with a great football mind: Dettmar Cramer (r) is still the only Bayern coach to win the European Cup or the Champions League twice.

Bottom: Two in a row: the Bayern team that denied Leeds United to lift the 1975 European Cup.

Munich tax office in which he said he would be forced 'to dissolve the club' if the authorities demanded their money immediately and in full.

You only rarely hear about this backdrop to the story of Bayern's third European Cup triumph and even the vast majority of German fans are not aware of how grave Bayern's financial problems were. Most people assume the club was rich because it earned a lot of money. Yes, it did. But it also spent freely. Neudecker and business manager Robert Schwan were acutely aware that they had been lucky in more sense than just one when Bayern defeated Leeds United. The team had finished the Bundesliga season in tenth place and would have been out of Europe – and all that much-needed extra revenue – if the team had lost the final in Paris.

But the 1975–76 season didn't seem to be going much better. In late February 1976, Bayern were still in mid-table, way off the pace. The club could hardly afford a season without games in Europe. 'The persons in charge,' says Havemann, 'were up to their necks in water.' They must have wiped quite some sweat off their brows when the authorities allowed the club to pay the tax debts in instalments. It didn't solve the money problems but it bought some time.

The great irony of it all was that Neudecker and Schwan had already made the deal that would one day save the club – but didn't know it. A bit over two years earlier, in late 1973, the former 1860 Munich coach Max Merkel had been alerted to a unique talent. Merkel was between jobs and hoped he might be given the Bayern post in the near future because Neudecker rated him highly. That's why he alerted Bayern to an eighteen-year-old kid from Lippstadt, 360 miles north of Munich, and then urged the boy to sign with Bayern. Although he had offers from sixteen different clubs, among them Schalke and Bielefeld, Karl-Heinz Rummenigge followed Merkel's advice and joined the Reds for all of 17,500 marks, then the equivalent of £3,000. (To make the story even more bizarre, Max Merkel then didn't join Bayern – but 1860 again.)

Beckenbauer christened Rummenigge Rosy Cheeks, because of his resemblance to the child whose face adorned the bottles of

Rotbäckchen, rosy cheeks, a popular children's juice. But the painfully shy kid was growing up fast. In one of his first training sessions with the team, he nutmegged Roth. 'A few moments later, Gerd Müller was running past me,' Rummenigge remembered many years later when I was profiling his club for a magazine, 'and from the corner of his mouth he said: "If I were you, I wouldn't do that again."'

Rummenigge had done well in his first season and was now, in his second, a regular. Exactly two weeks after Bayern had received the alarming letter from the Munich tax authorities, Rummenigge even scored a goal against the great Benfica from Lisbon. Yes, it was only a deflected shot and Bernd Dürnberger and Gerd Müller both scored a brace, but the 5-1 win got Bayern into the semi-finals of the European Cup, so Karl-Heinz Rummenigge had every reason to feel good about himself.

It was this semi-final, more so than the eventual final, that turned out to be a great team's last hurrah. It was all new and exciting for rosy-cheeked Rummenigge (so exciting that Dettmar Cramer gave him two shots of cognac to drink before the final to soothe his nerves), but the core of the team had been playing together for more than ten years. They had been through the occasional lows and the many highs, under constant pressure to perform; they were now battered, bruised and tired and they instinctively knew it couldn't go on for very much longer. Breitner was gone, Hoeness was limping, Beckenbauer was about to leave, Müller had retired from the national team in a huff, Roth and Maier were now in their thirties. But none of it really mattered, because the true hallmark, the real quality, of this fabled Bayern team was not individual class. Yes, of course many of these players were among the greatest of their generation. But what made them truly special was their unerring ability to rise to the occasion – as a team. No matter what life threw at them, Bayern said *Mia san mia* and dealt with it.

What life threw at them in the semis was Real Madrid. It would have been a football fan's dream tie come true even without all the extra baggage. And that baggage was remarkable. For one, the games reunited Bayern with Breitner, who was playing for Real, together with Günter Netzer. Then there was the fact that Real had eliminated none other than Gladbach – coached by none other than Udo Lattek – in the quarter-finals under scandalous circumstances. In the second leg, in Madrid, the Dutch referee had disallowed two perfectly legal Gladbach goals, one for a non-existent offside, the other for a highly dubious foul. The outrage in West Germany was so intense that Bayern, irony of ironies, were called upon to revenge Gladbach and help justice prevail.

Which is why Walter Fembeck, still Bayern's club secretary after all these years, couldn't believe his eyes when he arrived at Säbener Strasse on the last Friday in March 1976. People were queueing for hundreds of yards; some of them had spent the night in front of the building; the police were out in force to clear the area of cars that had been parked in the middle of the street. 'I have never seen anything like this,' Fembeck told a reporter. The whole of Europe wanted tickets to Bayern's home game against Real. Fembeck had received letters from France and Belgium. Some people sent blank cheques and said they didn't care what sum he put in.

An inquisitive reporter from the nationwide newspaper *Frankfurter Allgemeine Zeitung* talked to a few people in the queue. They were going to these extreme lengths to get a ticket for the second leg, he said, but what if Bayern were beaten really heavily in Madrid, say 4-0? One man replied: 'Then we're going to score five at our place.'

At first it looked as if this might indeed be necessary. After just eight minutes of the first leg, Bayern's left-back Udo Horsmann botched a harmless Netzer pass and suddenly Roberto Martínez was clear through on goal – he put the ball past Maier from the edge of the penalty area. Shortly before the break, Maier denied the same player, brilliantly blocking his shot from eight yards with his legs. While the television viewers were treated to a slow-motion replay of this opportunity, Roth set up Müller and the striker scored Bayern's equaliser.

In the second half, Martínez broke his nose in a collision with Maier and walked off the pitch in a blood-spattered shirt. There was more violence to come. A 26-year-old Spanish fan ran onto the pitch and made for the Austrian referee Erich Linemayr. He hit Gerd Müller along the way and threw a punch at Linemayr, before Hoeness and Maier wrestled him to the ground. 'Suddenly we were surrounded by police,' the goalkeeper said. 'They began to hit us – the players – until the referee intervened.'

Despite the important away goal, Dettmar Cramer said the tie was still totally open, adding Real would have two key players available for the return leg who had missed the first game, José Pirri and Breitner. In front of almost 78,000 fans at the Olympic Stadium, Real did indeed come close to taking an early lead through Carlos Guerini after seven minutes, but Maier tipped his bouncing effort over the bar. Barely two minutes later, Müller scored with a first-time left-footed shot from nineteen yards. From this moment on, the hosts dominated the game. Hoeness and Schwarzenbeck went close, then Müller kept possession against two defenders in the box and made it 2-0 with his patented shot on the turn. There was still almost an hour to play, but Real were beaten.

Roth and Müller missed two fine chances each in the second half, while only a looping Breitner shot troubled Maier at the other end. In stoppage time, Real's captain Amancio kicked the ball away in frustration and was booked for the second time. Miljan Miljanić, Real's Serbian coach, later said his team had not been at the top of their game. He expressed disappointment over how mercilessly the Munich crowd had booed Netzer and Breitner. Then he marvelled at Müller, calling him 'a phenomenon'. Finally, Miljanić predicted: 'This incredibly strong Bayern team will win the final.'

Most people were convinced of this, because Bayern's opponents in the final were AS Saint-Étienne, who'd lost to the Germans in the semis a year earlier. John Greig, the Rangers legend, lauded the French for their 'excellent team' and their 'beautiful football', but added that he expected Bayern to win because of dangerous men like Müller and Hoeness up front (the reason Greig was asked to comment on the two finalists was that the game was played at Glasgow's Hampden Park).

Neudecker wasn't happy about this. He argued there wouldn't be enough interest in a match between French and West German sides in Scotland to sell out a big place like Hampden Park (at the time, the ground's legal capacity was 85,165). He was also worried about the scheduling. The final was played on 12 May 1976. Only three days later, Scotland were to meet England in the British Home Championship. Neudecker concluded Scottish fans would save their money and rather watch the international. As it turned out, he was right – only 54,000 came out to watch the final – but his concerns didn't exactly endear his club to the neutrals.

In an interview with the Sunday newspaper *Le Journal du Dimanche*, Saint-Étienne's president Roger Rocher said that his club respected UEFA's decision and found nothing wrong with Hampden Park. Acerbically, he added: 'Bayern are interested in making a profit from the final. Saint-Étienne are merely interested in winning the final.' He probably didn't know how desperately Bayern needed money. (Rummenigge now says: 'We had to win the game. For our prestige, but also for financial reasons.') In any case, Rocher easily won the hearts of the neutrals and so Bayern, supported by only 6,000 Germans in Glasgow, were up against Saint-Étienne, more than 25,000 French fans and probably also a great many Scots.

For the second year in a row, Bayern's opponents would consider themselves very unlucky to end up on the losing side. But also for the second year in a row, the final began with a controversial moment the Germans were unhappy about, with good reason. Eighty seconds into the game, Dürnberger won the ball deep in Bayern's half and went on a fine solo run that took him almost to the French penalty area. He set up Gerd Müller and the striker put the ball away from an angle. However, the goal was not allowed to stand because the linesman had raised his flag to signal for an offside. Although he was positioned very

well, the linesman got the decision wrong. Still, it's too harsh to say
Bayern were clearly robbed of a goal here, because the flag went up
so promptly – and referee Károly Palotai blew his whistle so quickly –
that centre-back Osvaldo Piazza stopped chasing Müller even before
the striker struck.

Apart from this early moment, though, Bayern generally appeared
static and lumbering during the first half, the French lively and quick.
Saint-Étienne often dropped very deep and then, upon winning the
ball in their own half, mounted swift counter-attacks. Their left-
winger Christian Sarramagna gave Johnny Hansen many headaches,
but it was midfielder Dominique Bathenay who announced the most
thrilling and ultimately decisive stage of the game – the fifteen minutes
before and after the interval.

On thirty-three minutes, Bathenay finished one of those fast French
breaks with a thundering left-footed drive from twenty-five yards. The
shot hit the crossbar. The ridiculously unmarked right-winger Hervé
Revelli tried to bury the rebound with a flying header, but Maier calmly
caught the ball. Abruptly, the game came to life, now it was end-to-end
stuff. Less than a minute later, Uli Hoeness went agonisingly close at
the other end – his shot from the edge of the box whistled past the left-
hand post. In the thirty-seventh minute, the French were lucky again:
A powerful Rummenigge shot from inside the box slipped through the
hands of goalkeeper Ivan Čurković; stumbling backwards, he somehow
kept the ball from trundling across the line with a desperate effort. Two
minutes later, Sarramagna went past Hansen for the umpteenth time
and Jacques Santini headed the cross against the bar from six yards.

The famously massive, bulky Hampden crossbars entered French
football parlance that night as *les poteaux carrés* – the square posts. They
became a symbol for the plucky underdog's undeserved defeat. As the
Scottish sportswriter Alan Pattullo explained a few years ago in a piece
about the French club's desire to display the Hampden woodwork in
their museum, the square posts 'have since slipped into Saint-Étienne
legend, and the phrase is even used to mock them by rival fans'. (Why

the French blame the posts when it was obviously the bar – *la barre* – that thwarted their best efforts is unclear.)

Three minutes into the second half, Beckenbauer attempted a cheeky chip and gave the ball away. Revelli crossed from the right flank and Sarramagna wasted a glorious chance from just a few yards out – the ball hit his shoulder rather than his head and went inches wide of the post. Having emerged unscathed from three moments of crisis, Bayern woke from their slumber and became a bit more adventurous. On fifty-seven minutes, Müller was about to collect a Beckenbauer pass when Piazza unfairly challenged him from behind. Palotai blew his whistle. Free kick. Maybe twenty yards in front of goal. Beckenbauer stood over the ball. Franz Roth was to his right.

'I often took free kicks and I often scored,' says Roth. 'So Franz told me: I'll put it past the wall and then you let rip.' (Many, many years later, another Bayern maestro would find himself in a not dissimilar position and famously tell his teammate: 'Just knock it in and then we'll all go home.') Having given Roth his instructions, Beckenbauer stood like a Roman statue, erect and gracefully still, waiting for the referee's signal. Finally, Palotai was happy with the French wall. Beckenbauer gently nudged the ball to his right. Roth took a short run-up. With the strength of a bull, he thumped the ball into the net.

For the third time, Roth had made the difference in a European final. The goal boosted Bayern's confidence while the French, perhaps because they lacked their opponents' experience at this elite level, abandoned their dangerous wingplay and began to attack through the centre of the pitch. Now it was the Germans who won balls and mounted counter-attacks. All of a sudden, what had been so very hard for almost an hour came easily to the players in white. On seventy minutes, Čurković bravely threw himself at the feet of Müller and both players had to receive treatment on the pitch. The dying moments were hectic. In the final minute, substitute Dominique Rocheteau dribbled past three Bayern players and set up Revelli, now unmarked inside the box. But the winger mishit the ball and Maier easily saved the side-footed shot from ten yards.

Sixty seconds later, another final was over. When UEFA president Artemio Franchi presented Bayern captain Franz Beckenbauer with the trophy both men were so familiar with, you could hear shrill catcalls from the French (and perhaps the Scots). But you could also hear the German supporters sing the popular carnival song 'Oh, wie ist das schön' – Oh, how beautiful is this. The next line of the ditty states that it's been a long time since anyone has seen a day as beautiful as this one. For Bayern in 1976, this wasn't true, of course. The club had now won the most valuable European trophy for the third year in a row, something only Real Madrid and Ajax had done.

However, the next time Bayern Munich's supporters sang this song in Europe, it was a different matter altogether. After 12 May 1976, a long time indeed would pass until any of them saw a day as beautiful as this one again.

As they always do, the inland revenue officers came early. Two days after Bayern had been held to a draw by Duisburg to find themselves a solid five points behind Gladbach in the Bundesliga standings, Franz Beckenbauer was just about to have breakfast in his villa in Grünwald, eight miles south of Munich, when the doorbell rang. The three gentlemen who introduced themselves as tax inspectors were friendly and courteous, but they also meant business. They had a search warrant for Beckenbauer's house and they were going to use it.

It's tempting to argue that the events of this day – 24 January 1977 – were the reason why Beckenbauer left Bayern and Germany only four months later to play across the Atlantic Ocean, for the New York Cosmos. Not unlike his club, Beckenbauer was having money problems on account of a tax-saving scheme gone wrong. The prospect of a lucrative Cosmos contract must have been very enticing to a player who would soon celebrate his thirty-second birthday.

In late April 1977, the renowned political monthly *Der Spiegel* headlined an article about Beckenbauer's move to the United States 'Sweeper on the Run', as many people felt his sudden departure smacked of a getaway. Well, that's because it was. However, he wasn't trying to get away from the tax authorities. He knew he couldn't. (Beckenbauer eventually settled out of court for 1.8 million marks, then the equivalent of £475,000). What Beckenbauer was trying to get away from was his life.

The problem with the inland revenue people was not that they searched his villa (and Robert Schwan's house), it was that you could read all about it one week later in the tabloid *Bild*. Meanwhile, another newspaper informed the nation that Beckenbauer was estranged from his wife and dating a sports photographer. Football was no respite from all that hassle. When he stepped onto a pitch, he was usually greeted by catcalls. 'Though Bayern are not so despised, particularly in Northern Germany, as they once were when they were winning everything,' Keir Radnedge reported in early 1977 for *World Soccer*, 'there were still whistles and jeers a-plenty for Beckenbauer and his team during and after their recent 5-0 thrashing in Hamburg.'

Beckenbauer was living in a goldfish bowl. More than a decade before West Germany at long last produced sports stars that weren't footballers – from Boris Becker and Steffi Graf to Bernhard Langer and Michael Schumacher – he was the nation's number-one athlete and one of its biggest celebrities. Everything the boy from Giesing did was blown out of all proportion. It's not much of an exaggeration to say that even things like growing a moustache, which he'd tried in November 1970, triggered a national debate, dubbed 'the beard war' by Ulfert Schröder, one of his numerous biographers.

So when things began to go thoroughly pear-shaped in early 1977, Beckenbauer probably thought back to the third Saturday in September. Bayern's away trip to VfL Bochum on this weekend had produced one of the wildest and most entertaining games the league has ever seen: after fifty-five minutes, the hosts held a seemingly unassailable 4-0 lead. But only twenty crazy minutes later, Bayern were 5-4 in front! Bochum then tied the game with ten minutes left, before Uli Hoeness netted a last-gasp winner to make Bayern the only team in Bundesliga history to have won a game despite trailing by four goals.

Watching this spectacle from the stands was Clive Toye, a former English sportswriter who worked as the general manager for the New York Cosmos. Three years earlier, he had famously told Pelé, who was considering offers from Juventus and Real Madrid: 'If you go there, all you can win is another championship. Come with us and you can win a country.' Pelé went and won (and bagged almost £1 million per year in the process). Now Toye was looking for more stars of Pelé's calibre and there weren't very many around, basically only Johan Cruyff and Beckenbauer.

Toye negotiated with Schwan during September about bringing the Kaiser to America, but Beckenbauer demurred. Then, three months later, a few days before Christmas 1976, Bayern Munich became the first German club to win the Intercontinental Cup, defeating the Brazilian team Cruzeiro from Belo Horizonte over two legs (2-0, 0-0). Beckenbauer had now won almost everything a footballer could win; only the still relatively recent UEFA Cup was missing from his list of achievements. Where could he possibly go from there? As he recently said about those months to explain why he thought about Cosmos ever more often and more intently: 'Our glorious Bayern team began to come apart at the seams. Some players had left, but the club didn't seem to want to invest in order to replace them adequately.'

Maybe it wasn't that the club didn't want to, maybe Bayern couldn't. A major source of income had finally dried up in March 1977, when the team's seemingly eternal run in the European Cup at last came to an end. Having survived sixteen consecutive ties in the continent's premier competition, Bayern were eliminated at the quarter-final stage by Dynamo Kiev. At first it seemed as if the Reds' proverbial luck on the European stage would hold. Nurturing a one-goal lead from the home leg, Bayern gave away a penalty forty minutes into the return game in the Ukraine. Sepp Maier, the man who almost never saved a penalty, palmed Oleg Blokhin's effort to his left, against the post. The rebound hit Maier's head, but instead of ricocheting into the net, the ball sailed just wide of the upright. Bayern tenaciously defended their narrow lead until the final seven minutes, when another penalty and a close-range header put Dynamo through.

So Bayern needed money and Neudecker demanded a transfer sum of 1.75 million marks from the Cosmos for Beckenbauer's services. When Toye refused, the whole deal hung in the balance until the player himself chipped in with 350,000 marks out of his own pocket. Yes, this was one expensive spring for Franz Beckenbauer, but it turned out to be a good investment. 'It was one of the best decisions I ever made,' he says today about joining the Cosmos. In the United States, Beckenbauer grew immensely as a person, he widened his scope and adopted a cosmopolitan approach to life that would stand him in good stead when he later returned to Germany and, eventually, to Bayern.

For the club, meanwhile, losing Beckenbauer was a bigger blow than even pessimists had thought. Quite apart from the fact that his departure underlined a general impression that Bayern were in decline and the rats beginning to leave the sinking ship, he was also sorely missed as a team leader. Six months after Beckenbauer had made his Cosmos debut, a Bayern team ravaged by injuries were dismantled 4-0 by Eintracht Frankfurt and dropped into a relegation spot. 'An era is over for good,' coach Dettmar Cramer said. 'The rebuilding has begun.' But he was not the one who'd do the rebuilding. Two days later, on 28 November, Bayern's board held an emergency meeting during which Cramer was relieved of his duties.

So far, so normal in professional football. But now Neudecker added a typically idiosyncratic flourish to the whole affair. He needed a new coach and felt that his two most recent ones, Lattek and Cramer, had been too soft on the players. He also knew there was a coach rumoured to be the exact opposite: the very man who had beaten his side on Saturday, Eintracht's Hungarian manager Gyula Lóránt.

Apart from his reputation as an autocrat, Lóránt was also known as an innovator – Frankfurt were one of only two Bundesliga teams at the time that used an early, simple form of zonal marking. (The other team was Brunswick, coached by Branko Zebec.)

Furthermore, Neudecker had been told that Frankfurt's president – a debonair university chancellor by the wonderful name of Achaz von Thümen – found Lóránt impossibly gruff and hard to get along with. And so Neudecker called von Thümen on Tuesday, just three days after their two clubs had met, and suggested nothing less than a swap: the sensitive Cramer to Frankfurt, the coarse Lóránt to Bayern. Less than twenty-four hours later, Lóránt (and, crucially, his assistant Pál Csernai) travelled to Munich to discuss details. On the following Saturday, the 54-year-old Gyula Lóránt, a former member of the fabled Hungarian team known as the Mighty Magyars, sat on Bayern's bench and guided the Reds to a much-needed 4-2 win over Kaiserslautern.

This managerial barter deal had long-lasting effects on Bayern Munich. In fact, you could say that unbeknownst to all involved, Neudecker's decision unwittingly catapulted the club from the 1970s into the 1980s and ushered in Bayern's second period of sustained domestic dominance. Two key figures in the club's rise from a regional phenomenon to a national institution and then an international superpower were already gone: Franz Beckenbauer and Robert Schwan, who had joined his protégé, client and friend in New York. But within just nineteen months of Cramer's sacking, Franz Roth would be in Austria, Gerd Müller in Florida, Sepp Maier in hospital and Wilhelm Neudecker in something approaching enforced retirement, while two footballers and close friends – in the words of *Der Spiegel* – 'took over the entire club' together with a new president who liked fizzy drinks almost as much as *Lederhosen* and is the reason Pep Guardiola had no choice but wear *Tracht* at the *Oktoberfest*.

Even for a fast-moving and constantly transforming club like Bayern, these were many crucial changes in quick succession. They began after the end of the 1977–78 season, still Bayern's worst

Bundesliga campaign. Although Lóránt had won his first two games in charge, the team soon reverted to type. On the last matchday, Bayern suffered a humiliating 5-0 defeat in Kaiserslautern and finished the season in twelfth place. For a team starring Hoeness, Müller, Maier, Schwarzenbeck, Kapellmann, Rummenigge and a very young Klaus Augenthaler, this was a totally unacceptable showing. The problem, many people felt, was that Beckenbauer had left behind a leadership vacuum. And so Neudecker concluded it was time to set aside personal animosity and approach the one player he knew had both the ego and the class to lead this Bayern pack – Paul Breitner.

Breitner had returned to the Bundesliga one year earlier and signed for Brunswick. It wasn't a happy year. 'There was just too much jealousy, envy and resentment,' Breitner says about his one season in what was a small, provincial place compared to Munich and Madrid. 'Some of the players said: we'd rather lose than link up with this guy and win.' The reason he had joined Brunswick instead of one of the more famous German teams was simple: only the club still bankrolled by Jägermeister boss Günter Mast could afford the 1.75 million marks Real Madrid wanted for the former left-back, who had reinvented himself as a midfield maestro. When Mast learned of Bayern's interest, he felt he was entitled to a little profit and increased the asking price to 1.96 million marks (then the equivalent of £510,000). Now, how was Neudecker supposed to raise this kind of money, especially ahead of the first season in eight years without any European games for his club?

The solution came from an unlikely direction – Uli Hoeness. For the past four years, Bayern's shirt sponsor had been Adidas, the sports clothing and equipment company based in the small Franconian town of Herzogenaurach, 120 miles north of Munich. The close relationship between Adidas and Bayern went back to the early years of Beckenbauer's career. The first-ever apparel produced by Adidas, which had been formed as a shoe company by Adolf 'Adi' Dassler, was a tracksuit model called 'Beckenbauer', presented in 1967. Over the years, Franz Beckenbauer became a close friend of the Dassler family. (Or more precisely: a friend of Adi's branch of the Dassler family. This fine distinction is necessary, because Adi's older brother Rudolf fell out with his sibling and founded Puma, Adidas's fiercest rival until the emergence of Nike.)

The shirt sponsorship deal with Adidas was earning Bayern 250,000 marks per year. Quite apart from the fact that it isn't ideal if your kit supplier is also your shirt sponsor, the club felt there had to be more money in this. Astonishingly, or perhaps tellingly, the man who found Bayern a much better deal was not Neudecker or someone like long-time treasurer Willi O. Hoffmann. It was their forward with the dodgy knee. Hoeness had connections to Magirus Deutz, a manufacturer of commercial vehicles based in his native Ulm. Magirus Deutz offered a three-year deal for an annual 600,000 marks. Neudecker seized the opportunity, while Hoeness pocketed a commission fee of 10 per cent. (Magirus Deutz was later absorbed by the Italian company Iveco, who became Bayern's shirt sponsors when the original three-year deal ended in 1981.)

The Magirus Deutz money allowed Bayern to bring Breitner back, but the desired effect failed to materialise. In September 1978, just six weeks into the season, second-division Osnabrück travelled to Munich for a second-round cup game and caused one of the greatest upsets in the competition's history. In front of only 8,500 fans in the Olympic Stadium, the unfancied visitors conceded no fewer than three penalties, all converted by Gerd Müller – and still won 5-4. The last two goals in the game were particularly embarrassing. They came within two minutes of each other. Both times an Osnabrück striker was outnumbered in Bayern's box. Both times he put the ball past Maier with an impertinent chip. It was arguably Bayern Munich's most humiliating day up until that point.

8. A SIMPLE FOOTBALL CLUB

It was obvious there was something wrong with the team. As the noted weekly *Die Zeit* said a few days before Christmas 1978: 'There can be no doubt that the Hungarian coach Lóránt has not done a lot to ease the tense atmosphere. After each unsatisfying result, the readers of Munich's five daily newspapers could expect to hear about the feud between the players, the coach and the president. Noticeable in this context was the aversion the coach developed to those players with *Abitur* [the rough equivalent of A-levels]: Jupp Kapellmann became a sub, Uli Hoeness went to Nuremberg, Paul Breitner hardly exchanged a word with Lóránt any more.'

Hoeness had indeed left Bayern in October, because Lóránt wasn't giving him a game. (Perhaps with good reason – five months later the player was forced to finish his career on account of his knee problems.) And so Hoeness missed the strange and perhaps fittingly spectacular denouement to the Hungarian's brief but turbulent reign. In early November, Bayern travelled to Amsterdam to play in Johan Cruyff's testimonial. As mentioned before, the Reds took Ajax to the cleaners, winning 8-0. Almost thirty years later, Karl-Heinz Rummenigge apologised on Dutch television, saying his team's emphatic victory must have felt like a slur to Ajax, not to mention Cruyff.

However, as an explanation for what happened, Rummenigge added that the team had felt unseemly treated by their hosts. And indeed, after Müller opened the scoring by volleying a long Sepp Maier punt past goalkeeper Piet Schrijvers, he seemed to be making a point of dedicating his celebration to a particularly hostile section of the crowd. (Many years later, Hoeness failed to sign a young Frank Rijkaard to Bayern, because the player was represented by the agent Cor Coster, who happened to be Johan Cruyff's father-in-law. Apparently, Coster still bore a grudge.)

Barely four weeks after this contentious game, Bayern played away at Fortuna Düsseldorf. After twenty seconds, a Maier punt didn't get quite as far as it had done in Amsterdam. It was intercepted by Fortuna's centre-forward Emanuel Günther. He laid the ball off for Klaus Allofs, who scored from twenty yards. After an hour, it was 4-1. With fifteen minutes left, it was 6-1. On eighty-seven minutes, a Günther header from a tight angle wrong-footed Maier for a final score of 7-1. The result is to this day Bayern's heaviest defeat away from home.

The television cameras captured Lóránt as he made for the dressing rooms. He was certainly unhappy and would later tell his assistant: 'Pál, this means trouble.' But he walked steadily and seemed light on his feet. Still, Bayern announced on the following day that Lóránt suffered from a severe meniscus injury (sustained, it seemed, while ice-skating with his young daughter), could hardly move and would be unable to be on the bench for the next game. As it turned out, he would never again be on any Bayern bench.

In order to gain some time, Neudecker did what football officials in his situation often do. Having sacked the number-one man, he promoted the assistant on an interim basis. So it came about that the very antithesis of Lóránt coached the team on the following weekend. Pál Csernai had never been a great player – spending six years at Kickers Stuttgart, mostly in the second division – or a successful coach. But the Bayern players liked him. He was polite, reserved and pleasant, though perhaps a bit too full of himself in a quiet way. He liked the music of Giuseppe Verdi and could play the violin. While Lóránt sat on the bench wearing a tracksuit top, Csernai prided himself on his dress sense; he was the Pep Guardiola of the 1980s. Search for *der Mann mit dem Seidenschal*, the man with the silk scarf, on Google and the first results all deal with Csernai.

In other words, he was certainly not the kind of man Neudecker wanted for the team. And you can't say that Csernai did a particularly good job of advertising his abilities. He lost two of his first three games in charge. The second of these was a match in Frankfurt on a foggy, depressing day in early February 1979. There was no score for seventy minutes, then the hosts found the target twice. Csernai told sub Norbert Janzon, a 28-year-old striker who'd been signed from Karlsruher SC, to get ready. Eight minutes from time, the coach brought Janzon on. For Gerd Müller.

You sometimes read that it was the first time in Müller's career that he had been taken out of a game. That's not true, of course. He'd come off with a minor ailment as recently as November. But Müller hadn't been subbed for either tactical or performance reasons and with a game still on the line since April 1971. That Csernai, a virtual unknown who had never won anything as a player or coach, dared to do this proved that he had a bit more steel than people thought, but it still earned him bad press. 'One may confidently assume that a coach who's considered a nobody in the business was trying to make a name for himself at the expense of a player of outstanding merit,' *Kicker* magazine said. The Sunday paper *Welt am Sonntag* published an open letter from former international Willi Schulz addressed to Neudecker. Schulz accused the president of 'standing idly by and watching' while 'Csernai orchestrated a campaign against Gerd Müller'. The coach himself countered the criticism by saying: 'I just don't understand why such a drama is made of the substitution. I was often subbed towards the tail end of my career. That's football. Only performance counts. Müller has been out of form for weeks.'

The striker regarded the substitution as an 'act of revenge' for having been one of the few loyal Lóránt men. Then he said: 'As far as I'm concerned, Csernai doesn't exist.' Ten days after the game, Müller sent Neudecker a letter in which he asked to be released from his contract with immediate effect – after 607 competitive games for Bayern Munich, in which he had scored an astonishing 566 goals. He was without doubt the greatest striker the club and the country, probably the world, had ever seen. But he was thirty-three years old and, as Csernai correctly pointed out: 'He lacks stamina and he isn't moving about as much as he used to.' The club relented and, in the first week of March, Müller announced he was going to join Fort Lauderdale Strikers in the North American Soccer League to play alongside George Best and Teófilo Cubillas.

On 23 April, while the Bundesliga season was heating up, Müller and his wife left Munich for Miami. After almost fifteen years in Bayern's red shirts, there was no formal farewell, no testimonial, not even a few words of gratitude or a round of applause from the fans. Sepp Maier publicly wondered why 'everyone except Rainer Ohlhauser left in anger. Andersson and Torstensson weren't given as much as a bouquet of flowers, while Franz even had to pay money to get out.'

There was indeed at the time a culture of ruthless professionalism at the club that could, and would, very easily cross into cold-heartedness. As Breitner once said: 'There was no room for feelings.' This would radically change under Uli Hoeness, but for Müller it meant he left the club he'd helped build in acrimony. 'I'm looking forward to Fort Lauderdale and finally playing football again,' he said. 'But I hope they don't think here comes the great magician who'll run rings round everyone. I'll certainly need time to adapt.' In his first season in Florida, Müller scored nineteen goals and set up seventeen in twenty-five games to finish third in the list of the league's most productive forwards.

Although Neudecker had backed the coach in the brief but fierce struggle for power with Müller, he still regarded Csernai as a man living on borrowed time. This is why the president rather than the coach decided who would be given the captain's armband, now that both Beckenbauer and Müller were gone: Sepp Maier (a choice the president would come to rue).

You could understand why Neudecker wasn't happy with Csernai – the results didn't improve. Quite the contrary. On 10 March 1979, Bayern were beaten 4-0 at home by relegation candidates Arminia Bielefeld. It was, and still is, one of the club's worst home defeats in league history. Needless to say, the Bielefeld debacle was the final straw and put Csernai in an untenable position; he would have to go. However, the players pleaded with Neudecker not to sack the Hungarian. Eventually, the president agreed to a bargain. Looking back on those eventful days and weeks, Sepp Maier says: 'Neudecker promised us that the coach could stay if we remained unbeaten in our next two Bundesliga games, away at Brunswick and Mönchengladbach.'

The deal alone tells you a lot about how powerful the players had become, especially since Breitner's return, and perhaps also that Neudecker, who was now in his mid-sixties and had been at the club's helm for almost seventeen years, was no longer as vigorous and authoritative as he used to be.

The first of the two matches in question pitted the Reds not only against Breitner's old team, Brunswick, but also against Werner Olk. The man who'd played 266 league games for Bayern and captained the team between 1965 and 1970 had replaced Branko Zebec as Brunswick coach at the beginning of the season. He was under a lot of pressure because his team hadn't won since October. But of course the same went for Csernai and his players. Maier was running a fever, Breitner had spent the week before the game in bed with the flu and lost over a stone, Rummenigge was suffering from ligament problems. But somehow they all hung in there and ground out an ugly scoreless draw. The press later called it 'the worst Bundesliga game of the entire season' and Olk was sacked a few days later. But Maier and Breitner were happy. The deal was still on.

Or so they thought. But when the squad arrived at Hannover airport to fly to Munich, a journalist informed Breitner there were rumours that Neudecker had signed a new coach – none other than Max Merkel, the notorious slave-driver and former 1860 Munich gaffer. During a stopover in Frankfurt, the players saw an interview with their president on television that confirmed their worst fears. According to Thomas Hüetlin's book about Bayern, Maier hissed: 'We were so glad he had sacked this arsehole Lóránt – and now he goes out and gets an even bigger one!' Talking to a reporter, the goalkeeper phrased his concerns a bit more diplomatically: 'Mister Neudecker tells us all the time that the club has to save money and now he goes out and gets a coach who doesn't come cheap, as we all know.'

For many years, the story went that Breitner and Maier called the team together on the airport and held a vote on how to proceed. Hüetlin says that the two team leaders couldn't find Klaus Augenthaler and second-stringers Peter Gruber and Willi Reisinger because the three had located a television set and were watching West Germany's national qualifying event for the 1979 Eurovision Song Contest. As much as I want to believe this story, not least because the event was won by an over-the-top Eurotrash band called Genghis Khan, Breitner and Maier both state there was no vote. They claim they just knew how the squad felt and which steps needed to be taken (which is a polite way of saying they were running this team). And so, thirty minutes before midnight on a long and busy Saturday, the goalkeeper called his president on the telephone.

'Mister Neudecker,' Maier said, 'as the captain of this team I have to tell you that we don't approve of your decision.'

Neudecker's neck veins bulged. Of course I wasn't there to actually see it, but if ever a man's neck veins had good reason to bulge, this was it. Struggling to contain himself, Neudecker replied that Maier was just an employee of the club and that the president most certainly didn't need his approval when making any kind of decision.

'If you insist on having a new coach,' Maier said, 'please meet the team at Säbener Strasse on Monday and explain why you reneged on your promise to give us two games. We will be there – but we will refuse to train.'

Now Neudecker's last remnant of composure vanished. He yelled at Maier, accused him of being an anarchist and said the goalkeeper sounded like a trade union leader threatening a strike. Maier hung up on him.

When the players arrived in dribs and drabs at the training ground on Monday morning, they were relieved that Max Merkel was nowhere to be seen; instead Pál Csernai was there and also board members Karl Pfab and Willi O. Hoffmann. But at the same time, the players were anxious. As far as they knew, no team had ever done anything like this, blackmailed their own president. How would he react?

Neudecker had had one day to think the situation through and calm down. He had done the former but not the latter, because when he opened the door to the conference room at nine o'clock, he was still visibly disgusted. His voice, though, was, all things considered, calm. 'Ah, the great chairman,' he said, shooting a contemptuous glance at Maier. 'Well, if that's how things stand, I resign from my post here and now.' Without waiting for a response, he turned around and walked out. The players looked at each other in stunned silence. Then they changed into tracksuits and did what footballers do on a Monday morning: they held a training session. Under Pál Csernai.

Two hours later, club secretary Fembeck distributed a personal press release from Neudecker. It said: 'Led by captain Sepp Maier, the team has come out against Max Merkel and thus also against myself. I cannot tolerate having the running of the club circumscribed in this manner. By stepping down, I draw the necessary consequences.' When Hans Schiefele – the former Bayern player turned journalist who all those years ago had told Neudecker to sign Čik Čajkovski – asked Breitner for comment, the player said: 'It wasn't primarily about Max Merkel. Basically, it was about having a new coach. We just don't see a reason for another managerial change. Mister Csernai is a good choice.'

Everybody wanted a piece of Neudecker on this day that had shaken the club to its foundations. That explains why it was hard for treasurer Hoffmann to get hold of the man who had been his president until the morning. Finally, at three in the afternoon, Neudecker answered the phone.

'Will you take back your resignation?' Hoffmann wanted to know.

'No way, I'm not even thinking about it,' Neudecker replied. If he was expecting his trusted fellow board members, Hoffmann and Pfab, to follow his example, what he heard next must have given him the rest.

'Okay, fine,' Hoffmann replied. 'If that's the case, then I'm going to run for president.'

According to Hoffmann, who says he and Pfab didn't have any problems with Maier or the rest of the team and thus couldn't see the need to resign from the board, too, his announcement left Neudecker speechless, which may have been a first. Bayern's 6,500 members soon received notice that the club had called an extraordinary general meeting for 24 April, during which a new president would be elected.

Meanwhile, the nation's eyes were on Bayern's players. These men had been under pressure to perform for many years and for many reasons. But during the days following Neudecker's resignation, they realised they were now under a form of pressure none of them had ever known. Just a few weeks after Müller's unfortunate sendoff, the country was in uproar over Bayern yet again. Most people sided with Neudecker and criticised the players' behaviour as outrageous insolence. National coach Jupp Derwall even refused to call up Maier for an upcoming qualifier against Turkey. There were no two ways about it: the team simply had to do well in their next game to prove they were no deluded insurgents but knew what they were doing. They had to prove that Csernai was indeed the right man. As if somebody had scripted all this, the next game was away at old rivals Gladbach. Who were coached by Udo Lattek.

So many things had changed in such a short time, so many Bayern icons had left. But on 24 March 1979, five days after Neudecker had stepped down, the players in red made it abundantly clear that they were still Bayern Munich – because they rose to the occasion like only Bayern could. None other than Hans-Georg Schwarzenbeck opened the scoring after less than ten minutes. Norbert Janzon, the man for whom Gerd Müller had come off in Frankfurt, scored a brace. And Karl-Heinz Rummenigge netted four goals.

At half-time, with the score 5-1, the designated new president Willi O. Hoffmann walked into the dressing room. Disregarding the fact that forty-five minutes of football still had to be played, he informed the team that he had just booked a posh Munich restaurant for the evening. 'We'll party until morning!' he promised. And they did. Hoffmann says that 'the champagne was flowing until seven o'clock'. It may have been the night he acquired his legendary nickname, because people still know him as Champagne Willi.

Bayern's 7-1 triumph not only signalled the end of Neudecker's austere regime and the beginning of Hoffmann's jovial reign. It also underlined that the end of Gladbach's golden age had come – and kickstarted the Reds' resurgence. Bayern went on a seven-game unbeaten run and finished the season in fourth place, a valuable UEFA Cup slot.

After the game, Breitner talked to a film crew that was capturing his team's season for a documentary that had been planned long before anyone could imagine how colourful the campaign would turn out to be. 'We had to play against God and man,' he told the camera. 'Everybody wished us the worst, because what happened had never happened in German football before. Opposing the coach and the president, doing something that by German standards was revolutionary, is something Germans normally don't accept. And certainly not from well-paid footballers who are not supposed to speak their minds.'

In April, Hoffmann easily won the vote and became Bayern's new president. (A professor of business administration by the name of Fritz Scherer followed him as the club's treasurer.) The son of a simple toolmaker, Hoffmann was not only a Bayern man through and through – he had seen his first game in 1938, when he was eight – but also a dyed-in-the-wool Bavarian. He was very fond of *Tracht* and you rarely saw him without his traditional hat, complete with the tuft of chamois hair known as *Gamsbart*. Only seven months after becoming president, in November 1979, he dressed the entire squad in *Lederhosen* and cardigans for a photo shoot (only Csernai put his foot down. He wore a dark suit). It was Hoffmann who started the tradition of the entire first-team squad's visit to the *Oktoberfest* in fitting attire.

However, the story of those truly revolutionary months during 1978 and 1979 – months that thoroughly and permanently changed Bayern Munich – did not really end with Hoffmann's election and the positive finish to the league season. It ended on 14 July 1979, during the summer preparations for the new campaign. On this Saturday, Bayern played a friendly against Ulm, arranged by sponsors Magirus Deutz. In his autobiography, Sepp Maier says his team won '7-0 or 8-0' and that he'd had a quiet afternoon in goal. It's not true. The game finished 1-1. But perhaps it's no surprise that Maier got this detail wrong. Driving too fast through a thunderstorm on his way back home from Säbener Strasse to his house in Anzing, fourteen miles east of Munich, he lost control of his Mercedes and crashed into an oncoming car carrying two women. He blacked out instantly.

Both women were severely injured, suffering multiple fractures. At first it seemed as if Maier had broken some ribs and an arm and sustained a cerebral concussion but nothing life-threatening. It was only on the next day that doctors diagnosed a potentially lethal diaphragmatic tear, necessitating immediate surgery. Maier was thirty-five years old. He had played 442 consecutive league games for Bayern Munich, which probably constitutes a world record. (The British record is held by Harold Bell, who made 401 league appearances in a row for Tranmere Rovers.) He never played another one. Maier made some attempts at a comeback, but the pain wouldn't subside. In November 1979, four months after the accident, he faced facts and announced the end of his career. That same month, Schwarzenbeck tore his Achilles tendon, which would force him to hang up his boots (and take over his aunt's tiny newspaper and stationery shop a stone's throw from the river Isar).

And so the decade ended with all the living legends that once were *Il Grande Bayern* scattered to the four winds. That is, not quite all of them. Breitner was still wearing red. And although Wilhelm Neudecker was much maligned during the chaotic last weeks of his long and fruitful presidency, it should not be forgotten that he saved one of his most important and inspired decisions until last. In February 1979, only five weeks before stepping down, Neudecker informed the public that he had finally found someone to replace Robert Schwan as the club's business manager: Uli Hoeness, barely twenty-seven years old.

Almost thirty-five years later, Hoeness was sitting in a meeting room at Säbener Strasse, reminiscing with Rummenigge about the old days and answering questions about the new ones for a feature I was researching. He was having serious legal problems, which dominated the country's headlines, but you wouldn't have guessed it from the relaxed, good-natured manner in which he talked about his first days as Bayern's business manager.

'When I started,' he said, 'we were a simple football club. Things like marketing and merchandising didn't play a role, there was very little television money. When the weather was good, people came to watch us. When the weather was bad, they stayed home. But we were totally dependent on attendances – 85 per cent of our revenue came from ticket sales. So I went to America to study gridiron and baseball, where they already made millions from merchandising.' (Bayern studied gridiron so well that, in 1984, president Willi O. Hoffmann would suggest a fourteen-team Bundesliga without relegation, 'modelled on the National Football League in the USA'.)

It wasn't long after Hoeness had immersed himself in the club's books that he found out the money problems were a lot worse than most people thought. Bayern's annual turnover was 12 million marks (then £3.15 million). The club's debts, meanwhile, came to seven million. About half of that sum was back taxes that would have to be paid soon. ,

All of which is food for an arresting thought. What if Neudecker didn't resign on the spur of the moment because of the players' coup? What if he preferred to be out of the line of fire when the house of cards collapsed, as it would inevitably do? And indeed, on at least one occasion Hoeness told a journalist that he suspected Neudecker had been using him as 'cannon fodder'. He explained: 'Neudecker sensed that everything was going down the tubes here.' If this theory is true, Neudecker must have been surprised that the novice business manager he installed not only kept the house of cards standing – but cemented it.

We'll never know for sure, because Neudecker died in 1993. Still, there are a few clues that suggest he wasn't quite that deceitful. For instance, Rudi Assauer – at the time Werder Bremen's business manager and later very successful at Schalke – always maintained that Neudecker offered him the job first. It was only when Assauer said he couldn't commit himself before the end of the season, what with Werder in the midst of a relegation fight, that Neudecker looked elsewhere.

Also, in all likelihood the major reason he finally offered the post to Uli Hoeness was not just that the player had brokered the Magirus Deutz deal, proving his business acumen. It was also that by getting Uli, Neudecker got someone else he may have wanted even more: Uli's younger brother Dieter. Less than a week after announcing that Uli would become Bayern's new business manager, Neudecker signed centre-forward Dieter Hoeness from VfB Stuttgart for just 175,000 marks – to replace Gerd Müller.

Dieter was unlike his brother, both as a person and as a footballer. Paula Hoeness, their mother, once said: 'Dieter was a lot more gifted in the fine arts. He painted and sang better than Uli.' And while Uli was fast, agile and had a fine first touch, his brother was tall, heavy, slow and technically limited. It was easy to dismiss him as strong in the air but little else. This, coupled with the ridiculously low transfer fee, is why a lot of people think Uli brought Dieter to Bayern as an act of nepotism. Nothing could be further from the truth. Stuttgart were desperate to keep Dieter Hoeness, who held down second place in the top scorers' table while the negotiations went on.

In fact, Dieter hesitated before signing for Bayern. As a contemporary piece in *Kicker* magazine pointed out: 'The times when Bayern was the desired destination for ambitious and business-savvy players are long gone. It's not surprising that Dieter Hoeness believes his chances of having sporting and, through that, financial success are greater in Stuttgart.' In the end, though, Uli convinced his brother. After all, he was also Dieter's agent and had advised him a few years earlier to have that low transfer sum, not even a tenth of his market value, written into the contract.

Both brothers were very successful in their first season together. While learning about the possibilities of merchandising and sponsoring, Uli Hoeness also continued Neudecker's and Schwan's tradition of organising profitable if arduous friendlies. In late October 1979, two days after a cup game and three days before a league match in Bremen, Bayern took a plane to Algiers to play against the Algerian national team. It earned the club 100,000 marks, but Hoffmann says that Csernai only agreed to the trip after Champagne Willi got him tipsy on three glasses of bubbly wine.

Dieter Hoeness, meanwhile, scored sixteen league goals. His most important probably came on the penultimate matchday and, as is so often the case in football, against his old club. Bayern were level on points and goal difference with a great Hamburg team starring Kevin Keegan. With two games left, Bayern travelled to Stuttgart, while Hamburg had a far easier away game in Leverkusen. Defender Horsmann scored twice to give Bayern a 2-0 lead, but in the dying stages the hosts pulled one back. It was only when Hoeness scored

Bayern's third with four minutes left that Bayern could be sure of an important two points. As the players came off the pitch, they heard astounding news: Hamburg had been defeated in Leverkusen. All of a sudden, Bayern were two points clear at the top of the table. A week later, the team beat Brunswick to claim the 1980 Bundesliga title, Bayern's first in six years.

However, the key men who orchestrated this unexpected triumph were not the Hoeness brothers. Two crucial roles fell to Pál Csernai and Paul Breitner, who would meet on the evening before every game to go through the line-up and the tactics. Thus evolved what the writers dubbed the 'PAL system' – the catchphrase referenced the old colour encoding system for television. Csernai himself once defined it as a 'practicable' version of the zonal defence Gyula Lóránt had introduced with mixed results. It was Breitner, as the undisputed team leader and midfield conductor, who brought the system to life on the pitch, where he struck up an almost telepathic partnership with Karl-Heinz Rummenigge.

The 1979–80 season was Rummenigge's breakthrough campaign. A year after being regularly criticised for wasting too many chances, the 24-year-old won the Bundesliga's top scorer trophy for the first time, with twenty-six goals. Six months later, he would also be voted European Footballer of the Year 1980, collecting more than three times as many votes as the men in second and third place, Bernd Schuster and Michel Platini. Soon, the press would coin the term *Breitnigge* to describe the unstoppable juggernaut that was Breitner and Rummenigge.

But there was another thing besides tactics and individual class. It was something that had been absent from the club for some time – harmony. Breitner was at pains to explain how the egotism and the infighting that used to characterise the team of the 1970s had evaporated. 'Back then it was dog-eat-dog and it only worked because the success was always there,' he said. 'But the friction killed the harmony.' Rummenigge echoed these sentiments, telling author

Dieter Ueberjahn how as a young man he had often thought about leaving the club, because the established players cold-shouldered him for a long time. 'I felt hard done by,' he said. 'I wasn't so naive as to think they would all welcome me with open arms, but it came as a shock to me when I realised it was only the craving for success and profit which kept those stars together.' According to Breitner, this had changed. He explained: 'Now we're vigilant about preventing egotistic and cliquish thinking.'

Whatever it was that propelled the new Bayern, it worked during the following season as well, though Hamburg were again a formidable opponent. The club had lost Keegan but gained an old acquaintance – Franz Beckenbauer. The Kaiser joined Hamburg during the winter break after three years in New York and for the first few months it seemed as if his return would be a triumphant one. In mid-March 1981, Hamburg were in first place, three points ahead of Bayern, when they hosted the Reds for a potential make-or-break match. 'This is the first time all season that we go into a game as absolute underdogs,' Hoeness said on television. 'It's a new situation for our players, and I think they are looking forward to proving all those people wrong who think the title race will be decided on Saturday.'

But Felix Magath gave Hamburg the lead, then Breitner, of all people, played a disastrous back-pass that gifted Horst Hrubesch another goal nine minutes into the second half: 2-0. Was this too deep a hole Bayern had dug for themselves? No. Because there was still *Breitnigge*. On sixty-seven minutes, Breitner won possession deep in his own half, went past three opponents and played a brilliant through ball into the path of Rummenigge, who scored from just inside the box. And with only seconds left on the clock, Dieter Hoeness outjumped two defenders and nodded the ball to Breitner, who fired home a first-time shot from close range.

Uli Hoeness had been right – and wrong. Because in its own way, this game did decide the title race. Somehow Hamburg couldn't mentally cope with having come so close to going a massive five points clear at the top. A week after the draw with Bayern, they suffered a heavy 6-2 defeat in Dortmund, then they were beaten at Schalke. When Beckenbauer's new team also lost to Stuttgart in mid-May, Bayern were, to all intents and purposes, home and dry. They claimed their second league title in as many years with a game in hand and four points ahead of Hamburg.

On the last matchday, the Bayern players arrived at the Olympic Stadium in *Lederhosen*, while a brass band played Bavarian folk songs, costumed groups wearing *Tracht* paraded across the pitch and whip-crackers showed off their traditional art. Hoffmann loved it all so much, he threw his hat into the crowd.

Numerous times during the game against already relegated Bayer Uerdingen, ecstatic fans ran onto the pitch. When Bayern made it 4-0 with only two minutes left, the crowd could be held back no longer. Thousands invaded the pitch and play was halted for more than ten minutes. Finally, the stadium announcer informed the supporters that if the game had to be abandoned, Rummenigge would be stripped of the two goals he'd scored and might not be able to defend his title as the league's top scorer. The fans left the pitch, positioned themselves on the running track, waited for two minutes and then, when the final whistle rang, invaded the field of play all over again.

The title was particularly sweet because it seemed as if Bayern had finally found a proper rival, the Barcelona to their Real, the Celtic to their Rangers, the Liverpool to their Manchester United. Hamburg were a tradition-laden club from a big, rich city. Like Bayern, their business manager was a former star player (Günter Netzer). And, like Bayern, they would soon have a foreign coach who was going to bring tactical novelties to the league (the great Austrian Ernst Happel, who pioneered the pressing game). But although Hamburg always finished in first or second place between 1979 and 1984, they could not sustain that success and would gradually fade away, to be replaced by a Bayern challenger every bit as unlikely as Gladbach had been in the 1970s.

What Hamburg did, though, was succeed in Europe. In 1983, Happel guided the team to an unexpected triumph in the European Cup over a star-studded Juventus side. For Bayern fans, this was deeply ironic. In the 1970s, the Reds often struggled in the league but excelled repeatedly in Europe, while their greatest domestic rivals were doing fine in the Bundesliga but found themselves dogged by bad luck under midweek floodlights. In the 1980s, it would be the other way round. Few events illustrate this better than those of May 1982.

On the first day of that month, Bayern met Nuremberg in one of the most memorable DFB-Pokal finals of all time. After barely a dozen minutes, Dieter Hoeness went up for an aerial duel with Nuremberg's Alois Reinhardt and sustained a bad cut. Like England defender Terry Butcher in a World Cup qualifier seven years later, Hoeness had his head-wound first covered with a bandage and then stitched up during the interval. Like Butcher, he would forever be associated with battling on despite the bleeding injury. Hoeness briefly considered coming off, but his brother pleaded with him to stay on. Bayern were not only trailing 2-0 but had also lost defender Bertram Beierlorzer, who'd torn his Achilles tendon only ten minutes after the Hoeness–Reinhardt incident, which is why Csernai was reluctant to make another substitution so early.

Eight minutes into the second half, a Wolfgang Dremmler cross from the right found Hoeness at the far edge of the six-yard box. Hoeness smartly headed the ball over to Rummenigge, who pulled one back for Bayern. Nuremberg were now coming apart at the seams, it seemed, while Bayern surged forward. But that left a lot of space for the opposition to exploit. On the hour, Nuremberg's Werner Dressel played a through-ball that bisected the Bayern backline, his teammate Herbert Heidenreich received the ball near the penalty spot and shot on the turn – only to see Dremmler throw himself into the path of the ball and deflect it against the left-hand post.

Five minutes later, Rummenigge hit the woodwork at the other end, but Wolfgang Kraus was there to put the rebound away and make it 2-2. Hoeness now became a pivotal figure in Bayern's attack, as Rummenigge and Breitner regularly used him as a partner for one-twos that split Nuremberg's defence. Of course he also made his main strength count: his bandaged head knocked the ball into the path of Kraus, who went down under a challenge from Peter Stocker to win a soft penalty. Breitner converted the spot-kick to put his side ahead after seventy-two minutes.

It was left to the man of the match to put the finishing touch on this classic cup final. With a minute to go, Breitner sent in a cross from the left and Hoeness headed home from seven yards for the final scoreline of 4-2. The sight of Hoeness with his blood-stained bandage, immortalised in print as his *Turban*, became one of the most iconic images of 1980s German football.

If you count the 1974 European Cup (which went to a replay) and the two-legged 1976 Intercontinental Cup as two finals, then the Nuremberg game had been the twelfth final in Bayern's history. All had been won. And just twenty-six days later, the team hoped to keep this streak alive when they prepared for big game number thirteen – the European Cup final in Rotterdam.

On a very warm Wednesday evening, the Reds faced English champions Aston Villa. In the previous season, Bayern had been knocked out by Liverpool on away goals in the semis, prompting a defiant Breitner to declare: 'We're the best team in Europe regardless. And we'll prove it.' Now, thirteen months later, here was their chance to do so. Brian Moore, covering the game for ITV, called Bayern 'the odds-on favourites, based no doubt on their greater experience in playing European football'. The odds became even better ten minutes into the match, when Villa's veteran goalkeeper Jimmy Rimmer came off with shoulder problems and was replaced by 23-year-old Nigel Spink, who'd made only one first-team appearance for the club.

And yet the English looked more comfortable during the first half-hour and dominated the match. Until *Breitnigge* got going. On thirty-one minutes, Breitner set up Rummenigge, who forced a fine save from

Spink before the follow-up from young Reinhold Mathy was blocked by a defender ten yards in front of an open goal. Thirty seconds later, Breitner crossed from the right and Rummenigge narrowly missed the target with a marvellous bicycle kick. It would turn out to be the blueprint for the rest of the night.

Looking back on the game, a philosophical Augenthaler says: 'What could go wrong, did go wrong. We were clearly the better team but wasted five or six excellent opportunities. They had two chances all night and scored. We kept moving forward, but that's football.'

On fifty-seven minutes, Augenthaler, who was having a fine night, embarked on a glorious sixty-yard run that took him past five Villa players, yet his shot from inside the box went wide. Then a Rummenigge flick-on sent Hoeness clear through on goal, but the linesman raised his flag to signal offside, perhaps erroneously. Another minute later, Spink denied Dürnberger. Now Augenthaler had another chance, but his header was nodded off the line by Kenny Swain. Then Hoeness failed to make contact with not one but two crosses right in front of goal in the span of only seventy seconds.

'But Villa still hanging on at nil-nil,' Brian Moore said after sixty-six minutes, sounding ever so slightly incredulous. Moments later, left-winger Tony Morley ran into Bayern's box with the ball at his feet, taking on sweeper Hans Weiner. Augenthaler, who was marking Peter Withe in front of goal, moved over to back up his teammate. In Pál Csernai's 'PAL system', somebody now had to take up Augenthaler's position and look after Withe. But nobody did. Morley delivered a low cross from the left and, from close range, an unmarked Withe prodded in by way of the post.

Just to prove what kind of night it was, Hoeness finally managed to put the ball into the back of Villa's net with two minutes left, only to see the goal (correctly) disallowed for offside. When the French referee Georges Konrath blew his whistle for the last time on this day, the side Breitner had called the best in Europe had become the first Bayern team in history to lose a final. Even the presence of Franz Roth, who had travelled to Holland hoping he would be the team's good-luck charm, hadn't prevented the spell from breaking.

While the squad quietly drove back to their hotel in Scheveningen, half an hour north of Rotterdam, Augenthaler and Dürnberger were still sitting in a caravan at the ground. The two had been randomly chosen for the mandatory post-match drug test but found it hard to deliver urine samples. 'The two Villa players came in, downed a crate of beer extremely fast and were gone again after twenty minutes,' Augenthaler recalls, 'but we were there for ever.' When he and Dürnberger finally arrived at the hotel, most of their teammates were drunk. A few chairs were hurled in frustration from the balcony, then everyone went to bed, knowing very well there was no sleep to be had.

The level of disappointment may be best gauged by what happened the next morning. Despite the defeat, the team was received by the mayor of Munich and various dignitaries. It was only during lunch that the players realised their coach was missing. Csernai had gone home directly from the airport. An angry Breitner said: 'Somebody who should be here isn't. If we lose, we lose together. A bit more decency would have been in order.' The coach apologised, blaming it on his 'frazzled nerves' and, unconvincingly, on a car that refused to start. This morning, more so than the previous night's game, marked the beginning of the Hungarian's end at Bayern. It had taken only two years for the harmony to fray.

One man who never shied away from a microphone or refused to answer a reporter's question said astonishingly little in the wake of the Rotterdam drama. There was probably a very good reason why Uli Hoeness restrained himself from criticising the team or the coach. Only three months before the final, he had learned that some things are more important than winning or losing a football match.

On 17 February 1982, Hoeness was going from Munich to Hannover, to watch Breitner and Rummenigge play in a friendly for West Germany against Portugal. He was travelling in a light aircraft – a six-seater Piper Seneca. The only other passenger, apart from the two pilots, was a good friend of his, a publisher. Somewhere over Nuremberg, Hoeness dozed off. Luckily for him, his seatbelt wasn't fastened. Because something went wrong during the plane's landing approach. The Piper Seneca brushed a few trees, crashed and broke in half. Upon impact, Hoeness was hurled out of the plane. The other three men died in their seats.

When the West Germany game ended, Rummenigge and Breitner were told what had happened. They immediately hurried over to the hospital, wearing their tracksuits. Hoeness was unconscious. The doctors feared for his life until the early hours of the morning. Then they told Rummenigge and Breitner that he wasn't as severely injured as they had first feared and would be fine. Still, Breitner refused to leave. He spent the night at the bedside, together with Uli's wife Susi.

At five o'clock, Hoeness woke up. He looked at Breitner and said: 'What was the final score?'

9. PULLING OFF LEDERHOSEN IS HARD TO DO

Very few German football fans would recognise Udo Scholz, now in his mid-seventies, if they met him in the streets. That's because his voice was more famous than his face. Between 1973 and 1994, Scholz was the stadium announcer at the most notorious Bundesliga ground, Kaiserslautern's Betzenberg stadium.

Visiting teams feared the Betzenberg, because at the time it was one of the few football-only grounds (another famous one was Dortmund's Westfalenstadion), which meant the fans were really close to the action. And these were passionate, not to say unruly fans. It's probably no coincidence that the first-ever Bundesliga match abandoned because of crowd trouble was staged at the Betzenberg. In November 1976, during Scholz's fourth season in Kaiserslautern, the game against Düsseldorf was terminated in the seventy-sixth minute after bottles were thrown from the stands and the referee felt threatened by the crowd.

Bayern found the Betzenberg particularly tough. We have already mentioned the Reds' legendary 7-4 defeat in 1973. That was almost par for the course. Between 1975 and 1983, Bayern couldn't win a single game in Kaiserslautern. It was so frustrating that after a 2-1 loss in March 1982, Paul Breitner famously said: 'Maybe it's best if we

stay home and just send them the points by mail.' But the following
year, business manager Uli Hoeness came up with a novel idea to end
the curse – he dressed the team not in their customary red or white
but in what came to be known as the 'Brazilian kit': yellow shirts, blue
shorts and white socks. Footballers being deeply superstitious beings,
Kaiserslautern countered this ploy by playing in their green away kit.
But the Hoeness mojo worked better. The home side wasted a penalty
(about which more later), then Augenthaler scored the only goal of the
game with a deflected free kick on the hour.

It's tempting to imagine Udo Scholz sang the song that would
soon become famous for the very first time on this day. The idea
for the song had come to him while on holidays in Murnau, a
picturesque market town in southern Bavaria. One day, Scholz
went to a country inn nestled deep in the forest. Late in the evening,
a group of young men walked into the restaurant. They wore
Lederhosen, but one of them had badly torn his. Scholz says that
somebody yelled: 'Pull off that boy's *Lederhosen*!' For some reason,
that phrase stuck in his mind. On the way back to his hotel, the car
radio played the Beatles ditty 'Yellow Submarine' – and Scholz put
two and two together.

A few weeks later, Bayern travelled to Kaiserslautern. As the visiting
players came out to warm up, Scholz began to sing '*Zieht den Bayern die
Lederhosen aus*' – pull off Bayern's *Lederhosen* – to the tune of 'Yellow
Submarine' over the tannoy. The fans immediately picked it up and a
new terrace anthem was born.

Scholz says all this took place 'in the early 1980s'. But that can't
be right; it must have happened earlier. Because in 1980, a jack of all
trades from Berlin by the name of Heinz Werner Schneider put out
a single. One of his trades was running the bohemian hipsters' pub
Hundekehle, meaning dog throat, so he used his nickname *Heinz die
Hundekehle* for the record. It was the year Franz Josef Strauss, the arch-
conservative prime minister of Bavaria, ran for chancellor, which West
Germany's art scene saw as a threat to liberalism. Thus the record

was a thinly-veiled satirical dig at the proud Bavarian Strauss. It was entitled: 'Zieht den Bayern die Lederhosen aus (Yellow Submarine)'.

When I stumbled over this obscure record, I suspected that Scholz might have heard it – instead of the old Beatles tune – on the radio and simply adopted it. However, then I tracked down Gregor Rottschalk, a Berlin radio legend and the man who produced the single. 'We went to see Hertha play Bayern,' he told me. 'And when the crowd started to sing this *Lederhosen* song, we said: Hold on, this is funny, maybe we should do something with it.' In other words, when Rottschalk penned some additional lyrics and then produced his anti-Strauss single in the summer of 1980, 'Zieht den Bayern die Lederhosen aus' had already reached Berlin, so it must predate 'the early 1980s'.

Whenever it came into being precisely, 'Zieht den Bayern die Lederhosen aus' spread like wildfire, became the most fervently struck-up football chant in the league and is probably still the first song any non-Bayern fan learns. It became enormously popular because the Reds dominated the 1980s so thoroughly that 'Anyone But Bayern' was the dictum of choice for most German football fans.

One reason for the club's domestic pre-eminence was that the Reds finally solved their goalkeeping problems. When Sepp Maier had to hang up his gloves, Bayern's number-one shirt went to a young, Hamburg-born goalkeeper by the name of Walter Junghans. He did well in his first season (making *Kicker* magazine's Team of the Year), but then he became as inconsistent as his stand-in, the veteran Manfred Müller.

Junghans made his last appearance for the club in one of the classic 1980s Bundesliga thrillers: the home match against Hamburg on 24 April 1982. The visitors scored three goals in the final twenty minutes to win the game 4-3 and settle the title race. It was Hamburg's number one, future West German international Uli Stein, who committed the worst goalkeeping gaffe of the game, while Junghans made no glaring mistakes. However, he seemed insecure throughout the match and most people felt a truly great keeper would have saved at least one, maybe two of the goals.

In early June, Uli Hoeness announced he'd reached an agreement with the Belgian club K.S.K. Beveren and would sign their 28-year-old goalkeeper Jean-Marie Pfaff for 800,000 marks (£190,000 at the time). Pfaff promptly conceded one of the craziest goals in league history in his very first game – away at Werder Bremen in August 1982.

Bayern dominated this match, but Bremen's excellent goalkeeper Dieter Burdenski denied them again and again. And so the game was still scoreless when, with a minute left in the first half, Werder won a throw-in deep in Bayern's half, only a few yards away from the corner flag on the left flank. Bremen's right-winger Uwe Reinders came running over – long throw-ins were his speciality. Even if you hadn't known this, it would have immediately become obvious from the way Reinders held the ball in only one hand and then walked back a few steps to take a short run-up.

As the ball sailed toward the near post, where Bremen's midfielder Rigobert Gruber was waiting for it, Pfaff left his line. However, he couldn't quite get to the throw-in, because Gruber was blocking his path and his view. The ball flew above the heads of friend and foe, but Pfaff probably didn't see this. All he saw was that the ball was suddenly above him and on its way into the goal. He desperately stabbed at it with his right hand. Although he made contact he couldn't stop the ball from crossing the line.

It was the only goal of the game. And of course it wouldn't have counted if Pfaff hadn't touched the ball, because you can't score directly from a throw-in. As the players sat in the dressing room after the final whistle, Csernai went through the roof. 'This is ridiculous,' he yelled so loudly that his words echoed down the hallway where the journalists were waiting, notepads at the ready. 'This is the worst goal we have conceded in three years!' And turning towards Pfaff, he hissed: 'You're no longer in Belgium!'

When I met Pfaff at a football gala in Düsseldorf in the summer of 2015, he said matter-of-factly his reaction to the goal had been a simple one: 'I realised that I had to work even harder and train even more now that I was in the Bundesliga.' In Belgium, Pfaff had been a semi-pro, because Beveren were a small club. He held down a regular eight-hour job at a bank and only trained in the afternoon. Of course all this had to change at Bayern and it did. Pfaff eventually became not only a firm fan favourite but was also recognised as one of the best goalkeepers in the world. It was Pfaff who saved the penalty in Kaiserslautern in late 1983, diving to his left and denying Andreas Brehme, which lifted Bayern's Betzenberg curse.

After that game, Pfaff himself explained his excellent performance with reference to the fact that he now had his own official goalkeeping coach – Sepp Maier. The Bayern legend's return to Säbener Strasse marked a watershed in the relationship between the club and its former players.

Hoeness certainly played an important role in this transformation. He would also begin to order Bayern's stationery not from a wholesaler but from a tiny, cramped store in Ohlmüllerstrasse, just a brisk walk from the public field at Schyrenstrasse where Bayern had played their first-ever game. The store was as nondescript as the street. A simple sign told you the owner was called Nitzinger. This was the name of Georg Schwarzenbeck's aunt Maria, who'd run the store until she felt too old to do the job. Now the man they all called Katsche stood behind the counter for eleven hours every weekday. When you asked him why he wasn't working for Bayern, he replied: 'I like to be my own boss.' He would talk about football if you prodded him in a polite way, but he preferred not to. 'Why don't you ask some of the others?' he'd say sooner or later. 'They're much better talkers.' (Schwarzenbeck closed the shop in 2008, blaming the Internet and big chain-stores for dwindling business. He continued to supply Bayern Munich, though.)

However, it wasn't Hoeness who had the idea of bringing Maier back. It was Jean-Marie Pfaff. 'Shortly after I joined Bayern in 1982,' he says, 'I asked the club to sign him as a goalkeeping coach. But back then they didn't want him. So for almost two years I drove to his place in Anzing two or three times a week to work out with him.' The reason the club didn't want Maier in 1982–83 had a name. After Pfaff won the game in Kaiserslautern almost by himself, Maier told a reporter: 'Jean-Marie is just as fanatical on the training pitch as I used to be. I would have loved to take him under my wing earlier, but at that time there was still one Mister Csernai at the club.'

That even the man who had brought down a president to save Csernai's job now uttered his name with something approaching contempt underlines how isolated the Hungarian had become at the club in the wake of the Rotterdam final. His time at Bayern was up in May 1983, shortly before the end of the season. Csernai struck just too many people as aloof and arrogant. The powerful Herbert Jackisch, CEO of Magirus Deutz and a member of Bayern's board of directors, had demanded the sacking of the coach for months. When Jackisch began to link Csernai's fate with that of Willi O. Hoffmann, publicly announcing he would prefer a return of former president Wilhelm Neudecker, Hoffmann had to act. He dismissed Csernai with three games left in the season, promoted his assistant on an interim basis and announced that a man would return in the summer whose name had been chanted by the fans at the Olympic Stadium increasingly often during the previous weeks: Udo Lattek.

Lattek was not a natural man-manager like Čik Čajkovski, not a radical if troubled genius like Branko Zebec, not a cerebral strategist like Dettmar Cramer, not a sophisticated tactician like Pál Csernai. As *Der Spiegel* put it in an obituary when Lattek died in February 2015: 'He always left being visionary to others. He was convinced you don't win trophies by imposing what you think is best on a team. You win by getting the best out of what is there in the team. If you will, this was the Prussian element in him.'

In other words, Lattek was the ultimate pragmatist. But of course that's not a bad thing. When he joined Bayern for the second time, he was, at only forty-eight, the most successful club coach in the world. During the eight years he'd been away, Lattek won the UEFA Cup with Gladbach and the Cup Winners' Cup with Barcelona. The only other manager who has managed to lift all three European trophies is Giovanni Trapattoni. But only Lattek pulled off this feat with three different teams, not to mention in two different countries. Bayern signed him to win, and win he did. In the four years of his second stint at the club he guided the Reds to three league titles and two domestic cups, while also coming very close to bringing the coveted European Cup back to Munich.

And so, in the summer of 1983, it was almost like the good old days again at Bayern: Hoeness in charge, Lattek on the bench, Maier cracking jokes at the training ground. It could have been even better – Breitner could have been on the pitch. But the 32-year-old midfield dynamo retired in the summer, after a difficult, injury-strewn season. His testimonial, which pitted Bayern against a World XI starring Zico and Mario Kempes, was a great spectacle. When Bayern took the lead in the twenty-seventh minute, the stadium announcer said the goal had been scored by Breitner, which raised a great cheer from the Olympic Stadium crowd. But it wasn't true. Franz Beckenbauer, playing for the World XI, had tried to clear the ball, but ended up putting it into his own net. This was, it has to be said, a bit of a speciality of his. After all, Beckenbauer had done the very same thing in his own testimonial the previous summer.

Lattek's first season back at the helm brought a lot of commotion on and off the pitch. It produced two of the most notorious transfers in league history and two of the most famous football matches. In a way, one of these big deals and one of those unforgettable games were even connected.

In mid-March 1984, while the club were in the midst of an unusually tight title race (only three points separated the top five teams), Bayern held a spectacular press conference. Facing hundreds of journalists, countless photographers' flashbulbs and even television cameras were, from right to left, Bayern treasurer Fritz Scherer, Karl-Heinz Rummenigge, Udo Lattek, Willi O. Hoffmann, Archimede Pitrolo and Gianni Sartori. The latter two gentlemen came from Milan and represented Italian giants Internazionale. Like everyone else at the table, they rarely smiled but listened earnestly while Hoffmann explained the deal to the assembled media. Rummenigge would become an Inter player on 1 July, the Bayern president said. The transfer sum was 10 million marks (then £2.6 million) plus all the revenue from a friendly between the two clubs to be staged in August. (Which is why the move eventually netted Bayern between 11 and 12 million marks.)

It was a breathtaking deal in every regard. Rummenigge was now the most expensive footballer in the world. Yes, he was great. Yes, British pop duo Alan & Denise had just immortalised his 'sexy knees' in song. But he was twenty-eight years old and there were concerns his best years might be behind him. As Hoeness once quipped: 'For that kind of money, we should have carried him to Italy in a palanquin.' (A couple of months later, Napoli pulverised this transfer record by paying a seemingly absurd £6.9 million for a 23-year-old Diego Maradona. All things considered, Napoli made the smarter deal.)

At one point during the press conference, Rummenigge said: 'What bothers me is that all everybody is talking about here is money.' That, however, was to be expected. Rummenigge probably felt as if he had been thrust under a magnifying glass for costing so much money and earning a big wage. But it wasn't really about him. As the noted writer Jürgen Leinemann said in a contemporary piece: 'Nobody envies him his money. He is modest, friendly, nice, dependable.' Rather, people wondered what Bayern would do with all this sudden income. No Bundesliga club had ever spent as much as 2.5 million marks on a player and now the Reds had pocketed at least four times this amount. In one fell swoop, the club's financial problems were solved – the debts had been erased and there was money to spend. *Kicker* headlined: 'Bayern's Millions Drive the Bundesliga Crazy'.

Exactly six weeks after the press conference, Bayern began investing the Italian money. Even though his contract stipulated that he had to inform his club about any journey exceeding 125 miles, a young Gladbach midfielder by the name of Lothar Matthäus furtively flew to Munich, took a medical supervised by Bayern's club doctor Hans-Wilhelm Müller-Wohlfahrt and then signed a three-year contract. Annoyed, Gladbach's business manager Helmut Grashoff said: 'It looks like our rules no longer apply to Lothar.'

The slightly surprising thing about the transfer was not so much that Bayern wanted Matthäus. Even though it would be a long time before he became the superstar we remember him as, he was certainly one of the most promising midfielders in the league. No, it was surprising that Matthäus wanted to play for Bayern. The young man was born in Herzogenaurach, the small Franconian town almost literally torn in half by the fierce rivalry between the original Dassler brothers, Adi and Rudolf, and their respective companies, Adidas and Puma. In Herzogenaurach, you are either an Adidas man or a Puma man, there is no middle ground. Matthäus's father Heinz was a Puma man, employed as a janitor. His mother Katharina did sewing work for the company from home. His first club, FC Herzogenaurach, was almost a factory team. (Adidas men would never play for FC. They used to run out for the town's other club, ASV Herzogenaurach.) A few years ago, Matthäus told *11Freunde* magazine that this was why he joined Gladbach in 1979: 'My dad worked for Puma. Puma was Gladbach's supplier. So Borussia was my club. Bayern were Adidas, meaning I wasn't interested in them.'

Five years later, though, ambition won the upper hand over principles and Matthäus joined Bayern for 2.6 million marks (but, needless to say, continued to wear Puma boots). While the player's impending transfer dominated the headlines, Bayern travelled to Gelsenkirchen, the industrial city in the western part of the country that is home to Schalke. The club, then in the second division, was about to host Bayern in a DFB-Pokal semi-final, the likes of which nobody had ever seen.

After only 130 seconds, Karl-Heinz Rummenigge put the overwhelming favourites ahead from seven yards. Barely nine minutes later, the 22-year-old Reinhold Mathy made it 2-0. (Mathy, now at best a faint memory, was considered one of the most promising German talents at the time but soon saw his career falter.) Schalke pulled one back within fifty seconds when Rummenigge's younger brother Michael, signed by Bayern a few years earlier, lost the man he was supposed to mark.

Then Schalke's local hero Olaf Thon made his presence felt. Thon would later win three league titles with Bayern and the World Cup with West Germany, but this cup game, staged one day after his eighteenth birthday, would forever be remembered as his greatest, or at least his defining, night. On nineteen minutes, Thon started a move near his own penalty area that he finished with a low strike at the other end, tying the game. Schalke's spacious and inhospitable Parkstadion ground was now a madhouse and not even the fact that Michael Rummenigge restored Bayern's lead with a great volley only fifty seconds later could dampen the electric atmosphere; this was now a highly dramatic cup game and up for grabs.

Bayern's left-sided midfielder Hans Pflügler forced a fine save from Schalke's goalkeeper, none other than former Red Walter Junghans. Then Täuber hit the post. Thon, who stood just five foot seven inches, tied the game on the hour with a header, towering high above the Dane Søren Lerby, who had been signed from Ajax for a lot of money to replace Breitner but was struggling to find his footing. Ten minutes later, another cross sailed into Bayern's box and again the only player who went up for it wore a Schalke shirt. His name was Peter Stichler and his header gave the hosts the lead for the first time in what was already an epic game.

Bayern sent on another striker, Dieter Hoeness. In the subtle but steady Gelsenkirchen downpour, the Munich giants now threw everything forward. Ten minutes from time, Michael Rummenigge found the target with a flying header after a defender had mistimed Lerby's cross: 4-4. Extra time. For a bit over twenty minutes, the match almost resembled a normal game. But as it turned out, it was only charging up its batteries for eight minutes of sheer craziness.

In the 112th minute, Junghans let a harmless ball slip out of his grasp, demonstrating why Bayern had let him go, and Hoeness nudged it across the line from a yard out. The television commentator said: 'This game has been decided.' Four minutes later, Schalke's veteran sweeper Bernard Dietz made it 5-5 with a first-time shot from a corner. Ninety seconds after Dietz's goal, Karl-Heinz Rummenigge spotted an unmarked Hoeness and played a lethal vertical pass. Hoeness was clear through on goal and coolly put the ball between Junghans's legs for the eleventh goal of the night. The television commentator said: 'Is this the deciding goal? It is. It must be.'

Two minutes and two seconds into stoppage time, the referee blew his whistle. But not, as some people thought, to end the game. Instead, he awarded Schalke a free kick twenty-five yards in front of goal. Thon shaped as if to shoot but stepped over the ball and ran into the box. Instead, Bernd Dierssen struck the ball. It hit various legs and thighs in the goalmouth, then Augenthaler headed it to his right – and straight into Thon's path. The kid smashed the ball into the far corner with a fantastic left-footed volley: 6-6. Replay.

Interviewed amidst ecstatic supporters, Thon stunned the nation – and, one assumes, shocked Schalke's fans – after the game by admitting that he was a Bayern fan and actually slept in Bayern bedding. (Which also tells you that Uli Hoeness had begun to implement a few merchandising ideas.)

This second game, the replay, has been overshadowed by the unbelievable 6-6 draw, but it was amazing in its own right. Bayern gave away a two-goal lead and Pfaff had to make a brilliant save to deny Thon, before Karl-Heinz Rummenigge scored the winner with a flying header, sending his team into the final. Against – how could it have been any different? – Borussia Mönchengladbach and Matthäus.

The game between the grand old rivals of the previous decade has gone down in history as one of the most memorable finals in this competition. Although it was a good, entertaining match, the game's fame is basically down to one single moment. Gladbach, coached by their former striker Jupp Heynckes, took the lead through Frank Mill and although Bayern created a whole slew of chances, the Reds had to wait until the eighty-third minute before the equaliser finally came: Mathy hit the post from close range and Wolfgang Dremmler rifled the rebound home from a tight angle. For the first time, a DFB-Pokal final went to penalties.

The first man up was, inevitably, Lothar Matthäus. Pfaff had a well-earned reputation as what Germans call an *Elfmetertöter*, literally a penalty killer. (In fact, the Belgian saved 64 per cent of the spot-kicks he faced in the Bundesliga, the best ratio in league history.) Perhaps that's why Matthäus tried to place his kick particularly carefully, aiming for the top right-hand corner. In a way, it was a good decision, because Pfaff guessed right, dived to his left and would've probably saved a low shot. In another way, it was a bad decision. The shot cleared the crossbar.

If you ask any Gladbach fan about this moment, chances are he or she will tell you that Matthäus intentionally missed his penalty. It's nonsense, of course, but the miss garnered him the unfortunate nickname 'Judas' in Gladbach and had many people wondering why Heynckes sent him out to take a penalty in the first place. The answer is simple: Matthäus was a good penalty-taker. He'd scored a number of goals for Borussia from the spot and felt comfortable. And there is another thing – there were many more penalties to come.

After the game, Matthäus was photographed sitting on the pitch and sobbing uncontrollably. It's another iconic image emblematic of 1980s football and maybe that's why many people assume that his penalty decided the match. It didn't. Four minutes after his miss, Augenthaler tried the old trick of hammering the ball into the middle of the goal. But Gladbach's goalkeeper Uli Sude wouldn't be duped and easily parried the shot. (Matthäus ran over to Sude in his socks and embraced the goalkeeper.) It was 4-4 in the shoot-out after the first round of penalties. While Matthäus told a reporter 'Missing this penalty is the biggest disappointment of my career,' the drama went on.

With the score 7-7, Gladbach's striker Frank Mill was supposed to step up, but he told Heynckes he wasn't feeling well. (Nobody knew it at the time, but Mill had sustained a concussion in an aerial duel with Dieter Hoeness.) And so substitute Norbert Ringels placed the ball on the white spot, took a long run-up – and made the left-hand post quiver. Pfaff triumphantly raised his arms, while Dieter Hoeness went looking for the ball, because it was his turn now. The reason he couldn't find it was that young Michael Rummenigge had grabbed the ball and was briskly walking towards the penalty spot. The twenty-year-old watched Sude dive to his left and coolly knocked the ball into the opposite corner. Before the ball had hit the back of the net, Rummenigge had turned and was racing towards his brother to celebrate. Karl-Heinz was the first player to face the cameras and talk about the game. 'My brother has made me the best possible present,' he said. Then he left the pitch – and the club.

Top: The Bull: Franz Roth delivers a powerful shot during yet another massive game he won for Bayern, the 1976 European Cup final against Saint-Étienne.

Bottom left: A young Karl-Heinz Rummenigge (l), Franz Roth (c) and defender Udo Horsmann celebrate Bayern's third European Cup triumph in a row. The club would have to wait a quarter of a century for the fourth.

Bottom right: September 1978: the scoreboard at the Olympic Stadium documents one of the most embarrassing defeats in Bayern's history, against second-division Osnabrück.

Top: Gladbach goalkeeper Wolfgang Kneib makes a great save to deny Bayern midfielder Wolfgang Kraus (l). Gladbach won this game in late 1979, 2-1, but the end of the decade also means the end of their golden era. Bayern's greatest domestic rival can no longer keep pace.

Bottom left: December 1977: it must have been a cold day in Munich, because assistant coach Pál Csernai (l) is not wearing his trademark silk scarf. Twelve months later, he will take over from Gyula Lóránt (r).

Bottom right: In November 1979, new president Willi O. Hoffmann establishes a tradition by dressing the entire squad in *Lederhosen* and cardigans. (Only Csernai, proud of being a dapper dresser, refuses to don Bavarian *Tracht*.)

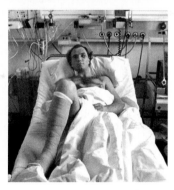

Top: Karl-Heinz Rummenigge (l) and Paul Breitner (r) strike up such a productive partnership that the press dubs the duo *Breitnigge*.

Bottom left: In 1980, the man who scored one of the most important goals in Bayern's history hung up his boots – and took over his aunt's tiny newspaper and stationery shop. For the next 28 years, Georg Schwarzenbeck would be behind the counter every morning at six o'clock. (His aunt is on the left.)

Bottom right: In February 1982, Uli Hoeness was the sole survivor of a plane crash. He later said: 'I survived, but the sunny boy in me died.'

Top: On the first day of the 1982–83 season, Bayern's Belgian goalkeeper Jean-Marie Pfaff concedes the only goal of the game at Werder Bremen from a throw-in. Still, Pfaff went on to be a hit (and a fan favourite) at Bayern.

Bottom left: On his last day in a Gladbach shirt, a 23-year-old Lothar Matthäus cannot hold back the tears after missing his penalty and losing the 1984 cup final against his new club Bayern.

Bottom right: Despite having sustained a head wound during the game, Dieter Hoeness heads home Bayern's fourth goal to put the 1985 cup final out of Nuremberg's reach.

Top left: Another Gladbach legend who went on to become a Bayern icon: Jupp Heynckes took over the Munich giants in 1987 – for the first but not the last time.

Top right: It's a good thing Bulgarian international Emil Kostadinov is between Jürgen Klinsmann (l) and Lothar Matthäus (r). The two men would soon engage in a famous feud that helped garner Bayern the nickname FC Hollywood.

Bottom left: July 1995: on his first day as Bayern coach, Otto Rehhagel needs a megaphone to be heard above the tumult and the shouting. Welcome to Hollywood!

Bottom right: Uli Hoeness re-enacts how Jürgen Klinsmann, furious at being subbed, once kicked a hole into an advertising pillar which now stands in Bayern's club museum.

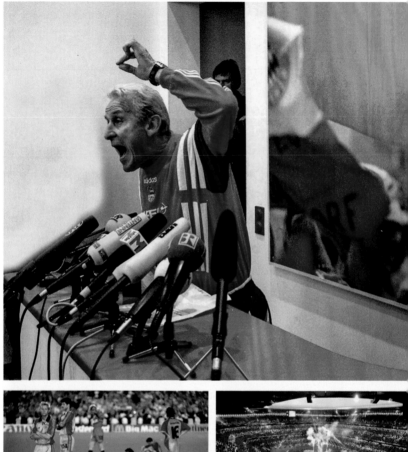

Top: The Day of the *Wutrede*: in March 1998, coach Giovanni Trapattoni, having lost patience with his FC Hollywood starlets, throws a tantrum that has gone down in history as the most entertaining three minutes and ten seconds in Bayern's press room.

Bottom left: On a traumatic night in Barcelona, Manchester United come from behind in stoppage time to beat Bayern and win the 1999 Champions League final.

Bottom right: A home of their own: in May 2005, Bayern open their new Allianz Arena with a game against the German national team. (Bayern win 4-2. Their fans chant: 'We're better than the whole of the country.')

Top left: Louis van Gaal was on the verge of becoming an honorary Bavarian, as he looked good in *Tracht* and lived the club's motto *Mia san mia*, we are who we are, to perfection. But when he started to think he was bigger than the club, his days were numbered.

Top right: It's still a Dutchman who finally delivers the elusive treble, though. A late goal from Arjen Robben (l) thrills Thomas Müller (r) and wins the 2013 Champions League final against new rivals Borussia Dortmund.

Bottom: Bayern's players urge Uli Hoeness to lift the coveted trophy. They know that nobody, not even Jupp Heynckes, has had a bigger share in this triumph.

Top: And so it comes as a massive shock to the club when Hoeness, who for all practical purposes *is* Bayern Munich, stands trial for tax evasion in March 2014 and is sentenced to prison.

Middle: The best team they ever had? Under Pep Guardiola, Bayern dominate the league to an unprecedented degree, set records at will and win domestic trophies by the truckload.

Bottom: And yet many fans are glad when Carlo Ancelotti arrives in Munich to take over the team. They think he'll have a better understanding of what makes this club special. Of what it means to be Bavarian.

10. BAYERN-DUSEL

In the late 1960s, when Bayern rose to national prominence, the club's biggest rival should have become Cologne. The Rhineland giants were progressive, efficient and professional. Their bustling, visionary president Franz Kremer had been a driving force behind the formation of the Bundesliga and he dreamed of modelling Cologne on Real Madrid. In the end, it never happened, partly because Kremer suddenly died of a heart attack in 1967. Instead, Cologne's much smaller neighbours Borussia Mönchengladbach emerged as Bayern's main competitors.

History repeated itself in the 1980s. Hamburg had all the makings of a perennial powerhouse but eventually couldn't compete on a consistent basis, maybe because first Netzer found the business side of the game too taxing and then Happel left for health reasons. Instead, a much smaller club, based sixty-five miles southwest of Hamburg, became Bayern's new and unexpected rival – Werder Bremen.

In many respects, Bayern and Bremen were polar opposites – even politically. Willi Lemke, Hoeness's counterpart at Werder, had served as the executive officer of the regional board of the Social Democratic Party in Bremen before becoming the club's general manager. He milked the two teams' contrasting images for all it was worth. Hoeness once called him 'a demagogue', adding: 'This man has stereotyped us as the enemy. That's class war, pure ideology. We are the arrogant millionaires, they are the league's underdogs.'

Demagoguery or not, portraying Bayern as snobbish capitalists certainly hit a nerve. In October 1989, when the Reds travelled to Hamburg to play St. Pauli, Hoeness was enraged when he saw the match programme. The cover was graced by a famous St. Pauli character known, for obvious reasons, as Tattoo Theo. He had his right fist raised to give the socialist salute. Above his head and below the fist was the headline. It read: 'Class War'. (Hoeness won an injunction that stopped the programme from going on general sale.)

The main reason for Bremen's unlikely rise was not Lemke, though. It was the coach, Otto Rehhagel. On occasion, Rehhagel had a good eye for talent, such as when he signed a young Rudi Völler in 1982 and then replaced him five years later with a 21-year-old Karl-Heinz Riedle. But Rehhagel's forte was working with experienced players who'd been around the block. On any given matchday, seven players in his starting XI had long since turned thirty. Most of them were desperate to finally win something, because they were nearing the end of their careers and, with the exception of the great Austrian sweeper Bruno Pezzey, hadn't much silverware to show for it.

But Bayern didn't let them win. Between 1985 and 1987, the Reds lifted three league titles on the trot for the second time in their history, not least because Søren Lerby finally delivered on his promise. It was the second of these titles that cemented Bayern's role as the Bundesliga's bogeymen and also gave currency to an expression whose origin is somewhat shrouded in mystery: *Bayern-Dusel*.

Dusel is an old colloquial German word for a fluke, a piece of undeserved, unexpected luck. *Bayern-Dusel* thus refers to the idea that the breaks will always go the Munich giants' way. The term is now so deeply ingrained in the collective German football psyche that it has its own Wikipedia entry. According to the article online, it goes back to the 1970s, when the team was not doing well in the

Bundesliga but somehow kept winning in Europe. Ten years ago, the writer Alex Feuerherdt, an expert on anti-semitism, held a lecture about 'German resentment towards Bayern Munich', in which he suggested that the myth as such is even older. He traced the idea of a perennially lucky Bayern back to the time when the club was regarded as a 'Jews' club', since anti-semites would denounce any Jewish achievement as unearned, acquired either through trickery, conspiracy or plain luck.

However, during the research for this book I have found virtually no reference to *Bayern-Dusel* as a generally recognised expression prior to 1990. So until proven otherwise, let's assume, if only for the sake of the argument, that it was the 1985–86 season that finally exasperated Germans so much that they became convinced unearthly forces had to be at work here.

It all began with violence and controversy. In November, Bayern and Bremen met at the Olympic Stadium for a much-anticipated crunch encounter. Only 37,000 were in attendance, because the weather was awful – large parts of the stands were covered in snow. As mentioned before, the otherwise beautiful stadium was not a pleasant place on such days. A week earlier, Katsche Schwarzenbeck had watched a World Cup qualifier from the stands and left after the first half because he was freezing to death. Now, for the Bremen match, he was clad in a thick leather coat and gloves. But he was still cold.

Maybe the people who stayed home had a sense of foreboding. The game was ugly. Early on, Bayern's Norbert Eder scythed down Völler from behind. When the referee whistled for a foul, Lerby complained and was booked. When the Dane then sarcastically applauded the yellow card, he could consider himself lucky to stay on the pitch. The same went for Augenthaler, the team's captain following Rummenigge's sale to Inter. In the sixteenth minute, he hacked down Völler, who had put the ball past him and would have been clear through on goal. Augenthaler was booked, too, though most observers agreed that he should have been given his marching orders. The referee later admitted it was 'a borderline decision', but explained that because Augenthaler was 'seeking to play the ball' he felt brandishing a red card would have been too harsh. It was a different matter a minute before the break. Pezzey brought down Matthäus and the Bayern midfielder retaliated by barging into the Austrian. Matthäus was sent off. Even though they were a man down, Bayern won 3-1.

Looking back on his club's great clashes with Gladbach in the previous decade, Schwarzenbeck wistfully said: 'There was a lot at stake during those days, too. Usually the league title. But back then we still played good football. It wasn't as tense and hectic as it is now and we didn't kick lumps out of each other.'

The game – and Augenthaler's foul – further fuelled the fires between the two clubs. Bremen's president, a normally soft-spoken anaesthetist by the name of Franz Böhmert, said he'd walked into the dressing room at half-time to tell his players it was no longer about winning, only about 'getting home with our health intact'. Lattek defended Augenthaler by saying: 'Völler is quite simply so fast that sometimes you're late.' Rehhagel complained: 'I just don't know what to do with Rudi any more. Wherever we go, he is brutally fouled. Maybe I should stop playing him.' Which in the end he had to do, for sixteen long weeks – the widely popular Völler was sidelined as a result of Augenthaler's foul.

For the rest of the season, and beyond, Augenthaler was booed whenever Bayern played away from home. The catcalls never rang louder than on 22 April, a Tuesday evening. On the penultimate day of the season, Bayern travelled to Bremen. The Reds were trailing Werder by two points, so most people felt the match amounted to a final for the league title. And perhaps for more than just that. Venerable *Kicker* magazine, not normally given to hyperbole, spoke of 'the clash of the belief systems', adding: 'The role of the villains is reserved for Bayern.' When Rehhagel said 'the whole nation is behind us', there was no dissent. 'All sympathies are certainly with Werder,' admitted Bayern's veteran defender Eder.

When you go to see Bayern play at home these days, you will meet street vendors selling merchandise almost as soon as you step off the U6, the underground line that takes you from the city centre to the northern edge of town, where the Allianz Arena is. Shirts and sweaters that read *Euer Hass ist unser Stolz* are very popular – your hatred is our pride. Maybe that sentiment originated in those weeks and months during the mid-1980s when, as Otto Rehhagel pointed out, the entire country seemed to keep their fingers crossed for Bayern's rivals. It must be very hard to cope with such universal antagonism, but Bayern – fans and players alike – have turned it into an art form. At times you almost feel as if they relish these situations so much that they seek them out, knowing they possess the unusual ability to draw strength from hostility.

As they did on this electric night in April 1986. The buzz around the game was unlike anything the league had seen before. The match was shown live on a giant screen on Bremen Market Square, less than two miles west of Werder's relatively small ground. It was one of the first instances of what is now a German national obsession, the public screening of big football games, often attended by tens of thousands during major tournaments.

Amidst all that clamour, Bayern kept a cool head. Sweeper Klaus Augenthaler seemed totally oblivious to the insults hurled from the stands and Pfaff played a blinder, tipping a Pezzey shot over the bar in the first half when most people had already raised their arms to celebrate a goal. However, Bremen dominated the midfield so thoroughly that Bayern found it hard to create chances. Twice Matthäus went close with free kicks, but not much happened from open play.

With thirteen minutes left, a player wearing number thirteen came into the game. Exactly 150 days after Augenthaler's foul, Völler was making his comeback. He had to walk through more than a dozen photographers to step onto the pitch. Ten minutes later, with the game still scoreless, Völler took a step into Bayern's box and tried to flick the ball over Lerby. The ball hit Lerby's face and bounced towards the touchline. While the Dane chased the ball, the referee blew his whistle and pointed to the penalty spot. On television, pundit Paul Breitner exploded. 'Nothing! The face!' he said excitedly. 'It hit only the face!'

Bayern's players were every bit as indignant as Breitner. They protested the decision, which appeared to gift Bremen the title, so vehemently that more than two minutes went by before the penalty could be taken. Maybe they were so desperate because they knew Werder's designated taker was Michael Kutzop, a 31-year-old defender and spot-kick specialist. For Kickers Offenbach and Bremen, Kutzop had converted twenty-nine in a row. This man never missed, he was a penalty machine.

Kutzop took a long run-up. Just before making contact with the ball, he hesitated, to see if Pfaff was going to commit himself. When the Belgian made no move to dive to either side, Kutzop kicked the ball towards the far-right corner. Too far. It hit the outside of the post and harmlessly bounced across the byline.

As far as German football fans were concerned, it didn't matter that the penalty decision had been wrong. It didn't matter that the referee told Bayern secretary Karl Hopfner he would have ordered the spot-kick to be retaken if the ball had gone in because Kutzop had stopped at the end of his run-up. It didn't matter that Rehhagel told the reporters: 'We don't want any gifts. There would have been an uproar if the penalty had gone in. We are strong enough to win the league without gifts.' It didn't matter that Bremen were still two points clear at the top of the table. What mattered was the general feeling that Bayern had had incredible *Dusel* again.

To make matters worse in the public-relations department, Bayern played old rivals Gladbach off the park on the last day, winning 6-0, while Bremen suffered a shock defeat in Stuttgart. The Reds claimed the league title on goal difference. Bremen's frustrated goalkeper Dieter Burdenski probably spoke for the vast majority of neutrals when he called Bayern 'the most arrogant team in the league' and said it would have been better for German football if his own club had won the title. Bayern historian Dietrich Schulze-Marmeling says: 'Rarely has there been a champion who was hated as deeply as the one in 1985–86.' He added: 'That didn't dampen Bayern's good spirits – quite the contrary.'

Credit where it's due, the penalty trauma – and the fact that Werder had now finished as runners-up for the third time in four years, earning Rehhagel the unwelcome nickname King Otto the Second – didn't break the team. Werder would finally win the league in 1988 and continue to be a strong opponent and a bona-fide contender until the mid-1990s.

The key man in Bayern's triumphant 1986 side was Lerby. He was so crucial to the team's success that Bayern went to unprecedented lengths to have him on the pitch. On the afternoon of 13 November 1985, Denmark were scheduled to play a World Cup qualifier in Dublin. Six hours later, Bayern would meet Bochum away from home in the DFB-Pokal. Those six hours gave Uli Hoeness an idea. He asked Lerby what he thought of playing in both games. 'When he confronted me with that crazy plan,' says Lerby, 'I felt coveted – and also challenged as an athlete. Our national coach assured Bayern he would take me off once we held a comfortable lead.'

Hoeness travelled to Dublin with Lerby, prepared to drive him to the airport almost as soon as he'd left the pitch. But things didn't go according to plan. After barely six minutes, Tony Cascarino crossed from the right flank and Frank Stapleton buried a beautiful header. At half-time, it was 1-1 and Lerby was told to stay on the pitch. 'Uli was standing at the touchline,' he recalls, 'and staring at his watch in desperation.' But Denmark scored two goals after the restart to take a 3-1 lead and, on the hour, Lerby was at last substituted. He took a brief shower, then Hoeness drove him to the airport, where a chartered jet was waiting. After landing in Düsseldorf, thirty miles southwest of Bochum, they were picked up in a Porsche. Hoeness and Lerby had one hour to spare, but when they could already see the Bochum floodlights, the two got stuck in a traffic jam. 'I went ballistic in the car,'

Lerby remembers. 'Finally I got out, said "See you, Uli" and ran the last mile. I desperately wanted to start the game.'

He didn't, though, because the teams were already in the tunnel when he arrived. Still, Lattek brought Lerby on for the second half and the Dane came close to creating the winning goal when he set up Matthäus. Bochum's goalkeeper parried the attempt, though, and the game ended 1-1 after extra time. As far as I know, this was one of only three recorded cases in which a professional saw action in two proper, competitive games on the same day.

Bizarrely, the next man to do this was also a Bayern player. On 11 November 1987, striker Mark Hughes, just loaned from Barcelona, went the distance for Wales in a Euro 1988 qualifier against Czechoslovakia in Prague. Later on the same day he came on as a sub in Bayern's second-round cup game with Gladbach. That match went to extra time as well; Bayern won 3-2. (The third such case involved goalkeeper Jorge Campos. He won a cap for Mexico and then starred in a league game for his club, LA Galaxy, on 16 June 1996.)

After the dramatic end to the 1985–86 season, Bayern lost Lerby to Monaco, who paid 1.5 million marks for the midfielder. Having had such a good experience with a Dane, the club invested this money into signing Lerby's fellow countryman Lars Lunde, who had just won the Golden Boot in Switzerland and lifted the league title with Young Boys. In Bern, the 22-year-old enjoyed a reputation as a bit of a bigmouth. It was not unwarranted. Before he'd played a game for his new team he told reporters: 'If I do well at Bayern, I can practically choose which Italian club I want to play for.' And after his Bundesliga debut, a drab draw away at newly-promoted Blau-Weiss Berlin, he said: 'I can't understand why a club as big as Bayern is afraid of a team like that.' After barely a year, Lunde was loaned out back to Switzerland, to FC Aarau.

This, though, was not the end of Lunde's Bayern story. On 12 April 1988, the Dane suffered a horrible car crash when he ran a red light at an ungated level crossing and collided with a train. He was in a coma for more than a week and the only thing he remembered from those days was that his Aarau coach stood at his bedside wearing a red tie. (The name of that coach? Ottmar Hitzfeld.) When Lunde woke from the coma, his coordination skills were gone. He couldn't even sit on a chair without losing balance. When Uli Hoeness learned about Lunde's situation, he paid for all medical rehabilitation and invited his former player to spend a month at his home. 'I became part of the family,' Lunde told a Swiss newspaper. 'His daughter Sabine moved into a room with her younger brother to clear some space for me. Uli saw to it that I found a really good physio, who worked with me on my coordination.' Lunde recovered almost completely but was still forced to finish his career two years later. He now works as a nurse in a hospital in Switzerland.

The Lunde story is just as emblematic of Bayern under Hoeness as Burdenski's certainly not unfounded accusation of arrogance or the repeated public bickering with Lemke (and, as we shall presently see, another man with a sharp tongue). The club which Sepp Maier not so long ago had accused of alienating players of merit now even took care of those who had not been stars. Which is why former player Markus Babbel would one day say: 'Among the top clubs in Europe, Bayern are the most humane. They have always shown generosity when there were problems. Take Alan McInally, who became an invalid and didn't have any insurance. The club said: we'll give you severance pay. They practically gifted him the money. Our business manager is somebody you can talk to about such things.'

The Scottish forward McInally was signed in 1989 for a club record 3.3 million marks – then £1.1 million – but soon suffered a knee injury that would eventually curtail his career. In 2012, he told Sky Sports about his time at Bayern: 'I've still genuinely got affection for a club that's a massive global machine. I've always thought myself fortunate to be involved with it. It was definitely the right thing I did at the right time in my career.'

In the second half of 1991, while McInally was making his last, futile attempts at coming back from the knee injury, Sepp Maier was

regularly running out for the Uwe Seeler Tradition XI, a celebrity side
set up by the Hamburg legend to play charity games. Gerd Müller was
a member of the team as well. He had returned to Munich in 1984
and, in his own words, done 'more or less nothing' since. He didn't
look well. Maier noticed that his clothes smelled of alcohol. Sometimes
Müller would ask to be taken off early, faking an injury, so that he could
go into the dressing room and drink a few beers. Maier also heard
that Müller's wife had filed for divorce because she couldn't stop her
husband from drinking. Finally, in mid-September, Müller's condition
became public knowledge when he attended a Bayern training session
at Säbener Strasse visibly the worse for wear.

A few days later, Müller was sitting in Uli Hoeness's office, quietly
watching his former teammate call a number of rehab clinics. Somehow,
Hoeness had managed to do what neither Müller's wife, nor his daughter,
nor any of his friends had been able to do – convince the man they once
called the Bomber that he needed help. Hoeness sent him to Garmisch-
Partenkirchen, fifty-five miles south of Munich. 'On the very next day,
I left Munich,' Müller told a newspaper many years later. 'I spent two
weeks in hospital and then another two weeks at a health resort. They
asked me to stay for two more weeks, but I knew I had made it.' He
never touched another drink, though he also knew that abstinence was
only the first step. 'If I hadn't found a job,' he said, 'it would have started
all over again.' But he did find a job. In January 1992, Müller began
working for Bayern Munich as a scout. He later became an assistant
coach, first in the youth set-up, then with the reserves.

What is it about Bayern and the tax authorities? In March 1985, *Der
Spiegel* reported that club president Willi O. Hoffmann was in deep
water. Several of his real-estate deals had gone wrong, whereupon
one of his business partners decided to make a voluntary disclosure
of tax evasion to avoid civil penalties. The magazine said the public
prosecutor's office was now investigating Hoffmann on suspicion of
fraud and wondered 'if the president could ride out a lawsuit'.

Maybe he could have, but it didn't get that far. It soon transpired there were many more people who weren't getting the tax write-offs Hoffmann had promised them. They wanted their money back – lots of it. The man everyone still called Champagne Willi realised he might be forced to file for bankruptcy. There was no way he could run a club as big as Bayern with all these problems weighing on his mind. Hoffmann announced he would be taking a leave of absence from his post from 1 July. 'It hurts having to leave the club, especially now that things are going so extremely well in terms of both football and finances,' he said. For three months, treasurer Fritz Scherer took over the post on an interim basis. Then, during the club's annual general meeting in October, the members formally elected him Bayern Munich's new president.

This is why it was Scherer, not Hoffmann, who was sitting in the Marriott Hotel in Vienna on 26 May 1987, drafting his victory speech. On the next day and just two miles away, in the ground which today is named after Ernst Happel but used to be called Praterstadion, Bayern were going to win the European Cup for the fourth time and a good president had to be prepared. When Scherer was happy with his speech, he went to have a glass of wine at the bar. It was now past midnight. The day of the triumph had arrived. When somebody asked him what he'd do if they lost the match, Scherer curtly replied there was no need to worry about that.

Was this a case of astonishing hubris? Didn't the club know how strong their opponents – nine-time Portuguese champions FC Porto – had looked in the previous rounds? The fact that Scherer wrote his victory speech in advance is often cited as a typical example of Bayern arrogance. However, it should not be forgotten why we know about the speech that was never delivered in the first place: Scherer himself told the story during the muted post-match banquet. Looking at 500 empty, pained, frustrated faces, the president displayed grace under pressure by admitting he had been just as certain of victory as everyone else in the room. While he had been composing that speech, he said, his thoughts were: 'Who can possibly stop us?'

Scherer was not a man given to delusions of grandeur. He was a civil servant at the polytechnic in Augsburg, his hometown where he had once played youth football alongside the great Helmut Haller. The *Süddeutsche Zeitung* called him 'a cool tactician', while *Kicker* wondered if he might be 'too bland for media darlings Bayern'. The reason this careful, calculating man was convinced the Reds would win the final was the all-pervasive sense that Bayern were what Americans like to call a team of destiny. Uli Hoeness had even predicted 'the beginning of a new, great era'. Put simply, it just had to be Bayern's turn again.

In the previous years, the club had often been stopped by English opposition: Liverpool in 1981, Aston Villa in 1982, Tottenham in 1984 (UEFA Cup), Everton in 1985 (Cup Winners' Cup). But after the Heysel disaster, England's clubs were banned from Europe. What's more, Bayern had eliminated Real Madrid – starring such greats as Emilio Butragueño, Santillana, Juanito and José Antonio Camacho – in the semis. There was a feeling that the hardest part of the job had been done. Even though they would have to play the final without Augenthaler, sent off in Madrid but sidelined anyway with severe back problems, Bayern were determined to not let this once-in-a-lifetime opportunity pass by. Andreas Brehme, signed a year before from Kaiserslautern, simply said: 'Well, Lars Lunde will have to come through, then.'

As it turned out, Lunde didn't start the game because Lattek opted for a slightly more cautious approach. Still, his team dominated the first half. Many years later, Porto's Algerian striker Rabah Madjer would tell UEFA's website: 'When we got onto the pitch, looking at the Bayern players – Matthäus, Rummenigge – there were some great names on the pitch. Then it felt like I was blocked.'

Well, of course the Rummenigge on the pitch was not Karl-Heinz but his less glamorous (and less gifted) kid brother Michael. Matthäus, meanwhile, hadn't yet fulfilled his promise. Three days before the final, the writer Ulrich Kühne-Hellmessen, who would one day publish a biography of the player, said about Matthäus: 'The accusation still hangs in the air: strong games against weak opponents, weak games against strong opponents.' It turned out to be a self-fulfilling prophecy, as Matthäus came under heavy criticism after the game for having failed yet again when the chips were down.

You just have to say that there was a lot less individual ability in this Bayern team than maybe the club themselves felt. In fact, the only true world-class player was Jean-Marie Pfaff. Perhaps nobody epitomises this willing but limited Bayern side better than nippy left-winger Ludwig Kögl. He had joined Bayern three years earlier from local rivals 1860 Munich for a pittance: 70,000 marks plus the gate money from a friendly between the two clubs. Now, in the twenty-fifth minute of the final in Vienna, this local boy, who'd grown up only a few miles south of Munich, put Bayern ahead. Porto's midfielder Jaime Magalhães headed a throw-in from Hans Pflügler directly into the path of an unmarked Kögl, and the diminutive forward scored with what may have been the only diving header of his career. As Lars Lunde told Swiss television on the twenty-fifth anniversary of the game: 'We were the better team in the first half. During the interval, we all felt there was no way we could lose this game. But then, in the second half, Porto hit us on the break.'

The longer the game lasted, the harder Bayern found it to contain the skilful Paulo Futre, maybe because Matthäus was beginning to lose control of the midfield. Futre was supposed to be Porto's left-winger, but he kept dashing down both flanks, leaving Bayern's lumbering defenders in his wake. Even Madjer was no longer 'blocked'. On seventy-seven minutes, he tied the game with a famous backheel that was in equal parts bold and matter-of-fact. Seven minutes later, despite having just been treated for cramp, Madjer went past Eder on the left wing with ease and sent in a cross that the Brazilian Juary knocked in from close range to win the game 2-1.

For Bayern, it was a traumatic night in every regard. Both Uli Hoeness and Udo Lattek called it the worst defeat of their careers (of course, Hoeness had no way of knowing something much, much

worse would happen twelve years later). But in a way it also helped
the club climb to the next level. After all, if there's one thing Bayern
have always been very good at, it's learning from setbacks. Two days
after the Vienna debacle, Bayern were in another hotel, this time in
Homburg, not far from the French border, to prepare for a Bundesliga
game. After dinner, Scherer held another speech. 'We have to forget the
Porto game and present ourselves as a unit,' he addressed the squad.
Scherer added that while everyone was placing the blame firmly at the
feet of Matthäus, he felt very proud of a side that had won three league
titles in a row before 'falling short for forty-five minutes of football'.

You could say the defeat in Vienna made Bayern an international
club for good. There had always been players from abroad wearing the
famous red shirts, but they were few and far between, not least because,
prior to the Bosman ruling in 1995, the number of foreigners a team
could field was limited. In the twenty-two years between Bayern's
promotion to the Bundesliga and the game in Vienna, only sixteen
foreigners had made league appearances for Bayern.

In fact, barely a year before the Porto final, Fritz Scherer had said
his club would concentrate on keeping German stars in Germany.
This was a reaction to words of warning from Franz Beckenbauer,
who had taken over the national team after the disastrous European
Championships in 1984. So many West German internationals were
being lured to Italy and France, countries where football clubs were
often owned by men with bottomless coffers, that Beckenbauer was
afraid the Bundesliga would bleed dry. 'We need to have attractions
in the league,' Scherer agreed. He promised Bayern would try to keep
German players who were being courted by Serie A teams in the
Bundesliga. Scherer explicitly mentioned Frankfurt's stylish defender
Thomas Berthold and Rudi Völler, though the president admitted
the latter transfer would be difficult to make considering the level of
animosity between Bayern and Bremen.

Yet, in the wake of Vienna, Bayern signed eleven foreigners in
less than four years. And the club wanted even more. English striker

Mark Hateley, for instance, who went to Monaco instead. And especially the man who'd scored the backheel. 'We will sign Madjer,' Uli Hoeness announced, 'no matter how high the sum.' Porto asked for three million marks and although Bayern had never spent so much money on a footballer before, Hoeness agreed. During the annual winter indoor tournament in Munich, Madjer even posed for the press in *Lederhosen*. Then he abruptly changed his mind and signed for Valencia. ('He's the greatest crook of all time,' Hoeness railed.)

But it seems a switch had been flipped in the business manager's mind. Between late 1987 and mid-1991, a dizzying array of players from abroad joined the Reds: Bernardo (Brazil), Harald Cerny (Austria), Johnny Ekström (Sweden), Mark Hughes (Wales), Erland Johnsen (Norway), Brian Laudrup (Denmark), Mazinho (Brazil), Alan McInally (Scotland), Radmilo Mihajlović (Yugoslavia), Allan Nielsen (Denmark), Jan Wouters (Holland). Most of these transfers, it has to be said, turned out to be monumental flops, especially the two Brazilians – which is why Hoeness changed his approach and later preferred to sign Brazilians who had already done well for another German club, such as Jorginho, who joined from Leverkusen in 1992.

And another critical shift took place after Vienna. In the summer of 1987, Bayern changed their coach. Udo Lattek joined Cologne as director of football. On his last day at Bayern, Scherer told him: 'You came as an employee of the club, but you leave as a friend.' That was quite an overstatement. Within a few months, the press gleefully delved into what *Der Spiegel* called 'a psychological war' between Lattek and Hoeness. But that was just the beginning. Soon the underlying tensions between the two clubs would escalate out of control. Maybe Scherer should have saved his line about an employee turning into a friend for Lattek's successor, because this man would indeed one day become a highly respected and much-loved member of the Bayern family: Jupp Heynckes.

Heynckes is such a Bayern icon today that it's almost forgotten how puzzling his appointment was in 1987. For one, he was a dyed-in-the-wool Mönchengladbach man. Heynckes had made more than 300 appearances for Borussia, his hometown club, and then coached the side for eight years. Of course this also meant he was a stout Puma man. It was strange indeed to see him on Bayern's bench, usually wearing Puma shoes together with a custom-made tracksuit top that bore the logo of his new club's shirt sponsors Commodore (the computer manufacturer had replaced Iveco in 1984) next to the brand name of Bayern's supplier's biggest rival.

Years later, Beckenbauer would make such contrary deals his speciality even while serving as the club's president. When Bayern cooperated with German car giants Opel, Beckenbauer endorsed Mitsubishi. While Bayern were sponsored by the Munich-based brewery Paulaner, Beckenbauer signed for competitor Erdinger. In March 2002, Bayern announced their strategic partnership with German Telekom. Six months later, Beckenbauer began to work for O_2 Germany. But, of course, he was the Kaiser, above mere mortals, whereas Heynckes still had to prove himself.

Heynckes was also an unusual choice because he hadn't yet won anything as a coach. The same was true of Pál Csernai in 1978, but in the years since then Bayern had grown massively. Finally, during those early stages of his managerial career, Heynckes was not at all the quiet-but-knowing, benevolent elder statesman he morphed into during his later stints at Bayern. For a long time, his image was that of a man driven by a slightly unhealthy ambition, such a stern disciplinarian that particularly younger players almost feared him, a man who was both quick-tempered and distant. So quick-tempered was he that one of his Gladbach players had dubbed him Osram, after the light bulb. Heynckes's face – reminiscent of Sir Alex Ferguson's at the best of times – would turn a deep red when he became agitated.

Rarely was his head as red as on 20 May 1989 – the infamous night when public-service broadcaster ZDF invited four men onto its Saturday sports magazine show to settle their dispute live on television. The participants in the discussion were Uli Hoeness, Jupp Heynckes,

Udo Lattek and Cologne's 35-year-old coach – a brash, opinionated man with a quick mind and a quicker tongue called Christoph Daum. Years before Alex Ferguson and José Mourinho became noted for playing mind games with opposing coaches, Daum had spent large parts of the season denouncing Heynckes. 'Watching the weather map is more interesting than talking to Heynckes,' he jeered. 'Heynckes could be endorsing sleeping pills,' he sneered. A particularly sly slur was: 'Heynckes has always been unlucky, misfortune follows him. Why should it change now?' Directed at one of the best players of his generation, and coming from someone who had never played the game professionally, this was a bit much. But it surely hit a nerve. Heynckes still hadn't won anything as a coach, having ceded the 1988 league title to Werder Bremen. He was under enormous pressure to succeed in this, his second season at Bayern.

Daum wasn't saying these things on the spur of the moment. He freely talked about how Lattek had taught him that the Bundesliga was a theatre stage and openly admitted a lot of his soundbites were 'kerfuffle', meant to 'wake the league from its stupor'. Like more than just a few observers, Daum thought the Bundesliga teams had been gripped by a mortal fear of the Munich giants and were held back by the deep-seated and irrational belief that Bayern would have *Dusel* whenever they needed it. So Daum began to systematically attack what he had made out to be Bayern's weakest link, Heynckes. And the coach was an easy target indeed. He wasn't a natural in front of cameras and microphones like Daum. In fact, when ZDF asked him to come onto the show, he initially declined. Heynckes only changed his mind when he was told an empty chair would be placed next to Hoeness as a visible reminder he was lacking the courage to face Daum.

One could understand Heynckes's reluctance. When the invitation came, table-topping Bayern had just been defeated by relegation candidates Kickers Stuttgart. Daum's team now trailed Bayern by just one point and the head-to-head game between the two sides on 25 May in Cologne was looming large.

Heynckes could breathe a little bit more freely when the show finally began at ten o'clock in the evening, because a few hours earlier Cologne were held to a draw in Hannover, so Bayern's lead was back to two points. Still, Heynckes was visibly ill at ease as the cameras started to roll. He left most of the talking to Hoeness – and thus began one of German football's great and silly but consequential feuds.

Hoeness accused Daum of having said Heynckes was 'totally on the rocks'. When Daum denied making such a statement, Hoeness produced a letter from the journalist who had printed the line and was willing to vouch for its authenticity with an affidavit.

'I know that the editor in question is friends with Hoeness,' Daum said.

'That's not true,' Hoeness replied, 'that's a lie!'

'That's just one of your ploys to make me lose my way,' Daum said. 'But I can guarantee you: you will fail.'

'I'm not even trying to,' Hoeness retorted, 'because next Thursday your way comes to an end, anyway.'

On and on it went, for almost twenty minutes, with Lattek and Heynckes hardly getting a word in. At one point the studio audience began to sing 'Zieht den Bayern die Lederhosen aus'.

'You're boundlessly overestimating yourself,' Hoeness said and pointed at a number of footballs suspended from the ceiling. 'Look up, that's a ball, not a halo!'

'I need to live to be a hundred years,' Daum shot back, 'to reach your level of overestimation.'

The result of the much-publicised spectacle was that the game five days later, on the day Catholics celebrate the festival known as Corpus Christi, was just as highly anticipated as the Bremen encounter in 1986. Even Richard von Weizsäcker, president of the Federal Republic, attended the game (as did Chris de Burgh). The match lived up to its promise. After twenty-five minutes, a majestic pass from Augenthaler found Stefan Reuter, signed the previous summer from Nuremberg, on the right wing. The youngster cut inside and hit the post with a left-footed shot from the edge of the box. The rebound fell to Roland Wohlfarth, who knocked it in from close range to open the scoring for Bayern.

Seven minutes later, a misunderstanding between Augenthaler and Raimond Aumann, Pfaff's successor between the sticks, gifted the hosts the equaliser. The sweeper expected the goalkeeper to leave his line and collect a long ball, while Aumann thought Augenthaler had things under control. Cologne's striker Thomas Allofs dashed between the two and chipped Aumann from six yards. During the interval, Daum told his players: 'I don't want to finish second. We can beat Bayern today!'

They couldn't. Five minutes from time, Ralf Sturm, who had been brought on for Thomas Allofs, lost possession to Kögl in his own half while his team was moving forward. Kögl looked up, saw an unmarked Wohlfarth in the box and delivered a perfect cross from the left wing. Wohlfarth is widely forgotten today, even though he found the net 119 times in the Bundesliga for the Reds. One of his most important goals came now. From the penalty spot, he headed the ball past Cologne's goalkeeper Bodo Illgner to win the game and the league title for Bayern. As soon as the ball hit the back of the net, Heynckes and Hoeness raced onto the pitch and celebrated with the players. Three minutes later, Bayern made sure after a swift counter-attack. Wohlfarth completed his hat-trick and gave his team a sweet 3-1 win.

After the final whistle, Daum faced the cameras and said: 'I would do it all over again. It was great fun. True, I suffered a setback, but I have always said it's okay to fall down as long as you get back up again.' Meanwhile, Heynckes commented: 'My aim was to win the league with Bayern, not to prove anything to anybody. I think my team played for their coach today.' At the press conference, the two men shook hands.

During the title celebrations, Bayern's fans in the Olympic Stadium's south curve rechristened their coach 'Seppl'. Heynckes's proper first name is Josef. In his native Rhineland, the familiar form is 'Jupp', whereas Bavarians will say 'Sepp' or, even more affectionately, 'Seppl'. The chant signalled that Heynckes had finally arrived in Munich. He became even more popular a year later, when he repeated the league triumph, again ahead of Cologne and Daum. Truth be told, though, the ease with which the Reds ruled the Bundesliga roost to win the 1991 trophy raised questions.

Yes, Bayern had more money in the bank than the competition. The club had sold Matthäus to Inter in 1988 for an impressive 7.5 million marks (£2.4 million). The sum was impressive, because many people felt the player wasn't worth it. Paul Breitner said: 'Matthäus has been stagnating for four years, it's best if everyone goes their separate ways.' The left-leaning political magazine *Der Spiegel*, always happy to take a swipe at Bayern or a Bayern player, called him 'an ageing prodigy who was never willing to take a risk in order to develop' and in so many words accused him of seeking one last, fat pay-cheque. (Ironically, of course, Matthäus did take a risk when he moved to Italy – and at long last did develop into an outstanding player.)

But, as mentioned above, Bayern didn't spend their money very well. The *Frankfurter Allgemeine Zeitung* newspaper began to call Munich 'the strikers' cemetery', because the club of Gerd Müller and Karl-Heinz Rummenigge couldn't find a consistent goalscorer any more. In 1989, Hoeness signed Mihajlović and McInally, from Dinamo Zagreb and Aston Villa, respectively, for a combined 5.1 million marks (£1.5 million). The press dubbed them Mic and Mac, but soon there was another nickname: *Chancentod*, death to scoring opportunities. The chronically underappreciated Wohlfarth had to come to the rescue again and finished as his team's best marksman once more. With just thirteen goals.

Perhaps Franz Beckenbauer's prophecy had come true, perhaps the league was bleeding dry. Cologne's best player was Thomas Hässler, but he was about to move to Italy as well, followed by Bremen striker Karl-Heinz Riedle. Rudi Völler, Jürgen Klinsmann and Thomas Berthold were already playing football in Serie A, despite Scherer's pledge to keep stars of their calibre in Germany.

And so the bitter reality was that Bayern were rich by German standards, but paupers compared to the giants of Italian football. Milan owner Silvio Berlusconi almost broke the world transfer record by spending £6 million on Ruud Gullit in 1987, then broke it when he signed Jean-Pierre Papin for £10 million in 1992. A few months later he paid Torino £13 million for Gianluigi Lentini. A non-commercial, community-based and member-owned club like Bayern simply had no way of competing in this particular arena. 'We signed Mihajlović and McInally because there were no alternatives,' Heynckes admits today. 'In the long run, it wasn't going to work with these two strikers. At the end of the day, they just lacked real top class.'

The situation left Bayern little choice. On the one hand, they couldn't afford foreign stars and they couldn't keep German stars in Germany. On the other, mediocre foreigners didn't live up to expectations. And so the Reds began to look for German players who had done well but weren't yet stars. Between 1986 and 1989, Bayern bought no fewer than four young and promising Nuremberg players: Stefan Reuter, Hans Dorfner, Roland Grahammer and Manfred Schwabl. For the second but certainly not the last time, the club was accused of poaching a domestic rival's best players to nip competition in the bud. (The first time such a charge was levelled at Bayern was in 1980, when the Reds signed Gladbach's Karl Del'Haye for what was at the time a club record sum and then put him on the bench for two seasons because there was no place in Pál Csernai's system for a classic winger like him.)

There was a silver lining, though. Commercial television had been banned in West Germany until the early 1980s, but the media landscape had changed. Now there were a number of stations that followed the example of ITV and, more recently, Rupert Murdoch's Sky Television and bid for the rights to televise German club football. In 1992, an agency controlled by the Bavarian media entrepreneur Leo Kirch acquired the Bundesliga rights for the next five years for 700 million marks (£260 million). One of Kirch's many stations – Sat.1 – now broadcast the league games. To recoup their investment, Sat.1 introduced novelties such as live coverage of a Sunday-night game. There was also the revamped European Cup, now called the Champions League, televised by another private station, RTL Television. The competition's new format assured the participating teams of a much higher guaranteed revenue.

The long and the short of this sea change in Germany was that the best football clubs suddenly made more money. A lot more. For Bayern, it was the long-awaited window of opportunity to close the gap on the Serie A teams. Or rather, it should have been. By a strange twist of fate, the most famous, most profitable and most business-minded of all German clubs went through a serious crisis just when success would have been most richly rewarded.

To be precise: a sporting crisis. Off the pitch, everything was dandy. At the 1989 annual general meeting, Scherer was re-elected, not least because he presented some impressive figures: Bayern now had 14,688 members. The turnover was 34.4 million marks, the club had made a profit of 1.2 million marks and there were more than 5 million marks in the bank. But money isn't everything. After winning the league a few months later, the team began to struggle on the pitch.

Astoundingly, Bayern lost the 1991 Bundesliga title to an old foe who hadn't finished in the top five since 1982: Kaiserslautern. When a late Stefan Kuntz goal gave Kaiserslautern a 2-1 win in the head-to-head game in late March and knocked the Reds off the top spot, stadium announcer Udo Scholz screamed himself hoarse and the fans sang 'Zieht den Bayern die Lederhosen aus'.

A month later, another mishap befell Bayern in the European Cup. In the final stages of the semi-final second-leg, away at Red Star in Belgrade, Bayern held a 2-1 lead that would have sent the game to extra time. In the eighty-second minute, Wohlfarth put the ball past the goalkeeper but watched it bounce against the left-hand post. With eighty seconds left on the clock, Red Star's Dejan Savićević whipped in a cross from the left. Augenthaler attempted a clearance but mishit the ball, sending it in a looping arc towards his own goal. Aumann, who probably should have prevented Red Star's goal in the first half, jumped in the air to tip the ball over the bar but somehow knocked it across the goal-line. *Bayern-Dusel*, anyone?

Schulze-Marmeling suggests the team underperformed during this period mainly because it was no longer 'a collective', no longer the unit Fritz Scherer had invoked on that night in Vienna. 'With the arrival of Effenberg and Laudrup, a cliquishness began,' writes the club historian. Stefan Effenberg, who had joined Bayern from Gladbach, and former Uerdingen player Brian Laudrup were very good friends. ('If he was a woman, I'd marry him,' Effenberg once quipped.) They were also young, flippant and lavishly endowed in the ego department.

Maybe Schulze-Marmeling is right and divisiveness spread through the squad like a disease. Or maybe it hit the team very hard that club institution Klaus Augenthaler finished his professional career in the summer of 1991, after 404 league appearances for Bayern. In any case, the following season was a nightmare. The Reds, whisper it, flirted with relegation (in December, they were just two points above the drop zone) and eventually finished the 1991–92 season in a preposterous tenth place. The league title went to VfB Stuttgart, coached by Christoph Daum.

However, in the funny way in which football history sometimes works, it would turn out to be much more important – for German football and for Bayern Munich – who finished second: Ottmar Hitzfeld's Borussia Dortmund. The reason why finishing as runners-up turned out to be a blessing in disguise for the club was that a new (and short-lived) system was in place during the 1992–93 season. While RTL Television had the Champions League, the ties in the other European cup competitions went to the highest bidder. But the Bundesliga clubs dropped like flies. By March, they had all been eliminated – except Dortmund. Borussia went all the way to the final and pocketed an amazing 25 million marks (then £10 million) from this one UEFA Cup run.

Of course Bayern were acutely aware how important it was to not get left behind in German football's first proper race for the television jackpot. Before the 1991–92 season began, president Scherer had said: 'Reaching a UEFA Cup slot is absolutely imperative, from a footballing perspective but also economically.' Maybe this explains why the club panicked when the Reds suddenly found themselves in the lower third of the table. In October, when Bayern suffered a humiliating home defeat against Kickers Stuttgart, some parts of the crowd chanted 'Heynckes out!' Bayern's most faithful fans, the supporters in the south curve, felt differently. They knew that Hoeness and Heynckes had become good friends and they had come to like the strait-laced but honest Jupp/Seppl.

But the pressure was becoming too much. On the Monday after the game, 7 October, Heynckes discussed the situation with the board members and admitted that terminating their relationship might be the best solution. Later that day, Scherer met Franz Beckenbauer in Munich's Sheraton Hotel and offered him the coaching job. The Kaiser declined, saying prior commitments made it impossible for him to be immediately available. And so Bayern contacted another former player. On Tuesday, the club announced that Heynckes was no longer Bayern's coach and would be succeeded by Søren Lerby.

More than ten years later, Uli Hoeness looked back on those weeks and months during a conversation with a Sunday newspaper. 'Parting ways with Heynckes in 1991,' he said, 'was the biggest mistake I ever made in my business life.'

11. THE DREAM TEAM

Quite a few nicknames for Bayern Munich have already been mentioned in this book. I even skipped one, as it's nearly forgotten these days, despite the fact it used to grace some of the club's early merchandise: *die Bullen*, the bulls. Sadly, that was not a reference to Franz Roth. Instead, the heavy Magirus Deutz trucks were known as 'the German bulls' and one of the company's slogans was: 'The Bulls Are Coming!' Since the so-called vintage look is en vogue now, and not only among football hipsters, Bayern offered a retro range two years ago, which prominently displayed the old moniker on hooded sweaters or track tops. (The club's website informed foreign fans and Germans too young to remember the name: '*Die Bullen* – the iconic synonym for the team of FC Bayern in the late 70s.')

During the 1990s, Bayern were slapped with two more nicknames, though chances are the reader is familiar only with the second of these – FC Hollywood. As the *Guardian* once said, the name 'was not intended in a good way, even if it came to chime with the glitz and glamour of Bayern Munich, the irresistible draw of Germany's No. 1 sporting institution'. Indeed, the FC Hollywood tag was meant to taunt and lampoon Bayern and nobody at the club liked it. In July 1996, Uli Hoeness told *Sport-Bild* magazine: 'Let's quickly forget this name. FC

stands for football club. That's what we want to be again. That's why
we'll batten down the hatches.'

To understand why Hoeness felt Bayern were no longer a football
club around this time (and what hatches had to do with all this), we
have to look at the other nickname, which came from the earlier
portion of the 1990s – the Dream Team.

Needless to say, the term was on everyone's lips during the early
years of that decade because of the 1992 United States men's Olympic
basketball team. It became known as the Dream Team due to the fact
that it was the first to feature bona-fide NBA stars, after the amateur-
only rule had been scrapped. The sobriquet soon spread into other
sports. Barely a month after the 1992 Games had ended, Juventus
owner Giovanni Agnelli labelled the Milan side assembled by his rival
Silvio Berlusconi as 'a dream team'.

In April 1994, *Kicker* first mentioned that the Munich giants were
trying to build what the magazine called the 'FC Bayern Dream Team
2000'. At the time, the Reds had just spent 10 million marks (then
the equivalent of £4 million) on French striker Jean-Pierre Papin
and a 24-year-old goalkeeper called Oliver Kahn, while also putting
out feelers for Bulgaria's Footballer of the Year Emil Kostadinov and
Juventus midfielder Andreas Möller. (The first of these transfers would
become reality some eight months later, the second never did.) But
the catchphrase didn't really become popular until a year later, when
the arrival of the man who was supposed to be the best coach in the
country, and the influx of a large number of star players, made people
refer to Bayern's 1995–96 side as the Dream Team. Or at least they did
until the team collapsed. Then came the inevitable 'nightmare' puns.

However, the true roots of all this – the Dream Team tag and the
FC Hollywood slur, the 'glitz and glamour', the 'irresistible draw' and
the nightmares – predate the signing of Papin and even the 1992
Olympics. Funnily, or maybe logically, it began with the sacking of
Bayern's most down-to-earth, unpretentious, dutiful and just plain
simple coach since the club had dissolved its contract with a decent

but lacklustre man called Helmut Schneider to sign the voluble Čik Čajkovski in 1963. It all started with the sacking of Heynckes.

Even before Heynckes's successor Lerby turned out to be the wrong choice (he managed to lose a UEFA Cup game away at Boldklubben 1903 in Copenhagen by the deeply embarrassing score of 6-2 and didn't coach beyond March), Fritz Scherer and Uli Hoeness were coming under heavy criticism for the harrowing experience that was the 1991–92 season. In October, shortly after Heynckes had been sent packing, even the club's *éminence grise* suddenly let his voice be heard – Robert Schwan.

Bayern's original business manager and Franz Beckenbauer's agent was just a few weeks away from his seventieth birthday, but as busy as ever. (Among other things, he handled money matters for Markus Wasmeier, then one of the continent's best alpine ski racers.) Schwan's tongue hadn't slowed down, either. In an interview with *Kicker*, Schwan tore into Scherer for having offered the coaching job to Beckenbauer, arguing it was just a PR measure orchestrated by a president desperate 'to save his own position'. Schwan added Beckenbauer would be willing to help his club – but in another role: 'He is ideally suited for the post of president.' Having thus proclaimed a coup to bring down Scherer, Schwan suggested another rolling head for good measure: 'I can imagine some alternatives to Mister Hoeness as well, for instance a man like Karl-Heinz Rummenigge.'

Today we know that Hoeness weathered this crisis and would look after the club's business affairs for another eighteen years, but it was by no means a foregone conclusion. After all, an alarming proportion of his recent transfers had been duds. 'But people shouldn't forget what he has done for the club during the last twelve years,' his brother Dieter said, now working for VfB Stuttgart. 'He is still the best business manager in the league.'

Maybe Scherer and Uli Hoeness agreed with Schwan that something had to change and that icons like Beckenbauer and Rummenigge could indeed bring some expertise to the table. Or maybe they paraphrased an old adage and decided that if you can't beat them, make them join you. In any case, Beckenbauer and Rummenigge were invited on board. However, they could only wield some influence if they sat on the club's executive committee. That was made up of the president (Scherer), the vice-president (Hans Schiefele, the former player and journalist), the treasurer (Kurt Hegerich, a local businessman), the secretary (Karl Hopfner) and the business manager (Uli Hoeness). Put differently, there were no vacant posts for the two club legends. So Bayern simply added new ones. In late November, Beckenbauer and Rummenigge were named vice-presidents, too.

These developments not only made Bayern arguably the most star-studded club off the pitch. (Was anyone else run by two former European Footballers of the Year and a World Cup winner?) It also irrevocably altered the balance of power. Scherer had always gone along with anything Hoeness cooked up, but Beckenbauer and Rummenigge nurtured ideas of their own. Even before he had been formally appointed, Rummenigge said: 'In the old days, we may have had debts, but we were successful and popular.' Beckenbauer sang the same tune: 'All the millions in the bank are of no use if you don't have any points.' The writing was on the wall. Perhaps against his own deepest instincts, Hoeness would soon be asked to take risks and spend more generously.

Finally, bringing Beckenbauer and Rummenigge back into the fold unavoidably turned Bayern into a club with three times as many alpha males as before, not to mention three times as many celebrity officials the press could approach in search of headline-generating quotes. Borussia Dortmund's business manager Michael Meier predicted that 'now the whole club will be shaking whenever Franz coughs'. It was an exaggeration, though a moderate one.

When Günter Netzer heard about the return of Beckenbauer and Rummenigge, he couldn't resist a little banter and quipped their club needed them 'on the pitch rather than in the boardroom'. There was some truth to that. Even the new triumvirate at Bayern's helm couldn't stop the slide. Lerby finally had to go and the club, perhaps imbued with a strong spirit of innovation in the wake of all that upheaval upstairs, found his successor in a novel place – at their sponsors, Opel.

Erich Ribbeck had started his managerial career as an assistant to Hennes Weisweiler with Mönchengladbach in the 1960s. His biggest success was winning the 1988 UEFA Cup at Bayer Leverkusen. Now he was working for Opel's sports sponsorship department. In this capacity, Ribbeck was attending a table tennis match in Hannover between Germany and Sweden on 10 March 1992, when suddenly he heard his name over the PA. The announcer said there was an urgent telephone call for Mister Ribbeck. When he rose to make his way through the row of seats, somebody joked: 'That's Uli Hoeness. They want you to save Bayern from relegation.' The man was almost right. When Ribbeck picked up the phone, he heard the voice of his friend Franz Beckenbauer, who told him that Søren Lerby had been sacked and that Bayern needed help. A few hours later, Ribbeck was sitting on a plane to Munich.

Ribbeck, nicknamed 'Sir Erich' by the tabloids because of his impeccable manners, won his first game in charge, at home against Hamburg. The visitors had a legitimate goal chalked off, then Bayern went ahead two minutes from time. When he was asked if the proverbial *Bayern-Dusel* was back, he said: 'Of course our win was lucky. But luck is part of the game.'

However, neither luck nor Ribbeck could really repair the season, which Bayern finished in mid-table obscurity. In the off-season, the summer of 1992, the club finally went back to making good deals on the transfer market. Apart from signing soon-to-be key players like Mehmet Scholl, Thomas Helmer and Jorginho, the club also pulled off a major coup by bringing back Lothar Matthäus.

Truth be told, though, it looked more like a gamble than a coup at the time. Under Inter coach Giovanni Trapattoni, Matthäus had blossomed into such an outstanding performer that he'd just been voted FIFA World Player of the Year. But in April, against Parma, he had torn his cruciate ligament. This is still considered a very serious injury; back in the early 1990s, it often meant the end of a career, especially for a player who was thirty-one years old. In fact, shortly before Matthäus sustained the injury, Trapattoni's successor Luis Suárez advised Inter to get rid of him and Brehme because they were too old. Matthäus proved Suárez – and every other critic – wrong when he came back only five months after the injury. Nine weeks later, he scored against Leverkusen with a stunning volley that was voted Goal of the Year in Germany.

But even this much-improved team couldn't bring the league title back to Munich. The Reds held down first place uninterrupted for the first thirty-two matchdays, yet they finished second behind Bremen. 'We have now outstripped Bayern in footballing terms,' Werder's business manager Willi Lemke gloated, 'while Dortmund have done so financially.' Of course that was just the usual ballyhoo between Bayern and Bremen, still the best of enemies, but it was not entirely without foundation. Bayern had now failed to win the league for the third year in a row, while Dortmund were indeed showing signs of becoming upwardly mobile, having brought back Stefan Reuter and Matthias Sammer from Italy.

This was particularly galling because Bayern had just published a musical statement that by and large declared second place to be unacceptable. It was the brainchild of Uli Hoeness. He approached a Bronx-born pop singer by the name of Andrew White with the idea of releasing an official club anthem. Six years earlier, White had relocated to Europe to get his career off the ground and found a job entertaining guests at the Madrigal Piano Bar in Munich. That's how he came to the attention of FC Bayern, who hired the singer to perform during their 1986 title celebrations.

White hooked up with a producer and composer from Munich called Harald Reitinger and the two composed a Bayern song. On his website, White says: 'In 1990 I wrote the very famous FC Bayern soccer team an anthem called "Forever Number One". I produced the song and sang together with the entire team. The song sold a half million copies within two weeks and entered the top 100 hit chart at number 22 and rose to the top 10 two weeks later.'

Not quite. White and Reitinger wrote the song in 1992 and it came out the following year. It sold 150,000 copies and peaked in the charts at number 16 in June 1993. However, even with these amendments the song is still the most successful German club anthem. The chorus, sung in English, is a rallying cry that Bayern will remain just that: forever number one.

Maybe that's why Bayern decided to take corrective action when the team went four games without a win in November and December 1993, and dropped into second place. Going into the winter break, the Reds were still in contention, just one point off the pace, but there was a feeling that Ribbeck had lost the dressing room. The Dutch defensive midfielder Jan Wouters openly accused him of using outdated methods and when Ribbeck, perhaps in an attempt to refute such accusations, tried to teach his team a flat back-four, his players struggled to adapt. (Most Bundesliga clubs used the tried and tested, typically Teutonic sweeper system until well into the next millennium.) Wouters then underlined how troublesome the job of Bayern coach had become since Beckenbauer and Rummenigge joined Hoeness at the management level when he told Ribbeck: 'You're the only one at this club who doesn't know football.'

Three days before 1993 was over, Bayern relieved Sir Erich of his duties. The new man at the sidelines, signed to run the team on an interim basis until the end of the season, was Bayern's first Munich-born gaffer – in fact, the first Bavarian to hold the post – since a man called Georg Bayerer coached the side in 1953–54. None other than Giesing's own Franz Beckenbauer himself took over. And the Kaiser delivered, winning the 1994 league title. However, in the process of doing so, he had what some people regard as the most outrageous case of *Dusel* ever recorded.

On 23 April, with three games left in the season and Bayern two points ahead of Kaiserslautern, the Reds met old rivals Nuremberg, mired in the relegation fight, at the Olympic Stadium. After twenty-six minutes, Bayern won a corner on the right side, taken by Marcel Witeczek. His cross was flicked on by Oliver Kreuzer, one of three former Karlsruher SC players now wearing red. The ball sailed towards the far post, where Helmer somehow bundled it into touch from two yards out. While Nuremberg's keeper Andreas Köpke patted Helmer on the back to console him for missing such a sitter, referee Hans-Joachim Osmers indicated a goal kick.

But there was still Jörg Jablonski, a career soldier working for the German army. For some reason, Jablonski thought Helmer had knocked the ball into the net instead of putting it wide of the post. He wasn't the only person at the ground to make this mistake. Some fans whose view was obstructed by the posts briefly celebrated until they saw the ball rolling into touch and hitting an advertising board. But Jablonski was one of only two people at the ground carrying a linesman's flag. He waved it to signal for a goal. While referee Osmers had seen Helmer miss the target, he trusted his assistant, supposing the ball must have crossed the line before Helmer made contact. Despite fierce Nuremberg protests, Osmers allowed a goal that had never happened to stand.

When the referee and his linesmen walked into the dressing room at half-time, Osmers said: 'Are you sure this was a goal?' Jablonski replied: 'Don't worry, the ball definitely crossed the line.' But as they came out for the second half, they walked past a monitor that was showing a replay of the scene. Osmers's heart sank. He knew he and his linesman had made a horrible mistake, maybe the most blatant in league history. He also knew the second half would be the most difficult of his career. There was a part of him that wanted Nuremberg to come back and reduce the importance of his blunder, but of course he couldn't let this colour his judgement. He just had to get on with business.

On sixty-five minutes, Helmer scored again, this time a legitimate goal. With eleven minutes left on the clock, the Swiss striker Alain Sutter pulled one back for Nuremberg. And, barely sixty seconds later, Helmer tried to dispossess Christian Wück in Bayern's penalty area. This was unwise, because the Nuremberg player had a reputation for going down easily. Helmer missed the ball, Wück made the most of it, Osmers gladly blew his whistle. Manfred Schwabl, who had joined Bayern at the Under-12 level but was now playing for Nuremberg, stepped up. He had never taken a penalty before as a professional. While Osmers reflected on how Helmer's foul had been a godsend, secretly keeping his fingers crossed for Schwabl to score, the player took his run-up. He put the ball to his left. But Raimond Aumann guessed right and parried the shot.

Almost immediately after the final whistle, people began to call for a replay of the game. They pointed towards a precedent. In 1978, a game in the second division had been restaged after video evidence showed that the referee had made a glaring mistake. However, the DFB was reluctant to go to such lengths again. After all, UEFA and FIFA were vehemently opposed to overruling a referee through technology. Whereupon Kaiserslautern's chain-smoking president Norbert Thines reiterated the often-heard claim that the governing body was protecting the Munich giants: 'There is a Bayern bonus, which is deplorable,' he said. 'When you have such an unequivocal case, the DFB should spontaneously spring into action.'

As the weekly magazine *Focus* said, Germany debated the issue 'as fiercely as if this was about the nation's destiny'. Public-service television changed its schedule and covered the incident with the sort of special broadcast normally reserved for political upheavals. It argued that Bayern had been gifted a crucial win in the title race. This sentiment was echoed by Freiburg's coach Volker Finke, who called Beckenbauer 'the Dusel-Kaiser'. This interpretation was not entirely conclusive. Bayern had been gifted a goal, yes, but the result hinged as much on Schwabl's penalty as on Jablonski's mirage. *Focus* said the uproar had to do with 'the Bayern factor', meaning the fact that 'the club from Munich has been dividing opinion for years'. Indeed, one wonders if the furore would have been the same if Nuremberg had benefited from a refereeing hallucination.

Whatever the reason for the public outrage, the pressure on the DFB was mounting dramatically. At the same time, UEFA – who were holding a congress in Vienna just as the debate reached boiling point – threatened the German governing body with severe penalties, including a ban from the 1994 World Cup, if Bayern's 2-1 win was annulled on account of video evidence. Still, on 26 April, the DFB did just that and ordered a replay for 3 May.

This second match was scoreless for forty-seven minutes, but then the levee broke and the Reds won 5-0. Four days later, they were crowned champions, one point and three goals ahead of Kaiserslautern. Nuremberg, meanwhile, went down on goal difference. Schwabl's penalty miss had turned out to be very costly indeed.

Six minutes before midnight on this last Saturday of the season, the guests who attended Bayern's victory party rose from their seats and honoured Franz Beckenbauer with a standing ovation, as these were his last few moments as the club's coach. 'Be careful,' the Kaiser said in jest. 'Maybe I'll be back.' Six months later, the club's members elected him their new president.

Finding a coach who could survive more than two years in this post would continue to be a severe problem for Bayern throughout the decade. Uli Hoeness was keen on a young, smart Frenchman by the name of Arsène Wenger. However, when Bayern's business manager enquired about his availability during the first week of April 1994, Wenger's club, AS Monaco, told him the coach would not be released from his contract. If Hoeness had been able to wait only five more months, he would have landed his man – and European football history would've probably taken a different course – because Monaco sacked Wenger in mid-September. But of course Hoeness couldn't wait, he needed someone to follow Beckenbauer, who had made it abundantly clear he had no intention of staying on as coach after the end of the season.

While Hoeness was headhunting, Lothar Mätthaus wondered whether to extend his contract. Giovanni Trapattoni, the man who had nurtured him at Inter, had made it very plain that he would like to work together with Matthäus again. Trapattoni was leaving Juventus after three years and toying with a move to Roma. But it came to nought, which is why Matthäus eventually signed a new contract with Bayern in the second week of April. 'I was constantly in touch with my former coach, Trapattoni,' he told the tabloid *Bild*. 'He desperately wanted to sign me. But when his move to Roma foundered, he advised me to extend my contract in Munich.'

You didn't need to be a genius to put two and two together. A famous, out-of-contract Italian coach, his favourite player Matthäus, and a club in search of impetus from abroad – they appeared to be made for each other. In the third week of April, Bayern's executive committee travelled to Italy and reached a general agreement with 'Trap'.

It looked like a match made in heaven. The 55-year-old Trapattoni was one of the most highly decorated coaches in the world. At a time when it was becoming painfully obvious that German football – still relying on two man-marking centre-backs and a sweeper at the back – was outdated, he had a reputation as a gifted teacher of tactics. The *Welt am Sonntag* newspaper even reported that Trapattoni was known in Italy as *il tedesco*, the German, 'because of his discipline and work ethos'. (Later articles traced the alleged nickname back to his playing days, when his hair was blond. Still, I have yet to meet an Italian who knows Trapattoni as *il tedesco*.)

But there were also some worrying signs. Trapattoni's wife, Paola, wasn't too keen on moving to Munich, not least because their seventeen-year-old son Alberto was in his final year at school. This is why Trapattoni eventually signed for only one year, just to see what would happen. Then there was the language problem. In mid-May, Trapattoni talked to a reporter from the sports television channel DSF and admitted he would be in need of an interpreter because his German was limited to the numbers from one to eleven. When he added he would be able to communicate with his assistant coach in English, alarm bells should have gone off. This assistant was Klaus Augenthaler – whose Bavarian accent was so strong many people couldn't understand him even when he spoke German. So it didn't come as a surprise that as early as August the papers quoted Bayern players who complained: 'When things become hectic, we don't understand a word he's saying.'

There were other cultural differences, too. In April, Bayern won an away game at Frankfurt in great style, 5-2. But Trapattoni had ruined it all after seventy-one minutes by bringing on a young Dietmar Hamann. At the time, Hamann hadn't yet signed a professional contract, he was what the rules defined as an 'amateur player'. A professional team could field three such players. Hamann was the fourth. 'I'm the only one who is to blame,' Trapattoni said after learning Bayern had forfeited the game. 'I should have known the German rules.' He dryly added: 'In Italy, they would have given me a bonus for winning an away game with four amateurs.'

Bayern finished the season in sixth place and Trapattoni didn't extend his contract. He confessed to the *Süddeutsche Zeitung*: 'My biggest problem was the language. I told the club: If I can't be 100 per cent Trapattoni, we should stop it here.' However, his first year at the club was not the fiasco some people made it out to be. The Italian did revolutionise the club's training methods, and not just on the pitch. He decided to close many sessions to the public. While that was something he was used to from Italy (and something Klinsmann and, more recently, Guardiola would reintroduce), it was highly unusual in Germany. Although 'Trap' failed to win silverware in 1994–95, almost everyone at Bayern still thought the world of him.

As the Trapattoni episode proved, it's rare for a football club to get the coaching decision absolutely right. However, it's equally rare to get it as monumentally wrong as Bayern did now. The club briefly considered replacing Trapattoni with Ajax gaffer Louis van Gaal. But then the triumvirate that ran Bayern hit upon a spectacular idea. In early February 1995, shortly after 'Trap' had informed the club he would leave in the summer, Rummenigge, Beckenbauer and Scherer (now a vice-president) travelled to a town near Munich called Ottobrunn, right next to Neubiberg, where Beckenbauer had once been slapped in the face by an 1860 player. Their destination was the house of Uli Hoeness, because that's where they were going in the dark of the night to secretly meet two surprise guests from up north: Bremen's coach Otto Rehhagel and his wife Beate.

When rumours of this unlikely coalition got out, people in Munich were puzzled. True, Rehhagel had been hugely successful in Bremen – winning two league titles, two domestic cups and the Cup Winners' Cup. But Bremen was not Munich. At Werder, Rehhagel had been an obstinate autocrat and it was always his way or the highway. At Bayern, he would have to answer to men who were at least as opinionated, knowledgeable and self-assured as he was. (Months later, Franz Beckenbauer would stand in a VIP lounge and say, loud enough for bystanders to hear: 'Do you know what the lunatic planned to do? He wanted to put Scholl in the stands! I prevented that.')

Then there was the media problem. In cosy Bremen, it sometimes felt as if Rehhagel only had to wiggle a finger for willing press people to sweep any undesired story under the carpet. Now, two days after the clandestine meeting in Ottobrunn, the Munich tabloids not only broke news of Rehhagel's late-night trip, they even knew every detail of the negotiations. When Werder travelled to Lohne, a town fifty miles south of Bremen, for a small tournament to prepare for the second half of the season, the crowd was in uproar. Cries of 'Judas!' rang out as Rehhagel came out of the dressing room. Some people called him a 'Bayern pig', others a 'turncoat'. The man had been solely responsible for the greatest era in Werder's history, yet this was all forgotten now. That he had signed for Bremen's fiercest rivals after fourteen years at Werder seemed incomprehensible.

The doubts and the antagonism gave Rehhagel even more reason to go out in great style. And in early May, with five games left, Werder did indeed climb into first place, one point ahead of Dortmund. From that moment on, the season headed towards its culmination, the final matchday, with the stark inevitability you only encounter in football and Greek mythology. Because what was Rehhagel's final game after almost one and a half decades in Bremen? Away at Bayern, of course.

Before the game, Helmer gave a revealing interview and predicted that Dortmund would win the Bundesliga, saying: 'We want to give our outgoing coach Giovanni Trapattoni a fine game as a parting gift. Also, Bremen have annoyed us in the past quite often.' After just fourteen minutes, a perfect Scholl free kick found Christian Ziege, who opened the scoring with a powerful header. There was nothing at stake for the Reds, but they played as if their lives depended on winning this match. With no regard for his own health, Oliver Kahn made a brilliant save from a free kick taken by Werder's wayward genius Mario Basler, colliding full force with the goalpost after having kept the ball out. Werder lost the game 3-1 and the league title with it.

Despite all those ominous portents, Rehhagel's short reign began with a lot of euphoria. More than 7,000 fans came out to watch his first working day at Säbener Strasse. Thirteen television crews and more than a hundred journalists covered the training session. Rehhagel brandished a megaphone to be heard above the tumult. Then he addressed the crowd and told them he couldn't make any promises but would be giving his all for the club every single day. Later he told reporters that all that hysteria was 'crazy', adding: 'I'm not Elvis Presley.' However, if he thought he was the main attraction, that all these people had come out to this Bavarian Graceland to see him, the famous coach, he was totally mistaken. (Bayern fan and journalist Thomas Hüetlin says Rehhagel was doomed to fail because he was 'caught up in his self-importance'.) It wasn't the coach who was the main reason for the fans' optimism and their interest. It was the team. The Dream Team.

During the summer, Bayern had spent 20 million marks on new players. (In the four years since Beckenbauer and Rummenigge had returned to the fold, the once fairly frugal club had laid out a total of 66 million marks, then the equivalent of £26.5 million.) The new arrivals were: MSV Duisburg's defensive midfielder Thomas Strunz, Kaiserslautern's Swiss playmaker Ciriaco Sforza, Bremen's Austrian playmaker Andreas Herzog – and a Tottenham Hotspur striker by the name of Jürgen Klinsmann.

These high-profile signings joined all the other well-known players who had arrived over the previous years, among them foreign stars such as Alain Sutter (Switzerland), Jean-Pierre Papin (France) and the Bulgarian Kostadinov. National coach Berti Vogts congratulated Rehhagel on what he called 'almost a Europe select XI', and *Kicker* magazine said: 'If Bayern aren't the deciding authority in the title race with this super squad, then they never will be.'

Alas, it all ended in tears. Almost exactly three months after Rehhagel's first training session, a newspaper from Hamburg headlined: 'The dream team is a nightmare.' And during the first months of 1996, Bayern were first dubbed 'a soap opera', then 'middlebrow comedy' and finally 'FC Hollywood'. Amidst the most mind-blowing media brouhaha German football had seen until that time, Rehhagel lost control (and Klinsmann's backing) and was sacked with four games left in the league season while Ottmar Hitzfeld's Borussia Dortmund won the Bundesliga again, and rather comfortably so.

How could the Dream Team implode so thoroughly? In a way, the time bomb had been activated as early as 25 January 1995. During a friendly match against third-division Bielefeld, Matthäus tore his Achilles tendon. It was his second very serious injury, following the cruciate ligament rupture. He was almost thirty-four years old. Again, many people presumed he would not come back. 'I'm not going to give up,' Matthäus said. And he didn't.

In the meantime, Helmer took over both the skipper's armband and the sweeper position from Matthäus at club level, while Dortmund's Matthias Sammer replaced him as the national team's *libero* to great effect, and Klinsmann was made the new Germany captain. For a while, it looked as if Matthäus might return as early as June, in that last game of the season, which pitted the outgoing Trapattoni's Bayern against the outgoing Rehhagel's Bremen. When Helmer was asked about this prospect in the same *Kicker* interview in which he predicted that Dortmund would win the league, the normally highly eloquent player suddenly became very tight-lipped.

Kicker: 'If Matthäus comes on during the game, who will play sweeper?'
Helmer: 'Maybe he starts the game.'
Kicker: 'Who will be the sweeper then?'
Helmer: 'Who used to be the sweeper of late?'
Kicker: 'So everything stays the same?'
Helmer: 'Guess so.'
Kicker: 'Will this be your last game as the captain?'
Helmer: 'If Lothar starts, the previous one was the last one.'

But Lothar didn't start and he wasn't brought on. In July, shortly after Rehhagel had arrived at the club, Matthäus suffered a setback and had to undergo a second operation. Now the end of his long career seemed a distinct possibility, but his incredible willpower prevailed again. In November, club doctor Hans-Wilhelm Müller-Wohlfahrt gave him the green light to take up training again.

At the time, Matthäus was quoted as saying that a comeback in 1995 was 'illusory' and that he was aiming for the end of the winter break in February 1996. However, he must have secretly hoped otherwise. In his autobiography, Matthäus says Vogts rang him up in December, shortly before a friendly between Germany and South Africa in Johannesburg, to inform him he wouldn't be called up. According to Matthäus, Vogts made it sound as if his position in the national team was safe and that the national coach just wanted to try out a few other players.

'Then, late at night,' says Matthäus, 'the phone rang. It wasn't a player but a good confidant from the national team set-up. He said: "Lothar, take care! They are undermining your position here."

'He said Jürgen Klinsmann and Thomas Helmer were the ringleaders of the revolt. Soon it was plain for every fan to see that the news from South Africa had been accurate. I wasn't called up for internationals any more.'

That Matthäus went on an unparalleled media rampage in the wake of this snub – whether it was perceived or real – is usually explained by his enormous ego and an uncontrollable urge to be at the centre of things, to talk into microphones and look into cameras. This is undeniably true. To this day, Matthäus is unhappy about the fact his coaching career never truly got off the ground, although few people on this planet have a deeper understanding of the game than he does. (There is no irony whatsoever in this sentence. I briefly penned columns for Matthäus and, whenever we talked, it never failed to amaze me how he seemed to be familiar with every player, coach, tactic or formation – past, present and, I suspect, future.) However, this is also the man who coached a team of nerds called *Borussia Banana* for a reality television show and invited cameras into his house for a multi-part personality documentary about his domestic life. You can understand why clubs are hesitant to sign someone who seeks publicity so compulsively.

Yet, as Matthäus himself pointed out at the time, there were also very tangible reasons why he resented being ousted by Helmer and Klinsmann. He said: 'I was the captain, the main contact person for the national coach and a crucial link to the DFB. While I was injured, Klinsmann took over all these roles. It's not just sporting considerations that make these positions so interesting. Happy-go-lucky Klinsmann is now the most powerful man in the DFB since the days of

Franz Beckenbauer.' In other words, he saw his influence erode – and with it perhaps a few lucrative deals.

Finally, maybe a simple yet forceful feeling such as jealousy played a role, too. Matthäus and Klinsmann had been members of the same Inter side and they had won the World Cup together. Of course they weren't friends during those years, they were way too different for that. But they got along reasonably well, as teammates tend to do. However, during the 1995–96 season, Matthäus might have felt marginalised – partly because of his lay-off – and also overshadowed. He was a protégé of Beckenbauer's, who had often called him the 'leader of the pack'. But now Helmer and Klinsmann, both bright and ambitious, seemed to be in charge. It was an open secret that one reason for Rehhagel's dismissal was Klinsmann's threat to leave the club in the summer if the coach stayed on.

Bayern needed Klinsmann more than they needed Rehhagel, partly because the player was a gold mine. These days, Klinsmann has such a bad reputation at Bayern – among officials and fans alike – that it needs pointing out how immensely popular he was during his first season. *Focus* magazine called him 'the darling of the masses' and marvelled how the Olympic Stadium would chant his name even when he missed a great chance against Bordeaux in the UEFA Cup. As had been the case at Spurs, his shirt with the number 18 flew off the shelves, earning the club almost ten million marks during the first part of the season alone.

In February 1996, Matthäus fired the opening round in the spat when he accused Klinsmann of putting his own interests first. The striker had publicly demanded Rehhagel should play two men up front, not just him. Matthäus said: 'He didn't ask for a striking partner when he scored four goals against Benfica.' Matthäus added: 'I don't have a problem with Klinsmann. I don't know if he has a problem with me.' Soon, accusations and complaints were flying back and forth. The club was unable to stop the bickering in public, not least because both Beckenbauer and Rummenigge were well-paid tabloid columnists themselves.

In March, Klinsmann said: 'Since the season began, we only play to 50 or 60 per cent of our potential. Football has become an afterthought here and half of the country is laughing itself silly at us.' Whereupon Matthäus challenged Klinsmann to a live debate on television to settle their dispute. Sarcastically, Klinsmann suggested they could do this 'in the balcony box of the *Muppet Show*'. The *Hamburger Abendblatt* said: 'It's a good thing that we have Bayern Munich. No other club fills the days between games in such an entertaining manner.'

In April, Klinsmann complained again about the constant ruckus. 'Sometimes it seems as if everything is important,' he said, 'except for the ninety minutes of football.' Strunz agreed, saying: 'There are so many sideshows here, we can't concentrate on the game any more.' This prompted a reaction from Beckenbauer, who claimed: 'At this club, we need turmoil. If you can't cope with that, you're free to leave.' And Matthäus riled: 'The conditions here are perfect. But Jürgen is only happy if he scores goals.' In June, he used the term *Hinterfotzigkeit*, two-facedness, to describe how Klinsmann had pushed him out of the national team.

It's hardly surprising that a team torn into (at least) two camps failed to win the league. What is surprising, though, is that it managed to win the UEFA Cup. Klinsmann certainly played a major role in this triumph. When the 1995–96 season began, the scoring record in a European cup competition stood at fourteen goals, set by Milan's José Altafini (also known as Mazzola) during the 1962–63 European Cup and tied by Ipswich Town's John Wark in the 1980–81 UEFA Cup. Klinsmann equalled this record as early as March, in the quarter-finals, when he scored from a Ziege pass at the City Ground in Nottingham to extend Bayern's lead to 5-0 (and 7-1 on aggregate).

However, when he failed to find the target in the next game, he seemed to be running out of time to better the record. That's because this next game was the semi-final first leg against Johan Cruyff's Barcelona. At the Olympic Stadium, the hosts – playing in Barça-styled shirts with vertical blue-and-red stripes, while the Catalans wore green – turned around an early deficit but were finally held to a 2-2 draw when a suicidal Markus Babbel backpass gifted Gheorghe Hagi an equaliser in the Bavarian sleet. Barcelona had been missing three defenders through suspension, which is why Cruyff played his 25-year-old central midfielder Josep 'Pep' Guardiola at the back.

Bayern now faced an uphill struggle but, two weeks later, they rose to the occasion yet again. Christian Ziege went close with a beautiful chip after twenty-five minutes, then Dietmar Hamann forced a save from goalkeeper Carles Busquets (the father of future Barcelona midfielder Sergio). Six minutes before the break, Busquets couldn't hold on to a curling Scholl shot and pushed the ball into the path of Babbel, who gave his team the lead.

After the restart, the hosts attacked with more determination than class and rarely troubled Bayern's defence. With six minutes left, Luís Figo had a good chance but saw his effort blocked by Kreuzer. The ball got to Scholl who immediately instigated a counter-attack and released Witeczek. The midfielder ran towards Barça's box with the ball at his feet. He feigned to cross for Klinsmann, then he accelerated and struck with his left foot. Defender Miguel Ángel Nadal deflected the shot, wrong-footing Busquets – 2-0. Iván de la Peña pulled one back in the eighty-ninth minute, but it was too little, too late for Barcelona. On the sidelines, Otto Rehhagel threw his arms into the air. He had no idea that despite taking his team to the final he wouldn't be on the bench for it. Less than two weeks after beating Barcelona, Bayern lost at home to Hansa Rostock and Rehhagel was sacked.

The man who took over was the man who always took over – the president, Beckenbauer. On the day before his second game in charge, away at Werder Bremen, a stray shot from Thomas Helmer during training knocked Beckenbauer's glasses off and gave the Kaiser a prominent shiner. It was symbolic. Bremen's business manager

Willi Lemke let it be known his club 'had not forgotten how Bayern wrested the title from us last year'. Werder won 3-2 and the race was over. However, there was still the UEFA Cup.

In its new incarnation, the Europa League, the competition has become little more than the Champions League's poor cousin. But in the mid-1990s it was different, partly because this was before the Champions League was expanded to feature more than just league champions. Even though none other than Beckenbauer himself had dubbed the competition 'the Losers' Cup', it was a precious prize. Especially because the pantheon of clubs that have won all three major UEFA trophies was (and is) very, very small. As Bayern prepared for the two-legged final against Girondins de Bordeaux, they would have known that only two clubs had managed to lift the Cup Winners' Cup, the European Cup/Champions League and the UEFA Cup: Ajax and Juventus. (To Bayern's dismay, in more sense than one, Chelsea joined this elite in 2013.)

Bordeaux were coached by Gernot Rohr, the grand-nephew of Oskar Rohr, whose goals had helped Bayern win their first national championship back in 1932. Gernot Rohr's team had famously eliminated Milan in the quarter-finals and was built around some great players such as left-back Bixente Lizarazu, the Dutch midfielder Richard Witschge, a young Christophe Dugarry and an even younger Zinédine Zidane. Yet the side also spent the larger part of their domestic season in the relegation zone, so Bayern went into the games as favourites. In Munich, a fine Helmer header from a Matthäus corner gave Bayern the lead. Jacques Offenbach's 'Cancan' – then the club's goal celebration music – sounded again on the hour, when Scholl dribbled past two defenders and fired the ball into the far corner.

The two-goal margin proved to be more than enough, though it should be said that the second leg was a lot closer than the eventual scoreline suggests. The atmosphere at the Parc Lescure was nothing short of electric and the French were unlucky when Kostadinov recklessly, perhaps brutally, took out Lizarazu, one of Bordeaux's best players, after half an hour. The Bulgarian was allowed to stay on – and proceeded to make the difference. In the fifty-third minute, he set up Scholl's opening goal with a great back-heeled pass; twelve minutes later, he capitalised on a goalkeeping error and headed home from a corner. Bordeaux pulled one back through Daniel Dutuel's long-range free kick. Then, with only twelve minutes left in the game, and thus the competition, came the moment Klinsmann had been waiting for since March, two months previously: Strunz went down the right wing and pulled the ball back for Klinsmann, whose first-time shot from the edge of the penalty area made the net bulge and set a new scoring record for a European cup competition.

At two o'clock in the morning, Beckenbauer rose from his seat at the banquet table and thanked the players 'for having led Bayern to European honours again after a twenty-year wait'. Neither he nor the next speaker, Fritz Scherer, mentioned Otto Rehhagel. Many years would pass before Beckenbauer and Hoeness admitted that sacking the coach with only four league games left and the UEFA Cup final coming up was unfortunate. The more elegant solution would have been to let Rehhagel win the UEFA Cup and then pull off the feat that was being discussed in the boardroom at least since March – invite Trapattoni to come back. Denying Rehhagel the opportunity to go out with his head held high, and a European trophy tucked under his arm, would inevitably lead to bad blood.

In 2009, Beckenbauer and Hoeness recalled how Rehhagel hadn't uttered a single word for seemingly endless minutes when they told him he was no longer wanted. Then he slowly said: 'Does this mean I can go now?' When the Bayern honchos nodded, the proud man left without saying another word and didn't even come back to pick up his belongings. That's why Franz Beckenbauer would one day pick Rehhagel's dismissal at this point in the season as the decision he regretted most. Hoeness added: 'It was idiocy.' Of course, by the time the two men finally came to this realisation, they knew Rehhagel had taken the most spectacular revenge in league history on Bayern.

12. THE GOLDEN AGE OF HOLLYWOOD

Towards the end of his first stint at Bayern, Giovanni Trapattoni confided in a friend that he had underestimated how complicated a language German is ('Oh, those verbs!'). And so, upon saying *buongiorno!* for the second time, 'Trap' told the Sunday paper *Welt am Sonntag* in May 1996: 'I will take an intensive language course during the next two months. Four hours every day. I'll be able to work without an interpreter.' He did and he was. And his German indeed improved. Relatively speaking.

Trapattoni's second expedition into the Bavarian jungle is generally considered to have been more successful than his first. For one, he by and large assembled the team that would win the Champions League, though many years later and for another coach. Trapattoni had already promoted the young Ghanaian-born defender Samuel Kuffour from the reserves during his first stay; now, during his second, he made him a regular. The Italian also signed Michael Tarnat, Thorsten Fink, Carsten Jancker, Bixente Lizarazu and Giovane Élber. And, of course, he finally won that elusive league title, claiming the 1996–97 Bundesliga trophy two points ahead of Bayer Leverkusen (coached by Bayern's old nemesis, Christoph Daum).

But, truth be told, that's not what most people remember his second time in charge for. Instead, the two years Trapattoni spent at Bayern's helm between 1996 and 1998 produced one of the most embarrassing upsets a Bayern team ever had to stomach and two incidents that are automatic choices for any highlight reel collecting the most memorable off-the-field moments in league history: the *Tonnentritt* and the *Wutrede*. Even the 1997 championship left a bitter taste of sorts, because four days after Bayern clinched the league title on the penultimate day, Ottmar Hitzfeld's Borussia Dortmund won the trophy the Reds had been futilely chasing since the mid-1970s, the Champions League. And where did they defeat a star-studded Juventus side to win the trophy? In Munich, in the Olympic Stadium.

The legendary *Tonnentritt*, pillar kick, happened on 10 May 1997. With ten minutes left, there was still no score between table-topping Bayern and last-placed Freiburg, partly because Klinsmann had missed a few good chances. Suddenly, the striker noticed that Trapattoni was preparing to make a substitution. Standing at the sidelines and waiting to come on was a 26-year-old player by the name of Carsten Lakies. He was a good, consistent goalscorer – for Bayern's reserves. Then Klinsmann noticed another thing. He was supposed to come off.

Although his feud with Matthäus was now a simmering conflict rather than open warfare, it had been another difficult season for Klinsmann. He had missed a crucial penalty against Valencia in the first round of the UEFA Cup (disobeying Trapattoni, who had ordered Matthäus to take the spot-kick). Meanwhile, FC Hollywood was still generating headlines and filling the back pages, not least because Bayern had signed another volatile, outspoken character – Mario Basler. On top of that, Klinsmann regularly found confidential details from his contract on the pages of the tabloids. The 'mole', as the informer came to be known, also revealed other internal affairs, such as who went out with whom's girlfriend, but Klinsmann was clearly his main target. Finally, Trapattoni's tactics were often cautious, not to say defensive, and the coach regularly took off one of his strikers as soon as Bayern had taken the lead. But that was not the case now. Quite the contrary: the Reds needed a goal.

Fuming with anger, Klinsmann walked off the pitch. He made sure he had himself under control until he had shaken Lakies's hand and crossed the touchline. Then he made a gesture that signalled 'That's it – *finito*.' He gave Trapattoni a mouthful as he passed him on his way to the players' tunnel and finally kicked a hole in an advertising pillar. It was an oversized battery bearing the logo of the Japanese electronics company Sanyo. Today, it's one of 500 exhibits in Bayern's museum. (The club archivist Andreas Wittner told me that 5,000 more are in storage.)

Lakies later said that he heard a crack as he ran onto the pitch but had no idea what it was. Klinsmann, meanwhile, painfully scraped his shin, as he hadn't expected the pillar to be so thin. But he was pumped up with adrenalin and only noticed the cuts when he sat down in the dressing room. A few days later, the striker signed a contract with Serie A club Sampdoria for the coming season. Klinsmann said he was glad 'the ordeal is finally over' and took one last swipe at Trapattoni when he explained Sampdoria were 'one of the most offence-minded teams' in Italy and would soon be getting a coach – César Luis Menotti – 'who preaches the attacking game'. (Lakies never played another game for Bayern. However, what you never hear when the story of the *Tonnentritt* gets told is this: three minutes from time, Mehmet Scholl sent in a cross and Lakies came agonisingly close to scoring what would have been the only goal of the game – his header cleared the crossbar by inches.)

The news quickly spread that Klinsmann was using a get-out clause in his contract to leave. (That clause was common knowledge thanks to the workings of the mole.) A local paper said the club had now become 'a madhouse' and compared it to those classic 1980s American television soap operas that centred around family intrigues: '*Dallas*, *Dynasty*, Bayern!'

There was one absurd punchline to Klinsmann's roller-coaster ride at Bayern. On the last matchday, Bayern played away at Gladbach. Shortly before half-time, a shot hit the knee of Gladbach's defender Hubert Fournier and bounced towards his own goal. Klinsmann scurried over and knocked the ball across the line. Then he gave Matthäus a grim look. Matthäus glanced over to the bench, where Uli Hoeness raised both hands, fingers spread apart to indicate the figure '10'. Whereupon Matthäus walked over to the linesman and asked him if he was absolutely sure that Klinsmann had touched the ball before it crossed the line.

The background to the sorry spectacle was this: Hoeness had predicted during the winter break that Klinsmann would score ten goals in the second half of the season; Matthäus wagered 10,000 marks that he wouldn't. The goal against Gladbach was number ten. Matthäus said the bet had been 'a lark', but when Klinsmann learned of the deal he apparently didn't find it particularly funny.

The *Wutrede*, rant or temper tantrum, took place in March 1998. For a crucial game away at Schalke, Trapattoni took Scholl and Basler out of the team and started Thomas Strunz. When Bayern's team coach arrived at the ground on Sunday, 8 March, everybody got off – except Scholl and Basler. Pointedly, the two sat in an empty coach for ten minutes before joining the rest of the squad. Bayern lost 1-0.

After the game, Trapattoni told the team the next training session would be on Tuesday. Then he drove to his house in Milan, where he took a pencil and eight small sheets of squared paper to draft a speech in German. On Tuesday morning, he drove to Munich. At the training ground, he changed into his coaching gear. While the players were sitting in the dressing room, getting ready for the training session, Trapattoni walked into the media room for the customary rundown of recent events.

'Are you ready?' he asked, staring at the journalists. Then he launched into German football's most famous speech. 'It is at the moment in this team,' he began, visibly trying to retain his composure, 'some players forgetting them professional what they are.'

It went on like this for three minutes and ten seconds. Trapattoni's German was garbled to begin with and it became more incoherent as his rage increased. Yet everyone understood every word. 'A coach not an idiot, a coach see what happen in pitch,' he said, pounding the table. 'In this game it was two, three or four players who were weak like a bottle empty,' he said. 'How dare Strunz!' he exclaimed. 'I have ready,' he said, and stormed off.

Of course he was widely lampooned. But he was also widely lauded for having read his FC Hollywood divas the riot act. Yet he must have known that he'd lost the dressing room for good on that afternoon. After this speech, his relationship with the team could never be the same again. Nine days later, he walked into Hoeness's office and asked to be let out of his contract, which had two years left to run. 'A coach has to know when the time has come,' he said. 'If I stay in Munich, I'll die.'

The Schalke game was the trigger for the *Wutrede*, not the cause. That was the way the season had been going. The tone was set on the first day, when Bayern hosted newly-promoted Kaiserslautern. Ten minutes from time, former Bayern player Ciriaco Sforza took a free kick on the right flank for the visitors. His inswinging cross was met by the Dane Michael Schjønberg, who left Kahn no chance from six yards. It was the winning goal. That was bad. Worse was that Kaiserslautern's coach raced across the entire width of the pitch after the final whistle to celebrate with the visiting fans. His sprint lasted only twenty-five seconds, but it must have seemed like an eternity to the Bayern supporters watching in agony. The name of the coach was – Otto Rehhagel.

Still worse was that Rehhagel's team kept getting results. No matter what the Reds did, they couldn't close the gap that Kaiserslautern had opened with that surprise win on the first day. When Bayern travelled to Kaiserslautern in December for the return match, they were trailing the promoted team by four points. A Hamann own goal gave Rehhagel's side the lead in the first half, a swift counter-attack in the final stages put the game – and, as it would turn out, the league title – out of Bayern's reach. Udo Scholz was no longer Kaiserslautern's stadium announcer, but his song was still alive and well. 'Zieht den Bayern die Lederhosen aus' rang around the ground at an ear-splitting volume.

Credit where it's due, Rehhagel had done just that, he'd pulled off his former team's *Lederhosen*. For the first and so far only time in league history, a newly-promoted team won the Bundesliga. It was a deeply humiliating outcome for Bayern. As if all that wasn't awful enough, the club also made all the wrong headlines again – even without Klinsmann. On the second day of April, the *Berliner Kurier* reported with hardly disguised malice: 'Oh no, FC Hollywood! What was supposed to be an April Fool's Day hoax turns out to be the truth. Yesterday, Uli Hoeness confirmed that the club has been monitoring their players' lifestyles by hiring private investigators.' The detectives' most worthwhile target, it turned out to nobody's great surprise, was Mario Basler, who liked a night on the town and was no stranger to the casinos.

Basler was incapable of toeing the line. Then again, he never pretended otherwise. When the man they called Super Mario – after the video game character – left the league to see out his career in Qatar five years later, the then national coach Rudi Völler said: 'I'd hoped he would admit to himself that instead of downing five wheat beers and smoking a pack of Marlboros in ten minutes he should have listened to his coach from time to time.' Basler replied: 'I never managed to drink five wheat beers in ten minutes. Just two. Maybe Rudi wouldn't talk such rubbish if he drank more beer himself.' Yes, he was a handful, was Mario.

If not even the combination of Hoeness and a bunch of private eyes could contain this unruly lot, which coach could? Who would be able to keep Basler in check? And Matthäus, who had been stripped of his captain's armband for publishing a tell-all book? And, for Christ's sake, Stefan Effenberg? Yes, as early as April the rumour mill whispered the midfielder was about to return to Munich.

Basler's valiant efforts notwithstanding, Effenberg was the league's most notorious bad boy, banned from the national team since he'd saluted the German fans with both middle fingers during the 1994 World Cup. The Munich paper *Abendzeitung* called him a 'divisive element' and reported that Karl-Heinz Rummenigge and a number of players were against bringing him back, six years after selling him to Fiorentina. They feared FC Hollywood would spiral out of control with Effenberg in the team. But the president liked the player. And it was also Beckenbauer who found the right coach for this rowdy bunch, for football's equivalent of glam metal band Mötley Crüe.

All through the first months of 1998, Beckenbauer kept bumping into Ottmar Hitzfeld. The reason was that the Kaiser was a pundit for RTL Television, which broadcast Dortmund's Champions League games, while Hitzfeld was now the club's director of football. However, he was missing the day-to-day work with a team and itching to get back onto the bench. Uli Hoeness would have loved to replace Trapattoni with his friend Jupp Heynckes, who was having a hard time at Real Madrid (and would indeed get the sack despite winning the Champions League). But he had known Hitzfeld since 1972, when they both played for the West German team at the Munich Olympics, and he was impressed by what the coach had achieved with Borussia Dortmund. In late March 1998, the 49-year-old Hitzfeld travelled to Munich to meet Beckenbauer, Rummenigge, Hoeness, Fritz Scherer and Karl Hopfner. The six men talked for only one hour, then everyone in the room had the same feeling: this is going to work.

And it did. In fact, it worked in a way that was beyond anyone's wildest dreams. Barely a year after Hitzfeld had put his name on the dotted line, the Reds literally came within seconds – and one penalty kick – of becoming only the fourth European team to win what is known as the treble. (The other clubs who'd done this by that point were Celtic in 1967, Ajax in 1972 and PSV in 1988.)

In retrospect, it seems logical that it would be Hitzfeld who finally tamed the lions. (Or maybe the tigers, this having been Effenberg's nickname since September 1994, when he sported an extravagant haircut – a tiger's face emblazoned on the back of his head.) Hitzfeld's man-management skills were unparalleled. The players called him the *General*, even though he never slammed doors or gave people the hairdryer treatment. Effenberg marvelled: 'No matter the situation, he never lost his composure and his aplomb.' This quality would soon be tested in a most cruel manner, but for the first nine months of Hitzfeld's first season, the team went from strength to strength.

One of the keys to success was Hitzfeld's rotation policy. 'At first we wondered what that was all about,' Helmer recalls. 'It was Hitzfeld's great achievement to humour everyone.' Only one season after Klinsmann had lost his cool after being substituted, Hitzfeld regularly benched even his biggest stars in the Bundesliga to keep them sharp and fresh for the Champions League. And nobody complained. Not even Basler. After more than two years of almost constant Tinseltown turmoil in Munich, this was as close to a miracle as a mere mortal could deliver.

Peace and tranquillity quickly yielded results. Bayern won the league with three games left (and by what was then a record margin of fifteen points) and reached the DFB-Pokal final. In March the Reds eliminated Rehhagel's Kaiserslautern from the Champions League by what must have been a deeply satisfying aggregate score of 6-0, then they knocked out a strong Dynamo Kiev side – starring Andriy Shevchenko, Kakha Kaladze and Sergei Rebrov – to make another final.

This one was played on 26 May 1999, at Barcelona's Camp Nou, a date and a place no Bayern fan will ever forget. Which, of course, also applies to Manchester United supporters, as Hitzfeld's team faced Alex Ferguson's former fledglings, now fully-fledged stars in their own right. The two coaches weren't yet the good friends they would one day – maybe on this day – become, but they knew and respected each other. Hitzfeld had eliminated United in the semi-finals two years earlier with Dortmund, but Ferguson's players had matured since then. It was difficult to pick a favourite. The teams seemed evenly matched, they were even both missing two near-indispensable key players: United were without Roy Keane and Paul Scholes, Bayern had to make do without Giovane Élber and Bixente Lizarazu. So Hitzfeld was probably right when he said: 'It's the form on the night that will decide the final. It will come down to nerves and absolute determination.'

Or rather, he was only half right. Because there's no denying his team had the better form on the night. In their book on United's history in Europe, David Meek and Tom Tyrrell say: 'Even allowing for the shock and distress of conceding . . . an early goal, United weren't playing particularly well.' Said early goal was scored by Basler. In the sixth minute, referee Pierluigi Collina awarded Bayern a free kick at the edge of the box for a supposed Ronny Johnsen foul on Carsten Jacker, which may have simply been an innocent collision. Basler stepped up and coolly curled the ball into the corner of goalkeeper Peter Schmeichel's net.

United had a few middling chances – the best of them was wasted by Jesper Blomqvist on fifty-six minutes – during the rest of the game, but they hadn't looked like scoring. Bayern, it has to be said, were far from scintillating, either, but they went very close four times in the final stages. First Schmeichel tipped Effenberg's left-footed lob over the bar with his fingertips (73'); then Scholl went one better and managed to chip the goalkeeper, only to see the ball hit the left-hand post (82'); the same player forced a fine one-handed save from Schmeichel with a shot from twenty yards (83'); finally Jancker's overhead kick rattled the crossbar (84'). Commentating for ITV, Clive Tyldesley said: 'Bayern Munich can't finish them off.'

And then the final minute began. The 30,000 German fans among the gigantic Camp Nou crowd made a deafening noise. In the VIP stand, UEFA president Lennart Johansson rose to walk over to the elevator that would take him down to the pitch for the victory ceremony. Passing Sir Bobby Charlton, he said: 'I'm sorry.' As the elevator door opened, two Germans stepped in together with Johansson: Franz Beckenbauer and Boris Becker, a devoted Bayern fan. Just as the door closed, Becker thought he could hear a cheer. 'Must have been the final whistle,' he told himself.

It wasn't. It was the equaliser. Thirty seconds into stoppage time, United won a corner, which David Beckham flighted in. Thorsten Fink mishit his clearance and the ball fell to Ryan Giggs. Giggs mishit his attempt as well. But that's how and why the ball reached Teddy Sheringham, who knocked it in on the turn. 'Bayern had their hands on the silverware,' RTL Television's commentator Marcel Reif stammered. 'I don't believe this.' A few moments later, he said:

'Another corner. We're in the ninety-third minute. Only Collina knows why.' This time Beckham's cross reached Sheringham, who flicked it on for Ole Gunnar Solskjær. From close range, the Norwegian super-sub scored the most unlikely and shocking of winners. At this moment, Becker stepped out of the players' tunnel and arrived at pitchside. 'Oh no,' he thought, 'they have tied the game.' Then he saw the result on the stadium's video screen: 2-1.

Basler, who had been substituted a few minutes earlier, took the opposite route. As soon as he saw the ball go in, he turned around and walked through the players' tunnel to the dressing room. He sat down on a bench and stared at the floor, while Collina ended the game and the tears began to flow. He was still in this position when the Bayern players received their losers' medals. Then the door opened and Beckenbauer walked in. He had just talked about the game in a strangely toneless and detached voice for RTL. He looked at Basler, then he sat down, too. Neither man spoke a word. The next person to enter the room was Rummenigge. He didn't say anything, either. Basler lit a cigarette. Then the room slowly began to fill. Finally, the entire Bayern delegation – plus various hangers-on – stood or sat around, at least forty people. But nobody said a word, nobody moved. Finally, Hitzfeld spoke: 'What happened has happened. From now on, fortune will favour us.' Then Markus Hörwick – Bayern's press officer since 1983 – made a motion with his head to remind Hitzfeld of the press conference. The two drove through the bowels of the spacious stadium in a golf cart to reach the press room.

After the end of the press conference, Hitzfeld told Hörwick that he would prefer to walk back to the dressing room, even though this would take a while because of Camp Nou's dimensions. As they were quietly marching down a long, narrow corridor, they noticed two other men in the distance. They were Alex Ferguson and Ken Ramsden, United's club secretary. Hitzfeld and Ferguson walked towards each other, while Hörwick and Ramsden kept their distance, like seconds for a duel. The two coaches exchanged a glance, then Ferguson opened his arms, embraced Hitzfeld and said: 'Sorry.' That was all. No further words were spoken.

A few hours later, at 1.20 a.m., a bell rang. The team and hundreds of guests were sitting in the banquet hall at the Hotel Barceló Sants, less than two miles east of Camp Nou. The bell indicated that the president was going to hold a brief speech. 'It's difficult to find the right words, but I'll try,' Beckenbauer said. As Scherer had done in Vienna, he praised the team and said he was proud of the players. Then he added: 'It's a game, it was a game, it will always be a game. We haven't lost a fight, we haven't lost a battle, we haven't lost our lives. We have lost a game.'

Seventeen days later, they lost another game. The DFB-Pokal final against Bremen went to penalties. With the score 4-4, Effenberg stepped forward. Since Kahn had saved one of the penalties, he was the last man up and all he had to do was score. His shot cleared the crossbar. A few minutes later, Matthäus missed his spot-kick, too.

Instead of winning the treble, Bayern had finished the season with two final defeats, one of which was traumatic. It could have broken the players, or at least destroyed the team. And there were indeed some worrying signs that the unity and solidarity that Hitzfeld had so masterfully created could come apart. During the last minutes of the Barcelona final, Helmer had made an obscene gesture because the coach didn't bring him on. And only a few weeks into the new season, Basler was involved in a pub brawl. In both cases, Hitzfeld made clear why they called him the *General* even though he didn't yell and scream. Neither man ever played for Bayern again.

Then there was the rekindling of the Lothar Matthäus debate. Many people blamed the Camp Nou drama on him. This time the charge was not that he'd choked again in a big game. Quite the opposite – he'd been one of the best men on the pitch. Rather, the accusation was that he had asked to be taken off with ten minutes left in the game. When Scholl gave a few autographs after the Barcelona final, a Bayern fan asked him why Matthäus had been substituted. With customary irreverence (and certainly a solid dose of frustration), Scholl replied: 'When the going gets tough, he always comes off. You should know this by now.'

The remark was overheard by a journalist. Scholl was slapped with a hefty fine and the tabloids were busy for a few days. In the end, though, it was just a storm in a teacup. While many fans are convinced Bayern would have won the final if Matthäus had stayed on, you can't argue with the point of view that it was simply the professional thing to do for a 38-year-old player who had run out of gas to tell his coach that the team needed fresher legs than his in the final stages. He was edging nearer and nearer to the finishing line, anyway. Less than ten months later, Matthäus left Germany to play the last few games of his long and illustrious professional career for the Major League Soccer team that later became the New York Red Bulls.

Having won three European Cup finals they maybe should have lost, Bayern had now lost three straight European Cup/Champions League finals they should have won. Not to mention that the last of these was lost in the craziest manner anyone had ever seen at this level – in 102 seconds of stoppage time. It would probably be taking things too far to say there was a wave of sympathy towards Bayern in Germany, but many football supporters did feel the team had been hard done by. (Not to mention that Hitzfeld was a universally liked man and people felt genuinely sorry for him.)

However, none of the countless writers or fans who had spent the previous years, decades even, accusing Bayern of getting all the breaks was willing to admit that they might have been overusing the *Bayern-Dusel* stereotype. Nobody said: 'Sorry, I was wrong.' At least not in public or in print. And it was just as well. Because, after having been almost uniquely unlucky, the Reds got up, dusted themselves off, knuckled down to the job . . . and, just as Hitzfeld had predicted, were showered with pieces of good fortune on a scale that left even jaded observers speechless.

First off was the *Wunder von Unterhaching*, the miracle of Unterhaching. The latter is a municipality of Munich, less than four miles southeast of Säbener Strasse. The local club there used to be more successful at winter sports than at football (the bobsleigh division produced Olympic medalists), but in 1999, SpVgg Unterhaching sensationally won promotion to the Bundesliga and spent two seasons in the top flight.

The last game of their first season was a home match against Bayer Leverkusen and Christoph Daum. The Rhineland side were in first place, three points ahead of Bayern. Hitzfeld's team had the better goal difference, but that didn't seem to be relevant. A meagre draw against lowly Unterhaching, comfortably nestled in mid-table, would give Leverkusen their first league title in club history. Nothing could go wrong. 'This is the last game, the last hurdle,' Daum said before the match. 'And we'll clear this one, too.' In the stands, visiting Leverkusen fans brandished a larger-than-life Daum image that declared him to be the 'Millennium Champion'. It was 20 May 2000.

In the twenty-first minute, Unterhaching's midfielder Danny Schwarz whipped in a cross from an inside-right position. A 23-year-old Leverkusen player by the name of Michael Ballack sensed that an opposing striker was making a run behind his back and tried to clear the situation by hoofing the ball into touch. But he didn't hit it cleanly and it ended up in his own goal. Just nine miles away, at the Olympic Stadium, Bayern were already leading old foes Bremen by three goals when the news made the rounds that whipping boys Unterhaching had scored. Hitzfeld, wearing his good-luck trenchcoat, clenched a fist. Hoeness grinned. The sell-out crowd cheered neighbours Unterhaching with a Mexican wave. Deep into the second half, a Munich-born veteran called Markus Oberleitner scored Unterhaching's second goal with a header from seven yards. The tiny ground erupted as if the hosts had won the league. Even a man wearing a photographer's bib wrapped his arms around Oberleitner.

When the final whistle came, it was half past four in the morning on the other side of the world, in Samoa. Franz Beckenbauer heard his mobile ring and briefly wondered who could possibly call him at this ungodly hour. It was his wife of ten years, Sybille. The Kaiser, trekking the globe to lobby for Germany's 2006 World Cup bid, listened to what she reported. Then Beckenbauer slowly said: 'Are you kidding me?' She wasn't. Hitzfeld had won the league for the second year in a row. When the news had sunk in, Beckenbauer raced out of his hotel room and danced down the corridor. Naked.

However, not everyone was so delighted. That same month, a song about Bayern did what Andrew White erroneously says 'Forever Number One' had done – it made the top ten, rising all the way to number eight. The tune was called 'Bayern' and the performers were the Düsseldorf punk rock band Die Toten Hosen. Needless to say, the single was not a club anthem. Instead, it stated: 'Ich würde nie zum FC Bayern München gehen' (I would never join Bayern Munich).

Maybe it's best we don't enquire how the band reacted a year later, when Bayern topped even the *Wunder von Unterhaching* by winning the most dramatic Bundesliga race in history in the most amazing manner imaginable – literally with the last kick of the entire season and at the very moment when, 225 miles away, another team was already in the midst of exuberant title celebrations.

Actually, it was even crazier than that, because when people remember the last moments of the 2000–01 season, when they recall how Stefan Effenberg said 'Just knock it in and then we'll all go home' and how Oliver Kahn ripped out the corner flag, they usually forget that the previous matchday had been almost as wild. Schalke were level on points with Bayern but topped the table on goal difference. Both teams seemed to be drawing their penultimate game: Schalke away at Stuttgart, Bayern at home against Kaiserslautern.

In the eighty-ninth minute, Hitzfeld sent striker Alexander Zickler onto the pitch. Sixty-five seconds later, Zickler collected a ball on the left flank. At this very moment, in Stuttgart, forward Sean Dundee attempted an impossible dribble against three defenders at the edge of Schalke's penalty area. In Munich, Zickler was racing down the wing with the ball at his feet. In Stuttgart, Schalke defender Tomasz Hajto dispossessed Dundee but couldn't properly clear the ball. In Munich, Zickler cut inside and struck. In Stuttgart, the loose ball rolled towards the Bulgarian Krasimir Balakov. In Munich, a Kaiserslautern defender blocked Zickler's shot, sending the ball skywards. In Stuttgart, Balakov fired a first-time piledriver into the far corner. In Munich, Zickler followed the flight of the ball with his eyes and when it came down, he volleyed it into the net from eleven yards. In the span of barely two seconds, Bayern had opened a three-point lead at the top of the standings. Now they only needed a draw on the final day, away at Hamburg.

Frankly, it was astonishing they were still in the title race at all. The Bundesliga trophy had clearly not been at the top of this team's list of priorities. Hitzfeld had been in a similar situation before, when he was coaching Dortmund. After winning back-to-back league titles, he knew the club was now aiming higher and all efforts were directed towards the Champions League. Bayern, of course, had always been aiming higher. Plus, the Barcelona trauma had become an integral part of the club's psyche. Though, surprisingly and maybe tellingly, not in a negative way. 'For me, that defeat was more like a motivation,' Effenberg says today. 'I told myself I'd probably get one more chance to win this trophy. And then nobody would take this cup away from us!' But when would he get this chance? The season after Barcelona, Bayern had been knocked out in the semis by Real. Now Effenberg was almost thirty-three. Like everyone else connected with the team, he subconsciously decided that this had to be it – Bayern had to reach the 2001 final of the Champions League, even if this meant throwing away a Bundesliga title.

With one exception, Bayern's determination on the European stage was almost palpable. This exception was a 3-0 hammering in Lyon. It triggered another famous *Wutrede;* this time the ranting and raving came from the Kaiser himself. 'This had nothing to do with football,' Beckenbauer addressed the team during the traditional post-match banquet. He compared the side to the Uwe Seeler Tradition XI, the charity team. Every single word stung – but the team never looked back. The quarter-finals reunited Ferguson and Hitzfeld. Ahead of the first leg, Sir Alex invited his German friend to a cup of tea. The two men talked about their families and current events. Then they wished each other the best of luck. Bayern won 1-0. A month later, they also took revenge on Real to reach their seventh final for the biggest trophy in European football.

But first they had this formality to get over with, the game in Hamburg. It may be unfair to say that Bayern tried to run down the clock as soon as the match had got underway, but it's not too far from the truth. While Schalke were winning their own game 5-3, the Reds were happy with earning the one single point they needed. With a minute left, Hamburg's Czech playmaker Marek Heinz crossed from the left. Two men went up for the ball. One was Hamburg striker Sergej Barbarez. The other was the best player on the pitch that day, Bayern's sweeper. He had been signed in the summer of 1999 from Gladbach. He was a Swede. His name was Patrik Andersson. And now he was late. Barbarez got to the cross first and scored with a header from seven yards.

Hitzfeld was not wearing his good-luck trenchcoat but a suit jacket. He straightened his tie and smiled. Then he looked at the stadium clock. While Kahn raced out of his goal to ask the referee how much stoppage time there would be, the thoughts were racing through Hitzfeld's mind. He was already thinking five days ahead, to the Champions League final against Valencia in Milan. If Bayern had lost the league title at any point during the previous weeks, everything would be fine now. But losing it in this manner, in the final minute, was bad news. 'I thought if we lost this game then we would be in trouble against Valencia,' the coach says today. 'The psychological ramifications would have been disastrous.' But the game wasn't lost yet. When the referee told Kahn there would be three minutes of injury time, the goalkeeper yelled at his teammates: '*Weiter! Immer weiter!*' Carry on, always carry on. 'The defeat in Barcelona had taught us that everything is possible in stoppage time,' Hitzfeld says.

When the game in Schalke ended, people were anxiously waiting for news from Hamburg. Schalke were one of the most tradition-laden and popular German clubs. They had last won the national championship in 1958, years before the introduction of the Bundesliga. Now it seemed the long wait was finally over. Three minutes after the Barbarez goal, a television reporter informed Schalke's officials that the Hamburg game had ended. Schalke had won the league. Thousands invaded the pitch, the players began to dance on the grass, Schalke's business manager Rudi Assauer was crying tears of joy. But the reporter had been misinformed.

Two minutes and thirty seconds into stoppage time, Hamburg's goalkeeper picked up what may or may not have been an intentional back-pass from a defender. The referee blew his whistle and awarded Bayern an indirect free kick in Hamburg's box, nine yards in front of the goal line. Effenberg waved Andersson over and told him to knock the ball in. Then the two men waited for well over a minute until the referee had positioned the wall, formed by eight Hamburg players plus the goalkeeper and a few red shirts trying to block a path for Andersson's shot. At long last, Effenberg heard the whistle. He gave the ball a gentle nudge and Andersson fired it right through that bundle of bodies and into the net.

Even though Kahn, knowing that Andersson's attempt would be the last action of the game and the league season, was just a few yards away from his teammates when the ball went in, he didn't run towards them to celebrate the goal that won the league. Performing what Konrad Lorenz would have termed a displacement activity, he turned around, raced over to the corner flag, ripped it out of the ground and fell on his back, manically pumping the flagpole up and down. Television commentator Marcel Reif said: 'Up in heaven, everyone must be wearing a red shirt. There is no other explanation.' He would be on duty again four days later. As would Kahn.

13. BUILDING AND REBUILDING

One November afternoon, I was wandering about in the bowels of Bayern's headquarters at Säbener Strasse. While there are seven football pitches behind the building, the house itself also boasts a spacious gym for sports like handball, basketball or gymnastics. (In fact, its walls are covered with English-language team rules for basketball — 'No lay-ups' or 'Be part of the solution, not the problem'.) A magazine was doing a photo shoot with a few Bayern players for their cover in this gym and I used the occasion to sit down and talk about what had changed under Pep Guardiola with Thomas Müller, Philipp Lahm and some other members of the team.

For unknown reasons, photo shoots always seem to go on for ever, so at one point I excused myself and went to the bathroom. On my way back, I must have taken a wrong turn. Because, when I opened a door, I suddenly found myself in a dressing room. A dozen or so teenage girls, clad in red Bayern kits, turned their heads and looked at me in a friendly but puzzled manner. I mumbled an excuse and beat a hasty retreat.

When I later called the club to find out who these girls had been, someone suggested they were NBA-style cheerleaders preparing for a training session. Bayern's men's basketball team, you see, is very successful. They won the national championship twice in the 1950s and then again in 2014. Bastian Schweinsteiger is a big fan and often rooted for the team from the stands even when they were playing in the second division. That's why his move to Manchester United in the summer of 2015 did not only leave a gap among the club's footballers.

Walking back from that dressing room to the gym, where a superstar like Arjen Robben was posing for the camera, I thought to myself that here, in these corridors, you could still feel the origins of Bayern Munich — a non-profit, charitable club that belongs to its more than 270,000 members and offers them a variety of sports, from table tennis to chess. In fact, when Mehmet Scholl finished his active career as a footballer in 2007, he switched divisions and became a member of Bayern's nine-pin bowling team.

However, this club is no longer the only Bayern. Since 2002, there have been at least two Bayern Munichs. One is the old club, founded by Franz John and shaped by Kurt Landauer and Wilhelm Neudecker. The other is a plc: Bayern Munich Ltd. This company is represented by the football team you see on television, full of glamorous star players and coached by a famous manager. The reason it came into being has to do with the massive remodelling of the European footballing landscape during the 1990s.

As was the case in Britain, football was nowhere near as popular in Germany during the 1980s as it would become during the following decade. In fact, as late as October 1990, the country's professional clubs agreed on a reform Uli Hoeness had suggested six years earlier: reducing the number of Bundesliga teams from eighteen to sixteen. Yes, at the very dawn of the great football boom, Germans felt there was not enough interest in the game any more to sustain so many professional clubs. (That great Bayern fan, Boris Becker, was partly to blame. His unexpected Wimbledon triumph in 1985 kickstarted a gigantic tennis craze in Germany.)

The plan to downsize the league was unceremoniously scrapped barely twelve months later, because suddenly attendances were soaring. After the 1990 World Cup in Italy, football blossomed all over

Europe; the Champions League gave the game more glamour, private television gave it a lot more money. Many people argued the German game – built on non-profitable clubs run by honorary officials – was ill-equipped to deal with these developments.

Still, change was slow in coming. When in June 1995 the *Hamburger Abendblatt* newspaper asked the DFB's president Egidius Braun when a big German club would be 'led by professionals rather than unsalaried amateurs', he replied that having the competence to do a job well had nothing to do with working full-time or being paid for it. Then he said: 'I don't think much of clubs as limited companies. Many of the Italian clubs that are plcs have such large debts that the government has to take action. They have to go into administration. We mustn't let this happen in Germany.'

Yet only six months later, there was another revolution: the Bosman ruling. It put an end to the old transfer system and the restrictions on the numbers of foreign players. This meant that one of the traditional revenue streams for German clubs was in danger of drying up while those teams that were owned by powerful corporations or rich businessmen could now sign (and play) as many stars from all across Europe as they liked. In order to remain competitive, there seemed to be only one solution: the Bundesliga teams had to become more professional and invite investors.

In October 1998, the DFB's general assembly decided to pave the way for the most dramatic change of the German game since the introduction of professionalism back in 1963. Clubs were allowed to turn their professional football divisions into limited companies, which meant they could sell shares or even float them on the stock market. However, in an effort to have their cake and eat it at the same time, the DFB added a statute that came to be known as the '50+1 rule'. It said that 50 per cent of a plc's shares plus one share had to remain in the possession of the parent club. The idea behind the rule was that companies or individuals could now invest in German clubs, even buy shares, but could never control or own them.

At the time of the rule change, in late 1998, twenty-five clubs in Europe were trading shares on the stock market. Following their example was a tantalising prospect. A club like Bayern could certainly expect to make hundreds of millions in one fell swoop. When Borussia Dortmund issued shares in October 2000 it earned the club 260 million marks (£93 million). Yet Bayern refrained from going public. One reason was that you can do this only once, another that you have no control over those shares once they are traded. Instead, Hoeness preferred to get a select few strategic partners on board.

In February 2002, Bayern's members voted in favour of making the football division a limited company. (At the time the club had 93,900 members. More than 1,500 of them attended the meeting, only 157 voted no.) Adidas then immediately acquired shares for 150 million marks. About ten years later, Audi and the Munich-based financial services company Allianz became shareholders as well, paying a total of 200 million euros, or £166 million. (The euro replaced the mark in January 2002.) At the time of writing, Adidas, Audi and Allianz each own 8.33 per cent of Bayern Munich Ltd. The parent club owns the remaining 75.01 per cent. (I said above that there are 'at least' two Bayern Munichs, because in October 2014, Bayern's basketball division was also turned into a company.)

However, there was a time when Bayern did entertain the idea of going public. The reason was the club's great dream – the Reds' own, football-only stadium. Since 1997, both Munich clubs had been clamouring for a new, modern ground. But the city hesitated, instead preferring to rebuild the Olympic Stadium. And so, in September of that year, Bayern's supervisory board decided to build a new ground, estimating the costs at 500 million marks. One option for raising so much money was by going public. However, it all dragged on. During the following years there was a constant to and fro as various plans were discussed, various sites considered.

Then, in July 2000, Franz Beckenbauer's tireless trips – such as his excursion to Samoa – paid off. Germany were awarded the 2006

World Cup and Munich hoped to be a host city. For that, though, it needed a modern stadium. In early 2001, Bayern and 1860 Munich agreed to set up a company that would build this new stadium, while the city promised to cover the development costs and the all-important infrastructure, such as expanding the underground railway network. In the summer of 2001, the three parties decided to build the new stadium in Fröttmaning, a district on the edge of town, some ten miles north of Säbener Strasse.

All of these massive changes were debated, organised and set in motion while the 2000–01 season was heading towards its dramatic finish: the Champions League final in Milan between Bayern and Valencia. But there was even more upheaval – the belated culmination of the conflict between Uli Hoeness and Christoph Daum. The latter was set to become Germany manager in June 2001, but nine months before that date, in late September 2000, a Munich tabloid published an article about Daum that mentioned rumours which had been making the rounds for five years, linking him with drug use, specifically cocaine. Five days later, an interview with Hoeness appeared in which he asked the DFB to reconsider appointing Daum as the new national coach. Hoeness said, among other things, that if a journalist could hint Daum was taking cocaine without being challenged, 'then that makes me wonder'. He went on: 'If someone can produce proof of this, I can't ignore it. Then Mr Daum cannot become the national coach.' Although this bit was rarely quoted, he also said: 'If all those charges are done with in three months, if it turns out that Mr Daum has been wrongfully incriminated, the contract can still be signed.'

In the words of Christoph Bausenwein, the author of a Hoeness biography: 'A wave of indignation swept through Germany, rolling across all newspapers and television stations.' Hoeness had not personally accused Daum of having a drug problem, but that's how his words were interpreted. Instantly, Hoeness was ostracised and became football's Public Enemy No 1. (This is no exaggeration. Dieter Krein, the president of Energie Cottbus, actually called him 'an enemy of the community'.) Hoeness was booed and attacked at grounds, then he received death threats. Bausenwein says: 'Particularly the editors of *Bild*, who regarded Hoeness as a thorn in their flesh because he'd always been critical of the tabloids, put Bayern's business manager in the pillory on a daily basis.'

This went on for almost three weeks. Who knows what would have happened if Daum – either deluded or simply misinformed – hadn't consented to a laboratory examination of a hair sample. On Friday, 20 October, the results arrived in Leverkusen. Early the next morning, 21 October, Daum boarded a plane to Florida before news reached the press that he had tested positive for cocaine. When Leverkusen's business manager Reiner Calmund called Hoeness to inform him about these developments, he marvelled: 'Guess what, the madman had the highest value they've ever measured at this laboratory.'

When Bayern won the 1996 UEFA Cup in Bordeaux, the club's fans had been impressed by a huge *tifo* – a choreography – displayed by the Girondins supporters. This led to the creation of Club Nr. 12, an umbrella organisation that represents the interests of Bayern's most active, committed fans and also organises *tifos*. One of their most famous choreographies greeted the Bayern players as they came out of the tunnel for the 2001 Champions League final. It is now sometimes reduced to the message written on a giant banner, but it was a lot more elaborate than that.

The *tifo* bathed San Siro's entire Curva Sud, normally the home of AC Milan's ultras but on this night the Bayern stand, in white and red. In the centre of the stand was a giant rendition of the European Cup. The trophy was framed by the date of the match – 23.5.2001 – in red on white. Below that was the famous banner. It read: *Heute ist ein guter Tag, um Geschichte zu schreiben!!!* Today is a good day to make history. And it was.

Though the game began, to put it mildly, inauspiciously. After less than thirty seconds, Giovane Élber collided with Valencia's defender

Roberto Ayala at the edge of the Spanish box. The Brazilian striker was trying to collect a long Stefan Effenberg pass and had his eyes on the ball when Ayala jumped into his back. Referee Dick Jol blew his whistle – and awarded Valencia a free kick. It was the first of many controversial decisions the Dutchman would make on this night. The next one was not too long in coming. With just eighty seconds on the clock, Jol pointed to the penalty spot in Bayern's box for a supposed Patrik Andersson handball. It was a highly dubious decision as Andersson, lying on his back, had actually done all he could to avoid touching the ball. Valencia's great playmaker Gaizka Mendieta put his side ahead from the spot. Oliver Kahn guessed the right corner but still had no chance to get to the ball. It was no surprise. Like Sepp Maier before him, Kahn cut a sorry figure at penalties. In late 2008, a group of German academics ranked him number 226 in the all-time list of Bundesliga penalty stoppers. (Maier finished dead last – in 280th place.)

Four minutes after Mendieta's goal, Effenberg went round Jocelyn Angloma in Valencia's penalty area and was brought down. Jol pointed to the spot again. Contact was certainly made, but most neutral observers felt Effenberg had been more than happy to go down when Angloma took the bait. Even Lothar Matthäus would say on the next day: 'The referee was a disgrace, not only because of the penalty decisions, all of which were wrong.'

Effenberg picked up the ball, then he gave it to Mehmet Scholl. That was no surprise, either. Scholl was one of the best penalty takers in Bundesliga history, converting eleven and not missing a single one. But now his nerves let him down, perhaps because Valencia's goalkeeper Santiago Cañizares stood right in front of him until being ordered to move between the sticks by the referee. Scholl didn't hit the ball properly and Cañizares easily blocked the shot with his knee.

Despite these two lucky breaks, Valencia never managed to hit their stride. The Spanish were strangely erratic and gave the ball away often. Bayern were clearly dominant, thanks in part to a courageous and spirited coaching decision. Ottmar Hitzfeld had started Owen Hargreaves, a twenty-year-old Canadian-born midfielder who had been playing for the reserves in the third division as recently as April. His job was to do the running for Effenberg in defensive midfield, which allowed the maestro to roam freely. Hargreaves did as he was told and then some, becoming the best outfield player on the pitch despite his tender age and almost total lack of experience at that level.

At half-time, Hitzfeld piled on the pressure by bringing Carsten Jancker into the game for French right-back Willy Sagnol. Four minutes after the restart, Élber went past Angloma and crossed for Jancker, lurking at the far post. The striker gave defender Amedeo Carboni a push as he went up, which is why the ball hit Carboni's arm. Jol awarded the third penalty of the game. This time Bayern's captain stepped up, Effenberg. With authoritative calmness, he buried his effort to level the score.

It was a tense game but a strangely uneventful final, a battle of attrition more than anything else. The match had shoot-out written all over it, perhaps because Jol had ruined it as a proper contest after less than two minutes. And so a European final featuring a German club went to penalties for the third time. The other two teams – Leverkusen in 1988 and Schalke in 1997 – had both won, which may have been a good omen. However, there was still the Kahn problem. How can you win a penalty shoot-out if your number one rarely saves a spot-kick? Six months earlier, Bayern had been knocked out of the DFB-Pokal on penalties by fourth-division Magdeburg because Kahn hadn't got close to any of the kicks.

The odds plummeted further when Bayern's very first taker, the Brazilian Paulo Sérgio, missed the target, blazing over the bar, while Mendieta and John Carew easily and confidently converted the first two Spanish penalties. But then, when it counted most, Kahn suddenly found the *Elfmetertöter* in himself. 'I told myself: if you want to win this cup, then do what you've always done,' he later said. 'Dive to your right.' He dived to his right against Zlatko Zahovič and although the penalty was well-placed, the goalkeeper made the save. Unfortunately, Andersson then wasted the very next spot-kick, which meant Kahn had to dive to his right again. For some reason, though, he didn't. As Carboni took his run-up, Kahn seemed glued to the goal-line. When he finally decided to move to his left, it was too late. It was a good thing. Carboni blasted the ball down the middle and Kahn palmed it onto the bar.

After the first five attempts by each team, it was 3-3 in the shoot-out. After the first six, it was 4-4. Then centre-back Thomas Linke sent Cañizares the wrong way. When the Argentine Mauricio Pellegrino stepped up for Valencia, it was 11.33 p.m. in Milan. Kahn dived to his right and blocked the shot with both fists. Then, for the second time in four days, he began to run. This time, though, he wasn't heading for the corner flag, as he had done in Hamburg, but for his teammates. A 25-year wait was over. Bayern had won the biggest trophy in European football for the fourth time. Hitzfeld had become only the second man (after Ernst Happel) to win the cup with two different teams. And there was another piece of trivia. In the thirty years between 1971 and 2001, only four finals in the European Cup or the Champions League had not been won by the team that got on the scoreboard first during regular or extra time. All four games involved Bayern Munich.

The magical Milan night did not herald a great new Bayern era. Although the club would go on to win the Intercontinental Cup later that year against Boca Juniors in Tokyo, the Champions League triumph in 2001 was the team's last hurrah and marked the beginning of another difficult period. Key players like Effenberg, Kahn, Scholl and Lizarazu were now thirtysomethings, while Hargreaves didn't fulfil his promise, to some extent on account of nagging injuries.

The decade that followed Kahn's heroics against Valencia, the noughties, were a strange time for Bayern Munich. Spectacular highs alternated with inexplicable lows in the Bundesliga, where the team would be described in hushed tones as the White Ballet, only to lose at St. Pauli or finish ten points behind a rather mediocre Stuttgart side a few seasons later. On the European stage, there were thrilling and close encounters with Real Madrid, but also two painful 4-0 defeats, one in Barcelona in the Champions League, the other in a UEFA Cup semi-final away at Zenit Saint Petersburg.

This inconsistency was partly due to the usual issues at Bayern – a few uninspired choices as regards the coaching position, disagreement over whether to spend big or not, a fundamental uncertainty as to whether the focus should be on the Bundesliga or the Champions League and, of course, good old disturbances. In 2002–03, for instance, Bayern tore through the league in an all-white kit that required getting used to but was easy on the eye in more sense than one. After years of a more cautious approach, the new cavalier style of a team led by former Leverkusen stars Michael Ballack and Zé Roberto thrilled the Bayern bosses, especially president Franz Beckenbauer. It also yielded spectacular results, such as five goals in little more than twenty minutes against an 1860 side that was plummeting down the standings worryingly fast.

Yet the approach proved ill-suited for Europe. Lothar Matthäus, now a columnist for the weekly sports magazine *Sport Bild*, castigated his former club so often that Hoeness lost his cool on television. 'He wants, and he always wanted, to become someone at Bayern,' Hoeness said. 'But as long as Rummenigge and I have a say here, he won't even become the greenkeeper at the new stadium.' Deeply hurt, Matthäus cancelled his honorary membership and even returned the parting gifts he had received when he left Bayern. A few months later, he sued the club, saying he was owed 500,000 euros from his testimonial. Meanwhile, Bixente Lizarazu lashed out at his teammate Niko Kovač during a training session, Kahn was heavily fined for breaking curfew and Samuel Kuffour, trying to punch Jens Jeremies, gave Thorsten Fink a shiner. Even the supposedly impeccable gentleman Hitzfeld made all the wrong headlines when he admitted to having had a long-term affair with a model half his age. As Bruce Springsteen would have observed, it's hard to be a saint in the city of Munich.

But not all of Bayern's problems were homemade. Maybe the Reds also began to appear a bit directionless because the club no longer knew who the opposition was. In England, Manchester United went into a season knowing Chelsea and Arsenal would be challengers. In Spain, Barcelona banked on the fact that if they finished ahead of Real they would win the league. But in Germany, five different clubs lifted the championship during the noughties. One was Dortmund, who were spending all those millions from going public on transfers and wages in a desperate, almost suicidal effort to keep abreast of Bayern. Soon the bubble burst and the club teetered on the brink of bankruptcy.

In 2004, Werder Bremen won the league-and-cup double. Three years later, Stuttgart triumphed and in 2009, Wolfsburg lifted the first Bundesliga title in its history, even though the team were a whopping eleven points away from first place in late January. There were no two ways about it – the German Bundesliga was crazy and unpredictable. The fans loved it, of course, but the lack of consistently dominating teams was not necessarily a good sign.

For the larger part of the decade, the German game went through an existential crisis, partly of its own making. Abroad, it was considered unsexy, unglamorous and, frankly, uninteresting. A key element here was certainly most football fans' traditional if often misguided obsession with the star player. In Germany, there weren't many, mainly because there was little money. When Bayern signed the Dutch striker Roy Makaay in 2003 for a then-club record of 18.75 million euros (£13 million), Hoeness said that with this sum, his club had entered 'a borderline area' in terms of what was sensible and practical. During the same transfer window, Real spent almost twice that amount on David Beckham while Barcelona landed Ronaldinho for £21 million. A year later, Didier Drogba joined Chelsea for £24 million.

The Bundesliga just couldn't compete in this arena despite the new rules allowing limited companies and despite the fact that the league boasted the highest average attendance in Europe: German private television hadn't turned out to be the bonanza the big clubs had hoped for. In 2002, the media group founded by entrepreneur Leo Kirch went bust, plunging the Bundesliga into a severe financial crisis, as money the clubs had relied on wasn't forthcoming. But even today, with a more stable and healthy partner in Sky Germany, the gulf is still enormous. In 2014, Cardiff City, the worst team in the Premier League, earned 74.5 million euros from television. Bayern Munich, one of the best teams in the world, made only half as much: 37.6 million euros.

One reason for the discrepancy is that Germans don't consider football an amusement or a diversion. It's part of the community fabric, a right rather than a luxury. Consequently, they are reluctant to pay top prices for it. That's why you can watch a lot of football on free television. (A public-service broadcaster shows highlights from all Saturday afternoon matches roughly an hour after the games have ended.) That's also why pay television in England has almost three times as many subscribers as it does in Germany, although the latter is a much larger country.

Another reason is that Bayern – unlike Real and Barcelona, who both pocketed four times as much from television as the Munich giants in 2014 – don't market their own television rights. Karl-Heinz Rummenigge periodically mutters threats to break away from the league's central marketing of broadcasting rights. (Bayern originally agreed to this in 2000. As it later turned out, the club received secret bonus payments from Leo Kirch for not seeking their own deals.)

It remains a double-edged sword, though. Since Bayern have been the only really big fish in the German pond since the 1970s, they eschew an awful lot of money by allowing the Bundesliga to negotiate for all clubs. In the summer of 2015 Rummenigge said the club stood to make 'four times as much as now' if they were marketing their own television rights, meaning he sees Bayern in the Real/Barcelona category. However, at the same time it's not in Bayern's best interests to widen the gap between themselves and their domestic opposition. The Reds need proper competition, if only because, as we shall see, it helps them stay sharp and provides an impetus to move forward.

This is a grave and fundamental paradox few other clubs face. Over the years, and coupled with Hoeness's well-documented willingness to help those in need, it has led to some unusual measures of support. In 2003, with St. Pauli in the third division and on the verge of going bust, Hoeness offered the old class-enemy a charity game that raised a much-needed 200,000 euros. (For perhaps the only time in his life, Hoeness was given a standing ovation away from home. He said it 'took some getting used to'.)

A year later, in 2004, Bayern did something even more unusual – they gave their biggest competitor money to bail them out. When Hoeness learned that Borussia Dortmund had such crippling debts they could no longer pay their players' wages, he loaned the club two million euros, essentially to keep a rival afloat. As Daniel Taylor marvelled in the *Guardian*: 'Imagine . . . another wealthy, powerful Premier League team sending a seven-figure cheque to Portsmouth or any of those other clubs who know what it is like to be bucket-collection skint. In England it never tends to happen. The rich get richer and the poor rattle their tins.'

The money was well spent, because, as we'll presently discuss, you could argue that Bayern went on to build one of the greatest teams in their history only because Dortmund's resurgence forced them to spring into action. Equally wise was the unplanned investment Bayern made in 2006. 1860 Munich, joint owners of the shiny new Allianz Arena, had been relegated from the Bundesliga and were financially in such dire straits that Bayern had to come to the rescue. The Reds agreed to buy their local rivals' shares in the stadium for 11 million euros and grant 1860 a right to repurchase. In other words, it was technically just a loan to save 1860 from going into administration. However, the Blues never got their finances in order and eventually waived the option to reacquire the shares. Which is why Bayern are now the sole owners of the Allianz Arena, while once-proud 1860 have become mere tenants.

However, having less money than many of the big clubs from abroad is nothing new in Germany. So why did the league fall into decline after 1997, when both the Champions League and the UEFA Cup were won by Bundesliga clubs, Dortmund and Schalke? The answer is probably complacency. Safe in the knowledge that a country so large and so football-mad would always somehow produce enough brilliant players, Germany had failed to adapt to changing times by modernising its youth set-up. The DFB realised this as early as 1998, when the German World Cup squad had an average age of 30.3 because there just weren't any good young players rattling at the doors. The wake-up call for the rest of the country was the national team's abysmal showing at Euro 2000. Now it was painfully obvious that Germany had lost an entire generation. In the crucial age group of players who would soon be in their mid-twenties, there was only one single player who deserved to be called outstanding: Michael Ballack.

In 2002, the DFB launched what it termed the 'Extended Talent Promotion Programme'. An enormous amount of effort and money now went into a complete overhaul of the youth set-up. The clubs played their part as well. In contrast to countries like England, where the FA has virtually no leverage when dealing with the clubs, the DFB held some power over the German teams and could force them to improve their talent development. Also, since money was drying up in the wake of Leo Kirch's downfall, the clubs slowly began to appreciate the value of homegrown players.

Funnily enough, the biggest and richest club in the land – the only team that didn't have a pressing need to invest in youth because money was tight – had modernised its youth set-up years before people realised there was something wrong with how talents were scouted and then schooled. Anyone who's interested in this fascinating but rarely told backstory of how a treble-winning Bayern team came about should spend an afternoon with the agent Roman Grill, who represents about half a dozen former or current Bayern players.

That's because Grill is more than just a business adviser. Twenty years ago, he was a veteran member of Bayern's reserves, playing under Hermann Gerland, the second team's iconic coach. Grill was one of those dependable players who were never really first-team material but who would teach the ropes to youngsters coming up through the ranks. 'In 1995, Uli Hoeness asked Björn Andersson to come up with a new youth-football concept,' Grill says. (Andersson, the reader may recall, was the player brutally taken out of the 1975 European Cup final by Terry Yorath.) 'I had a reputation as being very loyal, I captained the reserves. So after one year, Andersson asked me to become his assistant. Another two years later, he made me the head coach of the Under-19s. In my second year, we won the championship.'

This was in July 2001. In a close final that was staged in Leverkusen, Bayern defeated hosts Bayer 3-2. Grill's team included a few future Bundesliga players such as Zvjezdan Misimović and Piotr Trochowski. Amazingly, this was Bayern's first-ever title at the Under-19 level. Even more amazingly, the club had also won the Under-17 title the day before. A side coached by Stephan Beckenbauer and including quite a few players who would one day run out for Bayern's first team, such as Michael Rensing and Andreas Ottl, won 4-0 against Borussia Dortmund.

'At the time,' says Grill, 'the system we played throughout the youth set-up was a 4-3-3 with a number six, a number eight, a number ten and a number nine.' (Meaning: a defensive holding midfielder, a more creative holding midfielder, a central attacking midfielder and a classic target man up front.) He adds: 'Louis van Gaal played like that. But, as early as 2002, we switched to the Guardiola system. From that point on, our teams played with a three-man line in midfield and three versatile forwards.'

While it's tempting to linger over the thought that Andersson's revamped youth set-up anticipated the favourite formations of two famous future Bayern coaches by at least eight years, let's return to that weekend in 2001 when the club collected both the Under-19 and the Under-17 title. The defensive midfielder in Grill's team was a small but smart Munich boy about whom the agent says: 'He never made a mistake. He always found a solution.' The kid's name was Philipp Lahm.

Meanwhile, the attacking midfielder in the side coached by Stephan Beckenbauer was a boy who'd grown up fifty miles south of Munich, right on the Austrian border, and who'd only recently decided to concentrate on football and give up a promising skiing career. He was called Bastian Schweinsteiger.

Andersson's reformations at the youth level bore astonishing fruit. When Bayern won the Champions League in 2001, only two members of the squad had also played youth football for the club – Owen Hargreaves and Samuel Kuffour. (And both had joined Bayern fairly late, at sixteen years of age.) But when the Reds lifted the trophy the next time, in May 2013 at the new Wembley, the situation was markedly different. No fewer than six regulars had come up through the ranks: David Alaba and Toni Kroos plus the Bavarians Holger Badstuber, Thomas Müller, Lahm and Schweinsteiger. One could add Diego Contento and Emre Can, later of Liverpool, to this list, because both saw action in more than five competitive games during that treble season.

In the post-Bosman era, it has become very rare for a truly global club to rely on so many homegrown players, many of whom were even local boys. Barcelona come to mind, but nobody else. This is a source of great pride to Bayern's fans. It also explains why a certain section of the club's support was not exactly thrilled when Pep Guardiola began to bring in players from abroad, notably Spain, while marginalising someone like Mario Götze. (Götze was signed from Dortmund, under controversial circumstances we'll come to later, but he's an out-and-out Bavarian, having been born in the same city seventy miles west of Munich where Badstuber is from. When I asked him about his allegiance as a kid, he told me he grew up as a Bayern fan, just like his two brothers.)

Needless to say, breaking into the first team wasn't plain sailing all the way for those youngsters. When Lahm moved up to the reserve team, Gerland was reluctant to ask a player who was so young and so slight of build to control the crucial area in the centre of the pitch. Instead he played Lahm as a right-sided midfielder and finally – mainly because he didn't have anyone else who could fill this role reliably – at full-back. However, at that time this position was occupied in the first team by Sagnol and Lizarazu.

By 2003, Gerland felt that playing for the reserves in the third division was stunting Lahm's development. The coach phoned Bundesliga managers, offering them a player on loan who was a guaranteed hit. 'Hermann Gerland played a very important role in my career,' Lahm said when we discussed the early stages of his career. 'And of course that also goes for Felix Magath, who gave me my first game at the professional level.' Magath was coaching VfB Stuttgart at the time, the club that finally agreed to take Lahm on loan and where he did so well over two seasons that he won his first cap for Germany three months after his twentieth birthday.

This may sound as if Lahm's first years as a professional player were an easy ride, but that's not the case. 'While I was at Stuttgart, I first broke my foot,' he recalls. 'And then, just as I was about to go back to Bayern, I tore a cruciate ligament. This was a very serious injury at the time. When something like this happens to you at a young age, you are scared and you hope that everything turns out well.' It did. Bayern called Lahm back in the summer of 2005, to the delight of their new coach – Felix Magath.

On a Monday in mid-May 2004, Uli Hoeness invited Ottmar Hitzfeld and his wife for dinner to the terraced house in Ottobrunn where the business manager had been living for almost thirty years. Hitzfeld was in his sixth season as Bayern coach, longer than anyone else in club history

had managed, and his contract had another year to run. The Reds
already had a successor lined up, because the fifty-year-old Felix Magath
had agreed to take over the club in 2005. But the season wasn't going
well – Rummenigge and Beckenbauer felt that Hitzfeld was no longer
the *General*. He didn't seem to have the team under control any more, a
charge nobody had ever levelled against the stern headmaster Magath.

Over what Hitzfeld called 'a good Bavarian meal', Hoeness told the
coach with a heavy heart that the club would part ways with him at
the end of the season, contract or not. 'I have to accept this decision,'
Hitzfeld said. 'We had some great years and celebrated great triumphs.
The positive things will outweigh the rest.' Two days later, Magath
announced he would leave Stuttgart a year earlier than planned and
take over from Hitzfeld in the summer.

Magath was an odd choice. For most of his coaching career, he
was considered to be an expert at saving clubs mired in relegation
dogfights. He would come in during a season and turn things around
by instilling discipline – some said fear – and providing for supreme
physical fitness. (His former player Jan Åge Fjørtoft once quipped:
'Whether Felix Magath would have saved the *Titanic*, I do not know.
However, the survivors would have been in top shape.') His football
was considered to be as outdated as his training methods – Magath was
fond of workouts with medicine balls – or his habit of communicating
very little with his players.

But in recent years, Magath had worked wonders with a very young
Stuttgart team including, of course, Philipp Lahm. Also, after six long
years of Hitzfeld's benign reign, some people felt it was time to bring
in someone who was totally different to stir things up. Finally, there was
no obvious candidate besides Magath. Hoeness's old friend Heynckes
was under contract (at Schalke) and the same went for the two foreign
coaches Bayern had flirted with on and off over the years – Louis van
Gaal and Arsène Wenger.

Domestically, Magath's methods yielded impressive results. He
became the first, and so far only, coach in Germany to win back-to-back

league-and-cup doubles. To put this achievement into perspective: nobody at all has done this in England and Italy, only one coach in France (Saint-Étienne's Robert Herbin) and two men in Spain (Bilbao's Fred Pentland and Barcelona's Ferdinand Daučík).

The second of these doubles was particularly gratifying because it was Bayern's first season in their own Allianz Arena. As is always the case, when Bayern moved north some traditionalists mourned the good old days in the Olympic Stadium. It's certainly true that the futuristic, built-to-impress new stadium – the facade is made of inflated air panels that can be independently lit – is a long haul from the centre of town and, not unlike the new Wembley, can feel so slick, so clever and so perfect that it lacks soul. But anyone who has ever stood in a half-empty Olympic Stadium with a relentless sun burning the skin or icy sleet whipping the face must admit that the Arena is a brilliant place for watching football. Even the story of the sale of the naming rights has a certain charm. They went to the very company where Franz Beckenbauer, not yet fourteen years old, began an apprenticeship in 1959 as an insurance salesman.

The first Bundesliga game at the Allianz Arena was the opening match of the 2005–06 season. The new ground's first Bundesliga goal was scored by a player with an English passport, because after half an hour Owen Hargreaves put the hosts ahead against old rivals Gladbach. Even though Bayern were reduced to ten men before the break (defender Valérien Ismaël collected two bookings), Roy Makaay added two late goals for a deserved 3-0 win. The new stadium was an instant hit and sold out on a regular basis. Something, however, that is almost not worth mentioning. When Bayern travelled to Paderborn in February 2015, the club's website proudly announced that this was Bayern's 275th league match in a row in front of a sell-out crowd. 'It's been eight years,' the report read, 'since a Bayern game didn't sell out. On 30 January 2007, a cold Tuesday evening, "only" 60,000 came out to watch a home match against Bochum.' (The capacity then was 69,000. It's now 75,000. These figures refer to domestic games. For

European encounters, the standing areas have to be made all-seater, reducing the capacity by 6,000.)

This Bochum game in early 2007 finished scoreless. It's noteworthy not just because it wasn't watched by a capacity crowd but also because it was Felix Magath's last game in charge. Bayern fired him eighteen hours after the final whistle. The team had dropped into fourth place and was eight points short of an automatic qualification spot for the Champions League. 'The concern about reaching the Champions League has prompted this decision,' Rummenigge told the press. This was certainly true, but there must have also been some questions about Magath's man-management. In May 2005, after the coach had just won his first league title with Bayern, Hoeness told the *Frankfurter Allgemeine Zeitung* that although he was happy with Magath and his success, 'it would stand him in good stead if he could see more of a partner in a player. I think he may be stuck too much in the era of Happel and Zebec. He played under them when he was at Hamburg. That was a time when the main instrument was pressure.'

You can also gauge how uneasy Bayern felt about Magath's dictatorial approach by the fact that his successor was his predecessor, the great moderator and communicator Hitzfeld. His second stint at the club would not end quite as amicably as the first. In fact, it would produce many tears, literally and figuratively. But, in its own, strange way, it made the modern Bayern Munich. One reason for this is that Hitzfeld couldn't really save the 2006–07 season. The Reds finished fourth and missed out on the Champions League for the first time in eleven years. Obviously the problem wasn't the coach, apparently it was the team. Bayern decided to do something they hadn't done since the middle of the previous decade, when Beckenbauer and Rummenigge came on board and talked Hoeness into changing his time-tested ways. They decided to play with the big boys.

His biographer Bausenwein argues it's no coincidence Uli Hoeness had just exchanged his fairly modest terraced house in Ottobrunn for a spacious villa at the Tegernsee, the lake south of Munich that Wilhelm

Neudecker had circled after Bayern won promotion to the Bundesliga in 1965. 'Now he also displayed enjoyment at spending money in his role as the business manager,' said Bausenwein, 'and plundered the bank account.' This is probably too simple a conclusion, not least because it would later turn out that the private Hoeness had spent (and made) millions playing the stock exchange almost compulsively for a number of years. However, it's true that he had never gambled in his role as Bayern's money man. He did now. In the summer of 2007, Bayern spent 82 million euros (then £56 million) on stars like the French winger Franck Ribéry and the Italian marksman Luca Toni. *Kicker* magazine called this 'a turning point in the German game', because Bayern were now building a team for the Champions League rather than for the Bundesliga and did this by luring much longed for star players to Germany. The *Süddeutsche Zeitung* acknowledged as much when it dubbed the new team *die Galaktischen*, after Real Madrid's fabled galácticos.

The other reason why Hitzfeld's comeback unwittingly got today's Bayern Munich off the ground was that he soon threw in the towel, which led to a flurry of activity on the coaching bench. Now in his late fifties, Hitzfeld no longer had the strength and the patience to cope with the traditional turmoil at Säbener Strasse; he was simply tired of manoeuvring through shark-infested waters. The tipping point was a UEFA Cup game against, of all teams, Bolton Wanderers in November 2007. As was his wont, Hitzfeld rested a few stars and the Reds dropped two points in the group stage when Kevin Nolan chipped the ball past two opponents to set up Kevin Davies, who volleyed home with eight minutes left. After the game, Rummenigge blasted Hitzfeld's rotation policy: 'I'm miffed. It was so easy to win. 66,000 people had a right to see our best team. Football isn't mathematics, that's not okay.' The last line was a thinly veiled dig at Hitzfeld, a trained maths teacher. Less than two months later, in early January 2008, news broke that Hitzfeld would leave Bayern in the summer and exchange the day-to-day grind of running a club side for coaching the Swiss national team.

For the rest of the season – actually, well into the next season – the fans celebrated Hitzfeld. They chanted 'Ottmar, you're the best man in the world' during a warm-up match against the Chinese Olympic team in mid-January and they were still singing it eight months later, when Bayern played Internazionale during the pre-season preparations under a new coach.

They did this because they truly respected Hitzfeld, who went out in May 2008 with yet another league title won (his fifth with Bayern) and tears of deep emotion streaming down his face. For some reason, I never met Hitzfeld personally until we both appeared as pundits on a Sky Germany show in March 2013. When we parted company later that night, we were on first-name terms and I felt as if I had just rediscovered an old friend. So I can attest to Ottmar's knack of winning hearts easily. But, truth be told, the fans also sang his praises to let his successor know in no uncertain terms they didn't like him at all. It was none other than Jürgen Klinsmann.

The names of a few foreign-born candidates – specifically Marco van Basten, Frank Rijkaard and Rafael Benítez – had been bandied about in Bayern's boardroom. Hoeness, meanwhile, fancied a young German, Jürgen Klopp. Hoeness even went so far as to call the forty-year-old coach of second-division Mainz 05 and tell him that he might have a chance to take over the biggest club in the land. Yet Rummenigge suggested Klinsmann and convinced the others why this was a splendid idea. Which wasn't easy. Klinsmann had never coached a club side before. In fact he had coached for only two years in total, taking over the national team when nobody else wanted the job, in 2004, and stepping down after a surprisingly successful 2006 World Cup, a tournament that felt like a shot in the arm for the German game.

And that's what made him attractive. Rummenigge hoped for this same effect – a modernisation and rejuvenation of Bayern Munich. After all, the last coach who had brought new ideas and a novel approach to Säbener Strasse had been Giovanni Trapattoni during his first stint, more than a dozen years ago. Klinsmann promised all this and then some. The *Münchner Merkur* newspaper headlined 'The Pre-Announced Revolution: Everything at Bayern will change under Klinsmann'. And it did, as epitomised by the four stone Buddhas that graced the roof of Bayern's training centre when the new season began. To be fair, they hadn't been Klinsmann's idea. It was the interior designer who remodelled the building according to Klinsmann's demands who put them there, as decorative elements. But when the coach was asked about the Buddhas, he replied: 'They give us a certain energy flow.' (There were more Buddhas inside the building, some of them covered in gold, but the public never got to see those.) Three weeks into the season, the Buddhas on the roof were quietly taken down, partly because the Catholic Church – a powerful institution in Bavaria – made its irritation clear.

Many fans, meanwhile, had been sceptical long before they saw the Buddhas. A few of the older supporters had distanced themselves from Klinsmann during his second season in Bayern's colours, feeling he didn't really care about the club's culture and had only joined Bayern to finally win the league title that was missing from his CV. Many of the younger fans remembered very well how Klinsmann, as Germany manager, had first sacked Sepp Maier, the national team's long-time goalkeeping coach, and then demoted Oliver Kahn to the bench during the World Cup on home soil. There would be no embarrassing encounters between the three men, because Kahn had announced he would finish his career in June 2008, long before Klinsmann's name was first uttered in the boardroom, which in turn prompted the 64-year-old Maier to retire. Still, it did seem symbolic that two larger-than-life club icons were going out just as 'a culture shock in blond' was coming in, as journalists Patrick Strasser and Günter Klein called Klinsmann.

The funny thing is this: despite all the hullabaloo and media frenzy that accompanied his short reign, Klinsmann should today be nothing more than a footnote in Bayern's history, a coach in the category of Otto Rehhagel and Erich Ribbeck, less important than even Gyula Lóránt. And yet he plays a crucial if unwitting role in the tale of the modern club, because his departure ushered in a new golden era, a period of unprecedented dominance.

When Hoeness, Rummenigge and Karl Hopfner decided his position was no longer tenable, they needed an interim coach for half a dozen weeks. They needed somebody who would get the job done without asking too many questions and making demands. They needed a friend.

This was in late April 2009. Bayern were trailing Wolfsburg by two points, a team masterminded by the Munich-born Zvjezdan Misimović, who had once been the key player in Roman Grill's Under-19s. Wolfsburg's rise was worrying for Rummenigge, Hoeness and Hopfner – the board of Bayern Munich Ltd. Many years earlier, Hoeness had predicted that this club could one day challenge Bayern's monopoly and become a serious, permanent rival. The reason was money. Back when the DFB created the 50+1 rule, which limited the influence a company or an individual could wield, they granted two exemptions for historical reasons.

One was Bayer Leverkusen, which came into being as a sports club for employees of the Bayer chemical goods company. The other was Wolfsburg, which had similar ties to Volkswagen. Actually, the entire city only exists because of this car manufacturer! In 1931, an automobile designer by the name of Ferdinand Porsche began entertaining the idea of building a simple, good car that anyone could afford, in other words: a people's car, or, in German, a *Volkswagen*. Seven years later, Hitler himself laid the foundation stone for a gigantic car plant around which the city was planned and built.

Due to these exemptions from the 50+1 rule, Leverkusen are now fully owned by the Bayer company and the same holds true for Wolfsburg and Volkswagen. It also means that in theory Wolfsburg have access to enormous funds. In 2014, Volkswagen made a profit – profit, not turnover – of 12.7 billion euros. In practice, of course, the UEFA Financial Fair Play Regulations limit the club's options. Still, Wolfsburg's challenge came at a critical time. Later this year, in November 2009,

Hoeness was supposed to follow Beckenbauer and become the new president of the parent club while former player Christian Nerlinger was groomed to take over as the new business manager. Would the young man be able to cope with all these new threats?

Equally worrisome had been a defeat in Europe. In early April, Bayern were dismantled by Pep Guardiola's Barcelona. At Camp Nou, Bayern conceded four goals before the break. Beckenbauer said: 'Our performance in the first half was the most dreadful I've ever seen from a Bayern team. This was a demonstration, almost a humiliation. We've been given a masterclass in how to play this game.'

But, oh, how to play this game? This was the question now. Barça's football, based on ball possession and built around short passes, was clearly the way forward. One of the style's original architects was Louis van Gaal, who had coached Barcelona between 1997 and 2000. (Where his assistant was a Portuguese called José Mourinho.) Van Gaal had spent the last few years at AZ Alkmaar and was about to lead the unfashionable Dutch team to only the second league title in its history. In May 2009, Bayern's board announced they had reached an agreement with Alkmaar and were 'happy to have secured the services of an experienced coach like Louis van Gaal for Bayern'.

But who would warm the bench for the Dutch master until the end of the season? Hoeness called a place known as Casa de los Gatos, the house of the cats. It was a Spanish-styled country house in the Lower Rhine region, not far from the Dutch border. For more than two years, Jupp Heynckes had been enjoying retirement here, taking long walks with his dog Cando vom Finkenschlag, a German shepherd, in the woods near his farmstead.

When his friend Hoeness asked him to get back into the game on a temporary basis and guide Bayern through the last few weeks of the season, he didn't think twice. As soon as news of his comeback broke, *Kicker* magazine polled its readers. The question was: 'Is Jupp Heynckes the right man for Bayern?' 60,179 people cast their vote. 69.1 per cent of them said: no.

14. THE TREBLE

'I think it's fair to say that our focus on possession didn't start with Guardiola, that goes back to Louis van Gaal,' said Thomas Müller when we were hunched on one of those gym benches that are always too small. The lanky forward is normally one of the great entertaining interviewees, because he can be as unconventional in conversation as he is on the pitch. After all, this is the man who – having just scored a brace against England at the 2010 World Cup – waved into the television cameras and said: 'I would like to say hello to my two grandmas and my grandpa. That's long overdue.'

But when we talked about what had changed under Guardiola, occasionally casting glances at the various Bayern stars posturing for the camera, he was very serious and thoughtful.

'I mean, that whole Barcelona style goes back to the days of Johan Cruyff,' he said. 'So you always had that Dutch element in this school.' Then he added: 'The structures at this club are very strong, having grown over the years, so not too much has changed in terms of organisation. Of course Guardiola has very specific ideas about how football should be played. But generally speaking I don't think that Bayern are the sort of club that dramatically changes when a new coach comes in. The structures are very established, because the key figures have been here for so long.'

Müller knows this. Heynckes knew this, too. But Van Gaal didn't. Or maybe he knew it but didn't care. During one of his first public appearances, he said: 'The club is like me: self-confident, dominant, arrogant, honest, hard-working, innovative – but also cordial and familial.' The press lapped it up, and so one worrying sign went unnoticed. Van Gaal proudly quoted the club motto: '*Mia san mia*,' he said. Then he added: 'And I am who I am.'

To be fair, Bayern did not enter into the relationship dewy-eyed. They knew that the Dutchman possessed such an ego that even the close friends back in Noordwijk with whom he played bridge called him 'The King'. In all likelihood, the club had also heard that van Gaal's daughters addressed him in a formal manner, not unlike the way American children in the 1950s used to call their fathers 'Sir'. But the Bayern bosses probably suspected that some of those reports had been blown out of all proportion. Wasn't it a perfectly normal – if slightly old-fashioned – custom in Holland to speak to your parents in such a formal manner? And in any case, as chairman Karl-Heinz Rummenigge told the press: 'If we had wanted to sign everybody's darling, we would have gone for George Clooney.'

But at first it wasn't Van Gaal's ego that was the problem, it was the lack of results. Teaching the team the possession game took longer than the club had anticipated. By December, most observers felt that The King would soon put his head on the chopping block. He had alienated some players, specifically Franck Ribéry. Like all members of the squad, the Frenchman had got along very well with Heynckes during the few weeks he had coached the team. (Under Heynckes, Bayern had won four of the last five games to mount a late but ultimately fruitless title challenge.) Now Ribéry felt misunderstood and played out of position.

The press, meanwhile, criticised Van Gaal for being desperate to sign his fellow countryman Arjen Robben for 25 million euros (then £22 million) from Real even though the player was known to be highly injury-prone. Now Robben seemed to be constantly out of action with one thing or another. Finally, the team's ride through the Champions League group stage had been so bumpy that when Bayern travelled to Juventus, they needed a win to reach the next round.

Although they looked sharper and more lively than during any of the preceding months, they were trailing 1-0 after half an hour. Then Bayern's Croatian striker Ivica Olić was brought down in the box and the referee pointed to the spot. It was the first penalty the club had been awarded all season and the players looked at each other to see who had the nerves to take the most important kick in Bayern's recent history. The man who stepped up was none other than Hans-Jörg Butt, the goalkeeper. Butt coolly sent his colleague Gianluigi Buffon the wrong way and made it 1-1. In the second half, Bayern played Juve off the park to win 4-1. Suddenly it was a whole new season.

On that night in Turin, Bayern already resembled the team that would win the treble four and a half years later. Yes, van Gaal had spent a lot of money on Robben, but he also promoted homegrown players. He called up the twenty-year-old defender Holger Badstuber from the reserves and immediately made him a regular. The same went for nineteen-year-old Thomas Müller. (Before 2009 was over, van Gaal said: 'In my team, Müller always plays.') And he had also given Schweinsteiger a new lease of life. Coach after coach had played Schweinsteiger as a right-sided midfielder, though he lacked the pace and dribbling skills to shine in this role. Van Gaal simply moved him into central defensive midfield and was rewarded with a master strategist on the pitch. Five months after reinventing Schweinsteiger, van Gaal also called up a seventeen-year-old midfielder from the reserves and put him at left-back. When young David Alaba told a reporter that he was surprised to be used in this position, the Dutchman said: 'Even if he himself thinks differently, he is a left-back.'

When you look at all the crucial developments van Gaal instigated, you can understand why Philipp Lahm says: 'Van Gaal represents the crucial turning point. He introduced a specific idea of the game – a striker, two wingers, two defensive midfielders – and shaped the club with this philosophy.' However, when the Dutchman pointed out that much himself in 2013, saying that Bayern's signing of Guardiola 'bore the Van Gaal stamp', Uli Hoeness exploded. 'Only Louis van Gaal can say something like this,' he told the Dutch newspaper *De Telegraaf*. 'His problem is that Louis doesn't think he's God – but God the Father. Before the world came into existence, Louis was already there. But the world doesn't work the way he sees it.'

Well, in 2010, it very nearly did. Van Gaal won the eighth league-and-cup double in Bayern's history and also reached the Champions League final against Internazionale, coached by his old protégé Mourinho. In other words, the Dutchman was only one small step away from lifting Bayern's first treble. He felt on top of the world. During the league title celebrations on Munich's Marienplatz, he whipped the masses into such a frenzy that many observers would later remark how the spectacle reminded them of a Nuremberg rally. Dressed in *Lederhosen*, he declared: 'We are the best of Germany. And maybe of . . .' He paused, stared at the people below and raised his finger. 'Europe! Yeah!' He spread his arms wide and began to jump up and down as everyone went crazy.

Two days before the Inter game, the Dutchman disclosed in a newspaper column that he'd once dropped his pants in front of the squad. 'I wanted to make clear,' he said, 'that when I sub someone, I don't do it for my ego but for the team.' When Luca Toni retold the story a year later, he recalled the reasoning, not to mention the choice of words, slightly differently: 'The coach wanted to make clear to us that he can drop any player, it was all the same to him because, as he said, he had the balls. He demonstrated this literally.' (The Italian added: 'Luckily I didn't see a lot, because I wasn't in the front row.')

Van Gaal left out Ribéry for the final, but not to prove he had balls. There was no choice. The hot-headed French wizard had got himself sent off in the semis against Lyon for stamping on striker Lisandro's ankle. Three weeks later, on 25 May 2010, the Reds sorely missed their tricky winger. At the Santiago Bernabéu Stadium in Madrid,

Inter dealt with Bayern's new possession game the way they had dealt with Barcelona's possession game in the previous round: they put everyone behind the ball, sat back and waited for the right moment to strike. It came on thirty-five minutes. Inter goalkeeper Júlio César punted the ball upfield, the Argentine forward Diego Milito won an aerial duel, Wesley Sneijder returned the ball and Milito scored from ten yards.

The Reds would finish the match with 68 per cent possession, but they found it hard to create chances. Just twenty seconds after the restart, Müller wasted a glorious opportunity when he had only César to beat from ten yards. Müller's first-time shot wasn't well-placed, though, and the goalkeeper blocked the ball with his feet. In the seventieth minute, Milito collected a pass from Samuel Eto'o, dummied past Bayern's centre-back Daniel van Buyten and put the game out of the Germans' reach with his second goal of the night.

It was a disappointing if deserved result. But, unlike in 2001, the final didn't feel like the end of a ride, more like the beginning. Uli Hoeness, who had been elected president six months earlier, first comforted Müller, whose chance could have turned the game: 'Thomas mustn't fret, he's had an unbelievable season for such a young man.' Then he said: 'In 2012, the Champions League final will be played in Munich. So there's still a lot to dream of.'

That 2012 final – soon nicknamed *Finale dahoam*, Bavarian for home final – became a target, maybe even an obsession for the Reds. Since 1984, when Liverpool defeated Roma in Rome, no finalist in the European Cup or the Champions League had enjoyed home advantage. Amazingly, the dream would become real, though it wasn't The King who made it happen. Van Gaal had never been haunted by self-doubt, but in the wake of his great first season he went over the top. The straw that broke the camel's back might have been the Dutchman's launch of his autobiography in October 2010. Waving a copy in the general direction of Hoeness and Rummenigge, who were in attendance as invited guests, he addressed them like schoolboys.

'It's important for you, too, to read this,' he lectured the men who paid his wages.

A few weeks later, German football was treated to another *Wutrede*, this time live on television and from Hoeness. He was ranting, though not raving. In a calm but icy voice, Hoeness called Van Gaal 'advice-resistant', adding: 'A modern football club mustn't be a one-man show.' He also said that Van Gaal had alienated many players. He closed with: 'It's difficult to talk to him, because he doesn't accept other people's opinions.' In March the club told Van Gaal he would have to leave at the end of the season. Four weeks later, he was fired with immediate effect.

Of course it wasn't just his regal airs and graces that hastened the downfall of King Louis. Maybe Rummenigge and Hoeness would have gnashed their teeth and, who knows, memorised Van Gaal's memoirs if the results had still been there. But a young Dortmund team built by Jürgen Klopp was taking the league by storm, making Van Gaal's football look sluggish in attack and unsound at the back. When Bayern sank to fourth place, the club had to act. After all, you couldn't reach the *Finale dahoam* if you failed to qualify for the 2011–12 Champions League.

This was now the prime directive for Van Gaal's successor. But who could this be? In a long piece for the weekly *Die Zeit*, the writer Helmut Schümann attempted to find out why 'Bayern are using up so many coaches'. He listed a few obvious explanations, such as how it was almost impossible to not fall short of expectations in Munich, because 'it's virtually written into the club's statutes that they must win the league and the cup each year and also reach at least the semi-finals in Europe'. Schümann added that a Bayern coach was supposed to have his own philosophy, which at the same time had to be compatible with at least three other philosophies – Rummenigge's, Hoeness's and Beckenbauer's. (As most people tended to do, he forgot deputy CEO Karl Hopfner, who'd long since begun to wield more influence than Beckenbauer, now merely the club's honorary president.)

But then Schümann made another point. 'At Bayern, the human touch is important,' he said. 'Anyone who disregards this will be having a hard time.' There's some truth to that. The club's many detractors – the people who refer to the Allianz Arena as *Arroganz Arena*, and no prize for guessing what that means – always scoff at such notions; they call Bayern cold and ruthless and consider all that sweet talk about family mere lip service. True, Bayern can be ruthlessly professional and soon there would be an example of that. But they do have this other side to them. It explains why Hitzfeld, certainly the most humane among famous German coaches of the modern era, was able to stay for so long. It also explains why the other great conciliatory Bayern coach of the last thirty-five years was now entrusted with project *Finale dahoam* – Jupp Heynckes.

The project began with a small summer tournament in Munich in late July 2011. Hoeness and Rummenigge were sitting in a restaurant in the Allianz Arena, waiting for the game between Bayern and Milan to begin, when suddenly the coach of another participating team walked in — Pep Guardiola. The three men struck up a conversation, in the course of which it became obvious that the Catalan had spent the day gathering information about Bayern. 'And then, just as he was about to leave,' Hoeness recalls, 'he turned around and said: "I can imagine to work for Bayern Munich."' It was more than just a casual remark and none of the three men would forget it. (On the next day, Bayern lost the final of the tournament against Guardiola's Barcelona 2-0. Both goals were scored by the twenty-year-old Thiago.)

Heynckes's first full season back in charge produced great attacking football and at the same time brought new defensive stability – in the span of twenty-four days in August and September, for instance, Bayern scored eighteen goals in five games against Hamburg, Kaiserslautern, Freiburg and FC Zurich (in the Champions League qualifiers) while conceding none. The coach also delivered, according to plan, the *Finale dahoam*: Bayern knocked out Real on penalties in the semis to reach the final at their own Allianz Arena against a surprise team, Roberto Di Matteo's Chelsea.

And yet 2011–12 is remembered as the season when Bayern decided that serious trouble was brewing at home, that Christian Nerlinger was not the right man, that still another former high-profile player had to come on board and that the transfer record needed to be shattered. Not all of this had to do with the second-worst trauma in club history, the final at home. Rather, it was the fact that Dortmund first repeated their Bundesliga title and then also humiliated Bayern 5-2 in the German cup final that forced the Munich giants to step up efforts. They had now won only one league trophy in four years, their worst showing since the late 1990s.

'Competition is good for business, as they say,' Thomas Müller replied with a broad grin when I asked him if Dortmund's resurgence had made Bayern a better team. 'If you have strong competition, you've got to try harder. And that always helps you to develop and improve. That's a good thing for us, as a club, because having a strong opponent means you have to be more attentive.' And so, shortly after the end of the season, Bayern parted ways with Nerlinger and replaced him with the outspoken, opinionated Matthias Sammer, a fiercely ambitious and competitive man who's rarely pleased (as a player, he was called 'the Grouch'). Sammer – yet another former European Footballer of the Year in the club's corridors of power – then sat in on a meeting with Heynckes during which the future was planned.

Everybody present knew that the coach wanted Athletic Bilbao's defensive midfielder Javier Martínez. Everybody also knew that the player was way too expensive. He had a buyout clause of 40 million euros (£32 million) written into his contract. That was 10 million euros more than Bayern had ever spent on a player. At one point, Heynckes himself called Bilbao's president Josu Urrutia and asked him to lower the price for old time's sake. (Urrutia had once played under Heynckes.) There was nothing doing. Finally, Rummenigge looked at Heynckes and said: 'Let me ask you just one question. Will this player give us that little bit of extra quality which we need?' All Heynckes replied was: 'Yes.' Rummenigge looked at the others. They slowly nodded their heads. He said: 'Okay, if that's the case, then let's do it.'

This transfer, still Bayern's biggest in history, had nothing to do with Dortmund but all with the *Finale dahoam*, the Champions League final against Chelsea at the Allianz Arena. In Germany, people speak of the 'Bayern gene', something like a cross between winning mentality and the ability to snatch victory from the jaws of defeat. But the Bayern gene was not very much in evidence on 19 May 2012, when the Reds somehow managed to lose a game they thoroughly dominated and had won three times.

They first won it seven minutes from time, when Thomas Müller scored with a bouncing header from a Toni Kroos cross. It was Bayern's twenty-seventh attempt on goal of the match up to that point and many fans in the stands felt it was poetic justice that Müller, who had missed that glorious chance in Madrid against Inter, should score the winning goal. Only he didn't. With two minutes left, the Blues won their first (and only) corner of the night. Schweinsteiger later recalled how defender David Luiz, who had repeatedly told him 'Your team is better, but we are going to win' during the game, ran upfield for the corner and, passing him, said: 'Now a goal!' Seconds later, Didier Drogba met Juan Mata's corner at the near post and equalised.

Bayern won the game for the second time when Drogba brought down Ribéry with a reckless challenge and conceded a penalty just three minutes into extra time. Former Chelsea player Arjen Robben confidently stepped up, but goalkeeper Petr Cech guessed the right corner, plunged to his left and denied the Dutch winger. The Reds then won the final for the third time, when Mata missed Chelsea's first spot-kick in the penalty shoot-out. But even this lead wasn't enough. Cech saved from Ivica Olić and then pushed Bastian Schweinsteiger's penalty against the post with his fingertips. When Drogba converted the last penalty of the night, you had to fear for some of the Bayern players. Schweinsteiger in particular looked so devastated that you wondered if he would ever recover from what is now widely known as the *Fiasko dahoam*. And no prize for guessing what that means, either.

In the summer of 2012, Heynckes was the exact opposite of a man licking his wounds. He seemed to take the three second-place finishes as a challenge rather than as a set-back. The 67-year-old coach would call Rummenigge almost every day, even during the chairman's holidays, to discuss possible additions to the team and new systems on the pitch. But he wasn't the only one who called. In July, word reached Rummenigge that someone wanted to speak to him in Catalunya. Pep Guardiola was about to spend his sabbatical in America and requested a meeting before he left for New York.

Rummenigge travelled to Barcelona and the two men talked for five or six hours about what kind of club Bayern are – and what kind of person Guardiola is. The Catalan was the most coveted coach in the world and there was no doubt that many very lucrative offers would come in during his sabbatical. But Rummenigge got the impression that Guardiola wasn't really waiting for any offers – he wanted to coach Bayern. The two men agreed to stay in loose contact and wait until Christmas to see whether or not anything could come of all this.

In top-level football, the decisions about appointing coaches are the most important and the most difficult to make. Mainly that's because it's all about timing. If Arsène Wenger had been out of contract in the summer of 1994, Bayern's history would have been very different. If Ottmar Hitzfeld had been unavailable in the summer of 1998 – ditto. And so we can confidently assume that Rummenigge couldn't believe his luck when he travelled back to Munich to inform the rest of the board that they had a good chance of landing the most famous coach in the world, the guy who had perfected the van Gaal approach without thinking of himself as 'God the Father'. What's more, they could even have a smooth, clean transition, because Jupp Heynckes's contract would run out in the summer of 2013.

Of course, at the time nobody had any idea that while Rummenigge and Sammer (and, to a smaller extent, Hoeness) were getting all excited about the Guardiola development, Heynckes was building the best team in Europe and laying the foundations for the club's *annus mirabilis* – the treble. Yes, football is a funny old game.

Today, Heynckes says that he promised his wife in the wake of the *Fiasko dahoam* that he would retire for good in 2013. However, during the first half of what would be his final season it very often seemed as if he was waiting for the club to offer him a contract extension and felt slightly hurt it didn't come. From a professional standpoint, the club did the right thing, though – they opted for the future. In January 2013, Bayern proudly announced that Pep Guardiola would take over the team in the summer. Large parts of the foreign media appeared so startled by the Catalan's decision to forgo the Premier League for the Bundesliga that you could be forgiven for thinking Bayern had somehow been operating below their radar for years. This, after all, was a club that had reached two Champions League finals in three seasons. Oh no, make that three in four.

Bayern had finally become a well-oiled machine in which all parts interconnected, not least because Heynckes – whom many in the team regarded as a father-figure – had somehow taught his freelancing artists Ribéry and Robben how to track back. Occasionally, you could even see one of them – gasp! – tackle. The coach had also found his very own balance between van Gaal's possession game and the direct football Klinsmann loved. The team now had both: thrust and style.

In the Champions League semis, Bayern scored seven goals without reply against mighty Barcelona. As if this wasn't spectacular enough, Dortmund eliminated Real Madrid in the other semi-final to set up the first all-German final of the competition. It would be staged at, of all places, Wembley. Until those magical Spanish nights in April and May, the Bundesliga had been widely admired for the marvellous atmosphere at the grounds, thanks partly to affordable tickets and old-fashioned terraces, and the fact that the clubs were not rich men's playthings but owned by their members. Now those clubs were competitive, too. Suddenly, German football was hip. Dortmund, in particular, captured people's imagination, because Jürgen Klopp's young team had been built with very little money and seemed to epitomise the revolution: gone were the strong, rugged defenders that defined Teutonic football in the 1980s; now a typical German player was like Dortmund's young Mario Götze – lithe, elegant and silky-skilled.

While the two domestic rivals progressed through the Champions League, Bayern were already paving the ground for the Guardiola era. The Catalan wanted to sign two players, Thiago from Barcelona and the Brazilian Neymar from Santos. Hoeness and Rummenigge gave the green light for the first deal, but balked at the second. Bayern had broken their old rule of only signing Brazilians who had already proved they could adapt to Germany in 2008, when they bought São Paulo's defender Breno for a lot of money. It was another nightmare transfer (at the time, Breno was standing trial for arson) and so the club vetoed the Neymar plan. Instead, they sold Guardiola on a similar type of player: Götze.

The news that Götze would activate a get-out clause and join Bayern for 37 million euros (at the time that equalled £31.5 million) caused a furore in Germany. A tabloid broke the story shortly before Dortmund met Real, which fuelled speculation that Bayern had leaked the news to cause unrest in Borussia's camp. It also revived the old accusation that the Reds would purposefully poach a domestic rival's best players to stifle competition at home, the way they had signed Kahn, Scholl or Tarnat from Karlsruher SC and Zé Roberto, Ballack and Lúcio from Leverkusen. Although signing good players is not generally classified as a crime, those allegations made the Wembley final on 25 May even more explosive.

Bayern had already won the league by an absurd twenty-five points, so they went into the game as the popular favourites. However, in the previous two years, Dortmund had become the first team to win five competitive games in a row against Bayern and many felt they were now the Reds' bogey team. And indeed Borussia began the match like men possessed, dominating the game against a Bayern team that may have been gripped by fear of losing a third straight Champions League final. But Bayern's goalkeeper Manuel Neuer made five fine saves in the first thirty-five minutes and at last the Reds settled down to turn the final into a pulsating match worthy of the occasion.

On the hour, Ribéry played in Robben and the Dutchman found centre-forward Mario Mandžukić with his cross. From six yards, the Croatian striker gave Bayern the lead. Dortmund now seemed to be fading fast physically, but were handed a lifeline when Bayern's defender Dante recklessly conceded a penalty eight minutes later. İlkay Gündoğan equalised from the spot and the match seemed to be headed for extra time, as Bayern wasted excellent chances through Müller, Alaba and Schweinsteiger. But with only seconds left on the clock, Bayern's two resident geniuses produced a moment of rare magic.

At the edge of Dortmund's penalty area, Ribéry trapped one of Jérôme Boateng's trademark long passes. Keeping possession against two defenders, the Frenchman saw Robben make a diagonal run. Ribéry gently back-heeled the ball into Robben's path. With his first touch, Robben rode a tackle ten yards in front of goal. With his second, he evaded another defender. With his third, he pushed the ball past the goalkeeper. Without waiting to see if it would cross the line, Robben turned left and raced over to the touchline to celebrate the goal that won the Champions League.

Dortmund would later rue their bad luck. Götze, of all people, had missed the final with an injury and both Ribéry and Dante could have been sent off. But there was no denying the better team had won the game and after Barcelona in 1999 and then the *Finale dahoam*, it was simply Bayern's turn to be given a lucky break or two on the biggest European stage.

Heynckes acknowledged as much when he said after the game: 'It was time for the Lahm and Schweinsteiger generation, who are my

two captains, to win an international title.' Both men also won the
DFB-Pokal six days later to complete Bayern's first treble and would
then, twelve months on and alongside Neuer, Müller, Boateng, Kroos
and Götze, add the biggest title of them all, the World Cup. 'Without
the treble, Germany wouldn't have won the World Cup,' Heynckes
says now. 'This success has a special place in football history.'

And yet a cloud hung over the treble. When Bayern celebrated
their Wembley triumph at Grosvenor House on Hyde Park, the club's
new head of finances Jan-Christian Dreesen grabbed the microphone
at 2.15 a.m. 'There's someone missing up here on stage,' he said.
Then he led a chant of: 'We want Uli!' In contrast to Rummenigge,
Sammer and Heynckes, Hoeness hadn't addressed the 1,200 invited
guests but preferred to be seated in the background. Now, as hundreds
kept singing 'We want Uli!', he reluctantly rose and walked over to the
stage. He even forgot to put his jacket on. 'Uli's been through a difficult
patch,' Rummenigge said while Hoeness stood next to him. 'But it's a
mark of this club that we're all friends and stick together in difficult
times. So, Uli: good luck.' Then he looked at the rows of tables in the
elegantly designed Great Room and said: 'And now we party!'

In January 2013, only four weeks after travelling to New York with
a contract for Guardiola in his suitcase, Uli Hoeness turned himself
in to the tax authorities. He disclosed a secret Swiss bank account
and admitted to having earned considerable amounts of money from
shares and currency dealings for which he had failed to pay income
tax. This voluntary disclosure was made in the hope it would grant
him exemption from punishment, but eventually the Munich district
court decided Hoeness would have to stand trial regardless. Partly
because the voluntary disclosure was incomplete, partly because it had
been made while investigations were already underway.

The affair was a scandal of massive proportions in Germany and
it badly hurt the image of the man and his club. Hoeness explained
the account didn't exist to hide or launder money but purely for

gambling on the stock market. It had been set up in 2001 by the late Robert Louis-Dreyfus, the former CEO of Adidas, according to most reports, so that his friend Hoeness had what was referred to as 'play money' to recoup the losses he'd incurred during the previous year's stock market crash. Hoeness said: 'It was virtual, unreal money for me. It was like playing Monopoly.' All of which made the whole affair even more difficult to grasp for people who can't afford to treat even a few euros as Monopoly money, let alone millions of them.

During the trial, Hoeness then admitted to having evaded a lot more money in taxes than the authorities had suspected, 28.5 million euros. On 13 March 2014, he was sentenced to three and a half years in prison. One day later, Hoeness announced he would not appeal against this sentence and immediately stepped down as both president of Bayern Munich, the parent club, and as chairman of Bayern Munich Ltd.

Hoeness's fall from grace was particularly fascinating for the media because he used to be so widely lauded for his social conscience and charitable work. In early 2012, when Hoeness celebrated his sixtieth birthday, Rummenigge referred to him, not entirely tongue in cheek, as 'the Tegernsee Father Teresa and the Säbener Strasse Nelson Mandela'. He also, on a more serious note, said: 'You are the soul of our club.'

Now, two years later, Bayern's soul was behind bars. It's difficult to say how strongly this development affected Guardiola's first season in charge. It's equally difficult to say whether it was a success or not. Bayern won the domestic double again, and as the Spanish writer Martí Perarnau pointed out in his behind-the-scenes book about Guardiola's first year in Munich, the Reds became 'only the second team in history to have done so immediately after a treble-winning year (PSV Eindhoven did it in 1987–8 and 1988–9)'.

Perarnau was granted almost unlimited access for his book and so he's able to expand in great detail on Guardiola's coaching philosophy, his training methods and his lines of thinking. There is, however, very little about Guardiola as a person and sometimes you get the impression that the man's football obsession is too all-encompassing to leave room for much else.

Maybe this impression explains why a sizeable part of Bayern's support struggled to really warm to the Catalan. They understood that the club couldn't stand still – if there are fans who understand this basic fact of sporting life, it's Bayern supporters – and they respected the Catalan for being the brightest football mind of his generation. After all, they could see with their own eyes that he was making the team more versatile and flexible: sometimes Müller played up front as what is now known as a 'false 9', sometimes a more classic centre-forward like Robert Lewandowski, also signed from Dortmund, was in attack; sometimes Lahm played at right-back, sometimes he became what he had been under Roman Grill, a central defensive midfielder.

When I asked Lahm about this ultra-fluency, he replied: 'Football has changed. You'll hardly find a player any more who can play only one position. Modern footballers are very flexible. When you think back ten or fifteen years, you'd see many players who were strong, tall and rugged. But now that holds true only for goalkeepers and centre-backs, plus maybe for the central striker up front. Everybody else on the pitch is basically a midfielder.'

Guardiola was the future, there was no doubt about that. But some Bayern fans wondered if they liked the future. In September 2014 the club's match programme for the game against Stuttgart featured an editorial by Rummenigge. He harshly attacked what he called a 'shameful campaign' to question an increasing Spanish presence and influence at the club. 'I read about a "Spanish Armada" and a "Spanish invasion,"' he said. 'I think we all agree that such martial concepts have no place in sports.'

A few weeks earlier, Bayern had signed an ageing Xabi Alonso from Real Madrid, partly to replace Toni Kroos who'd taken the opposite route. The number of Spanish players in the squad now stood at five. But it wasn't only who came in, it was also who went out that made people uneasy. A few months later, following a defeat in the Champions League away at Porto, Bayern's doctor Hans-Wilhelm Müller-Wohlfahrt stepped down because, as his press release said, he felt the 'medical department was made primarily responsible for the loss for inexplicable reasons'. It was an open secret that Müller-Wohlfahrt didn't see eye-to-eye with Guardiola and while the resignation of a physio wouldn't mean much at most other clubs, it was a different matter at Säbener Strasse: Müller-Wohlfahrt had been working for Bayern for thirty-eight years and was as much a club icon as any player, coach or official.

The next legend to bow out was Bastian Schweinsteiger. After thirteen seasons with the Reds, during most of which the fans had yelled '*Fussballgott*' whenever his name was announced, he left the club for Manchester United in the summer of 2015, shortly after winning his eighth league title with Bayern, tying the record set by Mehmet Scholl. Schweinsteiger left because – true to the coach's mantra that games are won in midfield and that your best players should play in this part of the pitch – Guardiola kept adding midfielders to his squad, reducing the 31-year-old's chances of getting a game.

Of course the fans understood that the pressure on Guardiola was mounting, that soon it would no longer be enough to win the league by a record margin. Having been stopped in Europe in the semis twice, by Real and then Barcelona, Guardiola had to deliver in the Champions League and couldn't afford to be sentimental. But as they watched Schweinsteiger leave almost like Gerd Müller had left in 1979 – without a formal farewell and a round of applause from his fans – some people wondered if, with Uli Hoeness now reduced to a marginal figure due to his prison sentence, the club was changing too rapidly and too radically. A fan banner that appeared overnight at Säbener Strasse as early as July 2015 complained: 'Our identity is being destroyed.' In other words, some fans feared for an often overlooked but important element of this whole story. The human touch.

Maybe Guardiola sensed there was a gulf he would never be able to bridge, not least because he had no intention of trying. As early as August 2013, the Catalan had told the press: 'Winning titles is obviously nice, but that's not what it's all about in the end. What matters to me is that your players tell you at some point: "Coach, you have really helped me become a better player. I have learned a lot from you." That's what makes me happy.'

At the time, this statement was interpreted as an attempt to ease the pressure on himself after Heynckes had just won the treble. But of course Guardiola was absolutely serious. He was not interested in winning by all means necessary. In fact, he often gave the impression he would rather see his team execute his beloved *juego de posición*, the positional play, to perfection and lose the game than dumb down and win it.

At a club where winning forms part of the genetic makeup, this was an interesting approach – but not doomed to fail as such. The modern Bayern has moved on from the 1980s and early 1990s, when the club was often accused of cynicism and opportunism, on and off the pitch. The fans in Munich have come to appreciate flair, grandeur and style. Having lost as many finals for the European Cup or Champions League as they have won, five, they also know how difficult it is to snatch the big prize. So they will accept a valiant but ultimately fruitless effort as long as they feel connected on an emotional level. But as Guardiola's statement made clear, he wasn't interested in this, either. For him, football was and is only what happens between the white lines. For most people in the stands, however, it's a lot more than just that.

Thus few tears were shed when Bayern announced five days before Christmas 2015 that Guardiola would not extend his contract and move on at the end of the season. The following months promptly served to sum up his three-year reign. The Catalan won the league once more, making Bayern the first club in the 113-year history of the national championship to be crowned four years in a row, but again he fell short in the Champions League semi-final.

A sparkling Bayern team played an unashamedly defensive Atlético Madrid off the park and executed *juego de posición* to perfection. Or rather, to near-perfection. One single counter attack in the Reds' home leg gave the visitors the away goal that served to put them through. The bitter irony did not escape anyone watching. Guardiola had been denied an opportunity to equal Heynckes's feat by three different Spanish sides. First by his personal rivals, Real, then by his old flame, Barcelona, and now by what could be described as the only top-level team on the continent that stubbornly refuses to take any of Guardiola's teachings to heart.

On the next morning, a mild spring sun was shining down on Säbener Strasse. Although only those players who had not seen action against Atlético would be working out, thousands of fans came to watch the team. While the pitch was watered for the training session, a middle-aged man in a red Bayern sweater told a camera crew: 'Pep has given us good football that is easy on the eye but, unfortunately, not really successful. What's missing is winning in Europe. That's a pity.'

A few steps to his left, a bearded young man wearing sunglasses pondered how to express his feelings about the past three years without letting himself get carried away by the disappointment of the previous night. 'It was an exciting time, the team learned a lot and improved tactically,' he began. The muscles in his face were twitching while he weighed his words. Then he stated: 'But it lacked the human element, it was too un-Bavarian for me.' Grinning, he added: 'Oh well, now I'm looking forward to the next chapter.'

EPILOGUE

Klaus Augenthaler has spent twenty-two years at Bayern Munich. He was a youth-team player, then a reserve-team player, then a first-team player, then a youth-team coach and a reserve-team player again, then a first-team assistant coach and even, briefly, the first-team interim coach.

When you see him for the first time now, at fifty-eight years of age, you can't help but think that it tells. His hair is prematurely grey, his face is furrowed with deep wrinkles, his skin looks leathery. But sometimes there's a sparkle in his deep-set eyes that signals mischief and tells you he's nowhere near as gruff as he appears.

In fact, Augenthaler was behind one of the greatest football spoofs ever. On 29 March 1999, he held a surprise press conference. At the time, he was coaching Grazer AK, the tradition-laden Austrian club from Graz. His team were in third place and it was the day before their derby against Sturm Graz, so the assembled press pack was stunned when Augenthaler said he was going to resign with immediate effect. They were even more surprised when club president Peter Svetits then presented a totally unknown Lithuanian coach called Albertas Klimaviszys as the new man in charge.

The reason he was unknown was that he was a fake. In reality, he was a German comedian who was filming the entire, elaborate hoax for his new television show. Both he and Augenthaler were so deadpan, and stuck to their roles so stubbornly, that Austrian radio broke news of Augenthaler's resignation and the comedian even held a training session before the prank was explained.

And so it's fun to hear Augenthaler reminisce about all those years at Säbener Strasse. When he talks about his time as Giovanni Trapattoni's assistant, he says everyone understood the coach very well and that all this talk about not being able to follow the Italian's explanations was just a welcome excuse for some players. He says he retired even though he still had a year to run on his contract, because there were too many factions and cliques in the early 1990s team, people whispering behind his back that he'd become too slow. He says the team of the 1980s was able to cope with all the pressure and withstand the nation's antipathy (resulting in part from his foul on Rudi Völler), because the team-spirit and the camaraderie was unparalleled.

Finally, I ask: 'Well, how did you end up at Bayern in the first place?'

'The club I was playing for, FC Vilshofen, had a really good youth set-up,' Augenthaler replies. (Vilshofen is a Bavarian town 110 miles northeast of Munich.) 'When I was seventeen, we won the league and beat Bayern home and away. Because of that, four players from our small club were invited to Munich for a trial. So we went there in the summer. The trial lasted three days. Let me tell you, it was tough. I was knackered. But two of us were asked to join the club, Fred Arbinger and me.'

'So that was a trial with Bayern's Under-19s in July of 1975?' I repeat, taking notes.

'No,' Augenthaler says. 'A trial with the first team.'

For a moment, I'm speechless. Then I say: 'You mean they invite four seventeen-year-old kids from near the Czech border to Munich and then have them train with the Bundesliga side, the Beckenbauers and Müllers?'

'Yes,' Augenthaler says matter-of-factly. 'I think some of the big stars were still on holiday, because they had won the European Cup. But we trained with Bundesliga players I had only ever seen on television.'

While I scribble down a reminder along the lines of 'At Bayern, it's always sink or swim', Augenthaler corrects himself and mentions that he'd seen some of the players in the flesh before.

'I was at the European Cup final in 1974,' he says.

Now I'm speechless for more than just a moment. At last, I ask: 'In Brussels? You were at the final in Brussels? For the first game or for the replay?'

'For the first game,' Augenthaler says. 'I wasn't a Bayern fan at the time. I had a soft spot for Dortmund, because my best friend supported them. But of course there was a group of Bayern fans in Vilshofen. They chartered a coach to get to Brussels and offered people a ride. Well, I jumped at the chance. I was sixteen and thought I might never get to see such a big game again.' Chuckling, he adds: 'I can still tell you the price: 35 marks per person.'

I put down my pen. 'You know, this is amazing!' I exclaim. 'This is so great for the book I'm writing. Here's one of the true Bayern icons – and it turns out he was in Brussels and saw the very goal that more or less made the club a superpower, Schwarzenbeck's legendary piledriver. Fantastic!'

'I wish I had,' Augenthaler says slowly. 'Five minutes before the end of extra time, we left the ground to beat the traffic. None of us saw that goal.'

LIST OF ILLUSTRATIONS

1. Friedrich Ludwig Jahn, the father of German gymnastics (Imago/Arklvi); Kurt Landauer (Courtsey of Verlag Die Werkstatt, Göttingen, Germany); Grünwalder Stadion, 1927 (Courtsey of Verlag Die Werkstatt, Göttingen, Germany)

2. Zlatko Čajkovski and Franz Beckenbauer, October 1965 (Getty Images/Horstmüller/Ullstein bild); Sepp Maier and Petar Radenković, 1967 (Sven Simon/DPA/PA Images); Team training, 1966 (Imago/WEREK)

3. Gerd Müller and Jupp Heynckes, Bayern vs. Borussia Mönchengladbach, Bundesliga 1965–66 (Getty Images/Werner OTTO/Ullstein bild); Franz Beckenbauer, Footballer of the Year 1966 (Imago/Sven Simon); Bayern fans watching their team play Nuremberg in the DFB-Pokal semi-final, 1966 (Imago/WEREK)

4. Werner Olk with Werner Krämer, 1966 DFB Cup final (Imago/Horstmüller); Franz Beckenbauer with fanmail, August 1966 (Getty Images/Horstmüller/Ullstein bild); Wilhelm Neudecker, Čajkovski, Olk and business manager Robert Schwan parading the 1966 DFB Cup (Imago/Fred Joch)

5. Franz Roth scores the winning goal in the 1967 European Cup Winners' Cup final vs. Rangers (Schirner Sportfoto/DPA/PA Images); Franz Beckenbauer presents Bayern's first European Cup Winner's Cup to photographers (Imago/WEREK); Franz Roth and the Cup Winners' Cup his goal won for Bayern in 1967 (Sven Simon/DPA/PA Images)

6. Gerd Müller scores the winning goal in the 1969 DFB Cup final (Imago/WEREK); Gerd Müller posing as the King of the Goalscorers, 1969 (Imago/Kicker/Metelmann); Paul Breitner, 1971 (Imago/WEREK)

7. Udo Lattek celebrates Bayern's 1971 DFB-Pokal win with Robert Schwan (Imago/Sportfoto Rudel); Jupp Heynckes and Uli Hoeness, 1972 (Imago/WEREK); Uli Hoeness and Paul Breitner, 1974 (Imago/Fred Joch)

8. Dettmar Cramer and Robert Schwan, 1975 (Getty Images/Werner OTTO/Ullstein bild); Bayern celebrate beating Leeds United in the European Cup final, 1975 (Imago/WEREK)

9. Franz Roth, 1976 European Cup final against Saint-Étienne (Imago/Horstmüller); Karl-Heinz Rummenigge, Franz Roth and defender Udo Horsmann celebrate Bayern's third European Cup win, 1976 (Imago/Horstmüller); Bayern's humiliating defeat against second-division Osnabrück, 1978 (Imago/WEREK)

10. Wolfgang and Wolfgang Kraus, Gladbach vs Bayern Munich, September 1979 (Imago/Horstmüller); Pál Csernai and Gyula Lóránt, 1977 (Imago/Pressfoto Baumann); Willi O. Hoffmann's *lederhosen* photoshoot, November 1979 (Imago/Fred Joch)

11. Karl-Heinz Rummenigge and Paul Breitner, 1979 (Getty Images/Werner OTTO/Ullstein bild); Georg Schwarzenbeck in his aunt's shop, 1980 (Imago/Sven Simon); Uli Hoeness in hospital after his plane crash, February 1982 (Wolfgang Weihs/Picture-alliance/DPA/AP Images)

12. Jean-Marie Pfaff concedes the infamous throw-in on the first day of Bayern's 1982–83 season (Imago/WEREK); Lothar Matthäus after missing his penalty in the 1984 DFB Cup final (Imago/Sven Simon); Dieter Hoeness, during the 1985 DFB Cup final (Imago/Horstmüller)

13. Jupp Heynckes, Bayern's manager from 1987–1991 (Getty Images/Bongarts); Emil Kostadinov, Jürgen Klinsmann and Lothar Matthäus, 1995 (Imago/WEREK); Otto Rehhagel with his megaphone on first day of training, 1995 (Imago/WEREK); Uli Hoeness re-enacting Jürgen Klinsmann's off-pitch kick, 2012 (Imago/Ulmer/Cremer)

14. The Day of the *Wutrede*: Giovanni Trapattoni, March 1998 (Imago/Fred Joch); Despair after losing to Manchester United in the 1999 Champions League final, in the foreground: Sammy Kuffour and Thorsten Fink (Imago/Horstmüller); Opening of the new Allianz Arena, May 2005 (JOERG KOCH/AFP/Getty Images)

15. Louis van Gaal in *lederhosen* (Imago/MIS); Arjen Robben celebrate scoring the winning goal with Thomas Müller, Champions League final 2013 (Imago/Mika); Uli Hoeness is urged to lift the 2013 Champions League Cup, May 2013(Imago/Avanti)

16. Uli Hoeness at his trial, March 2014 (Imago/Future Image); Pep Guardiola celebrates the Bayern squad beating Borussia Dortmund to win the DFB Cup, May 2016 (Getty Images/Uwe Kraft/Anadolu Agency); Carlo Ancelotti during his inaugural Bayern Munich photoshoot, July 2016 (GUENTER SCHIFFMANN/AFP/Getty Images)

INDEX